Age of Anxiety

Politics, Literature, and Film

Series Editor: Lee Trepanier, Saginaw Valley State University

The *Politics, Literature, and Film* series is an interdisciplinary examination of the intersection of politics with literature and/or film. The series is receptive to works that use a variety of methodological approaches, focus on any period from antiquity to the present, and situate their analysis in national, comparative, or global contexts. *Politics, Literature, and Film* seeks to be truly interdisciplinary by including authors from all the social sciences and humanities, such as political science, sociology, psychology, literature, philosophy, history, religious studies, and law. The series is open to both American and non-American literature and film. By putting forth bold and innovative ideas that appeal to a broad range of interests, the series aims to enrich our conversations about literature, film, and their relationship to politics.

Advisory Board

Recent Titles

The Final Frontier: International Relations and Politics through Star Trek and Star Wars by Joel R. Campbell and Gigi Gokcek

Flannery O'Connor and the Perils of Governing by Tenderness by Jerome C. Foss

The Politics of Twin Peaks edited by Amanda DiPaolo and James Clark Gillies

AIDS-Trauma and Politics: American Literature and the Search for a Witness by Aimee Pozorski

Baudelaire Contra Benjamin: A Critique of Politicized Aesthetics and Cultural Marxism by Beibei Guan and Wayne Cristaudo

Updike and Politics: New Considerations edited by Matthew Shipe and Scott Dill

Lights, Camera, Execution!: Cinematic Portrayals of Capital Punishment by Helen J. Knowles, Bruce E. Altschuler, and Jaclyn Schildkraut

Possibility's Parents: Stories at the End of Liberalism by Margaret Seyford Hrezo and Nicolas Pappas

Game of Thrones and the Theories of International Relations by Ñusta Carranza Ko and Laura D. Young

Age of Anxiety: Meaning, Identity, and Politics in 21st-Century Film and Literature by Anthony M. Wachs and Jon D. Schaff

Published by Lexington Books
An imprint of The Rowman & Littlefield Publishing Group, Inc.
4501 Forbes Boulevard, Suite 200, Lanham, Maryland 20706
www.rowman.com

6 Tinworth Street, London SE11 5AL, United Kingdom

British Library Cataloguing in Publication Information Available

The hardback edition of this book was previously catalogued by the Library of Congress as follows:

Library of Congress Cataloging-in-Publication Data Available

ISBN: 978-1-4985-7518-8 (cloth) ISBN:
978-1-4985-7520-1 (pbk.) ISBN:
978-1-4985-7519-5 (electronic)

Age of Anxiety

Meaning, Identity, and Politics in 21st-Century Film and Literature

Anthony M. Wachs and Jon D. Schaff

LEXINGTON BOOKS

Lanham • Boulder • New York • London

Contents

Contents

political happenings of the day are reported next to, and oftentimes with less visual space, than trivial celebrity gossip and cat videos. Anxiety arises by not being able to coherently make sense of the irrelevant information that one can do nothing about, but one is ironically expected to take seriously as a responsible citizen, productive worker, and friendly neighbor. However, this cause of anxiety is masked by the fact that the information is often entertaining and is the substance of what others are talking about. One must have a "hot take" on the day's trending story in order to remain "relevant" and take part in what passes for public discussion.

When we shift our attention to the phenomenological—or qualitative personal experience—we will find that we are more anxious, busy, and distracted than ever before.[10] A neurotic anxiety defines our age, for we are disconnected from reality, and this is unable to coherently order and make sense of our lives.[11] At its worst, we are being socially engineered to care less about those physically close.[12] We are manufacturing a society of distracted multitaskers, which is a fragmented perspective akin to the experience of animals in the wild.[13] Distracted, we are robbed of real freedom as consent is manufactured within an increasingly "cheap democracy."[14] The possibility of coherently making sense of reality in this era of fragmented attention is becoming more and more difficult, for what is at stake is the question of what it means to be human.[15] However, there are distinct intellectual challenges to answering this question within the status quo. Specifically, the philosophical roots of the Age of Anxiety predispose members of society to uncritically reject solutions to the problem, because those solutions are opposed to the presumed truths, or first principles, of the age.

Adding to the problem is the fact that modern universities have all but abandoned their mission to teach wisdom and coherence in the minds of students. Knowledge itself has become extremely fragmented as the result of the knowledge explosion within the arts and sciences during the twentieth century.[16] Specialization within the sciences, the humanities, and the marketplace has fragmented the collective worldview, in that each of the various disciplines has its own truths and languages.[17] Students typically encounter knowledge in a hodgepodge manner, with no institutional encouragement to find a unifying purpose in their education. The general education package at most universities allows for numerous options with little to no direction as to why a student might choose one course rather than another. A university might require students take a certain number of credits in the humanities, but the number of courses that fulfill this requirement is so vast that it is difficult to ascertain what the humanities requirement actually accomplishes.[18] It is not unusual for a student to be able to graduate from a university without taking courses in history, literature, or philosophy. Certainly most American college students can easily graduate having read not a single line of Plato,

The Age of Anxiety, then, is not merely some philosophical construct drawn up by academics. It manifests itself in American society today. The burning question is why is it that the people who are so wealthy, so comfortable, so materially well provided for are so miserable, to use Eberstadt's term. There is a profound sense that despite our material prosperity there is something missing. What advanced societies may be experiencing is, in fact, the pathologies of affluence. With mere survival long since secured, the quest now is for more meaningful existence. In a society where simply surviving cannot be taken for granted, even small decisions become fraught with meaning as life or death may hinge on planting decisions, what kind of clothes you wear, a decision to travel a significant distance. In short, life of generalized poverty makes so many decisions meaningful by necessity. In an age of affluence, meaning must be generated. There is less pressing need for the community, the discipline, the religious faith that typify poor societies who must have these goods in order to fight life's battles. In one of life's paradoxes, that which makes life most meaningful (community, family, faith, work) are most needed when we are poorest. Thus, it may be inevitable that a wealthy people, finding less material need for these bulwark institutions of society, ends up anxious in its affluence. Life is more comfortable, but less significant. And we intuitively know it.

In order to analyze this phenomenon, we will first examine the certain sources of anxiety in our affluent society, including the state of information and knowledge in the public discourse. Then, we will look to the historical and philosophical origins of the anxiety, and by way of contrast to our current age, provide aspects of pre-modern life that made it worth living. Finally, we will show how these changes directly relate to the conditions of life within the Age of Anxiety.

FRAGMENTATION IN THE AGE OF ANXIETY

Anxiety typifies the modern experience as the fragmentation of a variety of once-stable narratives leaves individuals with little guidance as to how they might lead a meaningful life. One source of anxiety is the public discourse promoted by and maintained within the media. American public discourse is dominated by trivial information that is largely disconnected from meaningful social or political action.[9] Matters of public discussion are far removed and largely disconnected from the choices that make up one's daily life. Those matters that seem to be important and meaningful are in reality not matters that one can do anything about. Additionally, without a means to distinguish and judge the importance of information, the world becomes increasingly incoherent. This can be seen on any news website in which the

Preface

This book grows out of scholarship by numerous authors that has raised awareness of the existential, sociopsychological, and sociopolitical problems produced by modern understandings of the human person. The book draws upon the various works of Aristotle, Alexis de Tocqueville, Allan Bloom, Marshall McLuhan, Neil Postman, Francis Fukuyama, Alasdair MacIntyre, Charles Taylor, Wendell Berry, Sherry Turkle, Joseph Pieper, Walker Percy, Matthew Crawford, Douglas Rushkoff, C. S. Lewis, Thomas de Zengotita, and Nicholas Carr in order to show how the self has been displaced from its natural habitat of the local community and how the human person and society as a whole are affected by this displacement. These themes have manifested in the popular culture within both literature and film. By analyzing these artifacts, we intend to further develop understanding of the problem and provide potential solutions to the problem.

Since the Enlightenment, the human person has been predominantly understood as an autonomous individual or subject that ought to be free of external restraints and controls in its pursuit of happiness and meaning in life. This quest of self-fulfillment contains the notion that nature has no essential meaning and is simply material to be used for the convenience of the creative self. This approach has only become more dominant with the rise of postmodern critiques of modernism. The late Peter Lawler argued that postmodernism, as normally understood, is really hyper-modernism.[1] Communities once were the source of meaning and purpose within human existence, but the connection between the person and authoritative traditions is on the verge of complete dissolution. The vision of an autonomous self has evolved into a radical individualism that threatens not only communal life but also the individual self. We are living in an unparalleled historical moment in which the individual is thought to have the ability and, more importantly, the supreme right to define and create one's very self without reference to, and at the expense of, the greater sociopolitical-economic environment and communities to which one belongs. This freedom appeared to be and is promised to be absolute. In a very real sense, the self is thought to be both sovereign and sacred.

However, this has left the human person existentially paralyzed or incapable of living with a sense of meaningful purpose. Many feel existentially numb, skeptical of the inherent value of human life, and morally nauseous, to use Sartre's imagery. It is simply untrue that humans can "self-create" apart from a tradition or narrative. Selves, to use Charles Taylor's analysis, are by nature situated within the world, history, and local communities. The promise of finding fulfillment and happiness within an increasingly globalized society is showing itself to be an illusion. Americans live in one of the most affluent and technologically advanced societies, and yet it is one of the most heavily medicated societies in the world. Perceiving this void and the resulting discontent in the human experience, multinational corporations have swooped in to take advantage of this situation, stunting the human capacity of meaning-making through multimillion-dollar marketing, advertising, and branding campaigns directed at tying identity to consumption. Instead of deriving one's sense of purpose and identity from one's role and place within a community, the consumer has been deceived into thinking that their identity and purpose can be purchased through the meaning represented by the conspicuous consumption of brands. This line of thought was popularized in David Fincher's *Fight Club* when the Narrator asks, "What type of dining room set defines me as a person?"[2]

The authority of traditional, sociocultural institutions, which provided meaning, purpose, and direction to human life, has been undermined, and their influence in society has greatly diminished. Building upon these twentieth-century developments, the twenty-first century has begun with the default position that authority and power are identical and are derived from the majority. This is evident in the authority of consumption that rules the marketplace. The marketplace has no understanding of a human *telos* beyond the unlimited ability to consume.[3] Freedom of choice masks itself as meaningful, but without a sense of "enough" or satisfaction, the unrestricted fulfillment of desire leaves the person empty and wanting more. As we go through this "great disruption," which is done in the name of liberation and freedom, the self is being enslaved.[4] We must begin to ask whether we are free to choose or free to live within boundaries established by communities in which we live. To use William Cavanaugh's distinction, are we Augustinian selves who find freedom in conformity to a truth outside the self or are we Friedmanesque (as in Milton Friedman) selves who find freedom in unencumbered choice?[5]

The same phenomenon manifests itself in politics. A globalized world has undermined the meaning of local, state, and even national associations. The dislocation caused by a global marketplace has allowed multinational corporations to profit without being dedicated to, or responsible for, any particular place. More nefariously, corporations are programmed to extract wealth from local communities.[6] The oxymoronic "global citizen," often residing in a "global city," has more in common with other global citizens residing in other global cities around the world than with his fellow national citizens. This would not be an issue if it were not for the fact that public policy, especially in America, has been by, of, and for "the elite global citizen" rather than the "placed individual" who lacks the means, the ability, and the desire to uproot him or herself to pursue true cosmopolitanism. This change is witnessed by the admonishing of out-of-work coal miners to "learn to code" by members of the corporate media, an admonition that backfired when those journalists were told to "learn to code" during layoffs of early 2019. The Trump presidency, Brexit, and hyper-nationalization in Eastern Europe and places such as Scotland and Catalonian Spain are all extreme responses to the lack of localized, authoritative traditions to meaningfully guide human experience within a global world. In Donald Trump's infelicitous yet possibly true words, "A country is a country." To be American, Scottish, Polish, etc., must mean something. The decline of that meaning and its replacement by a consumer-self leaves many unsatisfied. In addition, the dislocation caused by the dynamism of hyper-globalization redounds to the benefit of the cosmopolitan self, while literally leaving others dislocated and behind. The rise of nationalism, or even localism, is a response to these pathologies.

Adding to the experience of angst and social instability, the rapid pace of technological development is driving an unprecedented faith in the malleability of human nature and, concomitantly, doubt in the existence of personness. Advances in neuroscience have left scientists to conclude that the self and consciousness are illusions created by the biochemical secretions of one's brain and the firing off of neurons. One's choices are not made by a will, whether it is free or bound, but rather are determined by neurochemicals and one's socioeconomic conditions. Additionally, many within the humanities have likewise undermined the human experience through the postmodern deconstruction of personness, the postulation of a self that is inherently fragmented, bodies with language. With both the sciences and the humanities rejecting personness as having objective existence, many are left without satisfactory answers to questions such as, "Who are we?" and "What makes us human?" Maybe we would be better off if our automated technologies and artificial intelligences would guide our daily choices, such as the most efficient route to work (Google Maps) or what time to wake up, based upon a Fitbit tracking one's sleep habits. Essentially, people are naturally gravitating toward allowing the self to be socially engineered. This development is being driven by a scientism that is looking forward to the merging of man and machine, an event called "the singularity" by futurists. This quasi-religious position is dangerous for, contrary to Sam Harris's thinking, science cannot provide the moral criteria necessary for true human progress.[7]

Humans by nature are social beings, and in the past that has largely meant being situated within local communities that contain and are defined by authoritative cultural traditions. With the rise of large nation-states, multinational corporations, and global NGOs, localized meaning-making is increasingly obsolesced. As such, human beings need to find meaning in alternative forms of communities, such as professional disciplines, that provide members with a sense of meaning. Along these lines, Alasdair MacIntyre's term for submitting oneself to a discipline is "practice." Developing a practice is what helps create a real, authentic self in opposition to a purchased self. The practice puts the individual into conversation with others within a community.[8] Contemporary philosopher Matthew Crawford makes a similar argument in his defense of craft and manual labor.[9] The submission to the discipline of organ making, to use one of Crawford's examples, is actually more meaningful and freeing than the notion of the self "liberated" from all external influences.[10]

We are looking at pieces of literature and films that speak to our age of anxiety that resulted from the decline of authorities and narratives that enabled an individual to feel a part of something and gave meaning to his life. Each chapter looks at paradigmatic exemplars from the popular culture. Each example is chosen because of its popularity and influence in the culture, and each relates to important aspects of the Age of Anxiety. Using Charles Taylor's terminology, we live in a social imaginary that has been disenchanted. That social imaginary is given witness in our popular culture, both literary and film. Using literature and film, this book both diagnoses the causes of the flatness of the late modern self as well as providing insight into how a better, more meaningful life can arise out of the debris of our disenchanted condition.

Popular culture often serves as a window into society's unconscious. The aspirations and fears of the people manifest themselves in art. In the modern age that means not just high art but art on a popular level, i.e., pop culture. The kind of stories people tell one another, the kind of stories that capture the public's imagination, tells us much about what is most important to a people. Popular culture in many ways manifests the anxiety of our age. We can use particular artifacts of popular culture to both diagnose and perhaps provide remedy for our ailments. Typically, academic study of popular culture is quite shallow, mirroring the crude ideological approach that is sadly all too typical of the modern academy. Popular culture studies often simply take an artifact, interpret it through a trendy ideological lens, culminating in a trite conclusion. This method is insufficient. If the purpose of studying popular culture is to gain a view of the collective mind, then the best interpretive structure is not through contemporary ideology, but through analyzing popular culture through the lens of the history of ideas. Popular culture by definition exists in the now, itself a manifestation of popular prejudices. To interpret popular culture via trendy ideology is to enter into a feedback loop. We best understand our times by getting outside our times, much as often the best way to understand one's country is by travelling elsewhere. Today the past is the true undiscovered country. We aim to place various artifacts of today's popular culture both within the history of ideas and by assessing popular culture through more contemporary thinkers who challenge the academy's ideological prejudices. Thus, we interpret pop culture using Aristotle, Thomas Aquinas, John Locke, Jean-Jacques Rousseau, and Alexis de Tocqueville, among other great thinkers. Among contemporary writers we assess pop culture within the philosophy of iconoclastic thinkers such as Charles Taylor, Alasdair MacIntyre, Wendell Berry, and Matthew Crawford. Using this method, we hope to create a dialogue between past and present and between our times and those who challenge the prejudices of our times.

INTERDISCIPLINARITY OF POLITICAL SCIENCE AND COMMUNICATION

At the outset of this project, the authors would like to situate this work in relation to their respective academic disciplines, outline the relationship between those disciplines, and discuss popular understandings of what those disciplines study. Of particular relevance to this project, both authors take a humanistic approach to the studies of communication and political science, which is in contrast to the social scientific narratives and methods that are predominant within both fields of studies. Both political science and communication are stereotyped not only in the minds of non-academics but also by academics in other disciplines. In terms of political science, the study is typecast as the social scientific study of polling and the historical and contemporary study of documents such as the Constitution. Indeed, in the basic Political Science 100 course, it is often taught that political science is the study of who gets what, how, when, and where. Similarly, communication is often confused with communications, with an "s," in that it is confused with the study of the transmission of information and the technologies that make this possible. In effect, communication studies messages and messaging. Given these norms, as well as the popular conceptions of these disciplines, many may wonder how it is that a political scientist and a communication scholar can work in an interdisciplinary fashion beyond the social scientific study of political communication.

In contrast to the normative forms of study and the stereotypes based upon those norms and conventions, the studies of communication and political science have a great deal in common, especially when approached from a humanistic perspective. In this sense, both studies investigate how human beings interact with one another, especially through the media of speech, law, and society. Indeed, it may be helpful to understand rhetoric as the medium that provides a common ground for political science and communication. In the Aristotelian schema, "politics" was the highest art, because it was the art of living justly in the *polis*, and was made up of ethics, rhetoric, and dialectic. Rhetoric, as the art of eloquent influence, was inherently political, and politics were inherently rhetorical in nature. Far from simply connecting used car salesmen and politicians in deceptive persuasive practices, rhetorical education was traditionally designed to produce good people who would dedicate themselves to serving and leading the public. This common ground and shared concern for the common good links these two disciplines and their distinct ways of approaching the world. These disciplines naturally function together to fruitfully assess the problems of the current historical moment and offer solutions to those problems. Along these lines, true political science "deals with questions that concern everyone and that everyone asks" and differentiates its answers from mere opinion because of the systematic analysis utilized to demonstrate truth.[11]

NOTES

1. Peter Augustine Lawler, *Postmodernism Rightly Understood: The Return to Realism in American Thought* (Lanham, MD: Rowman & Littlefield Publishers, 1999).

2. *Fight Club*, directed by David Fincher, written by Jim Uhls (Los Angeles, CA: 20th Century Fox, 1999).

3. *Telos* is a Greek term that is used in reference to a thing's purpose or essence. It is philosophically and metaphysically used in terms of the essential state of perfection of all categories of beings. In terms of classical Aristotelian and Thomist metaphysics, the human telos is that of happiness such that all human action is oriented toward happiness.

4. Francis Fukuyama, *The Great Disruption: Human Nature and the Reconstitution of Social Order* (New York: Free Press, 1999).

5. William Cavanaugh, *Being Consumed: Economics and Christian Desire*, (Grand Rapids: Wm. B. Eerdmans, 2008).

6. Douglas Rushkoff, *Throwing Rocks at the Google Bus: How Growth Became the Enemy of Prosperity*, (New York: Portfolio, 2016), 68–103.

7. Sam Harris, *The Moral Landscape: How Science Can Determine Human Values*, (New York: Free Press, 2010).

8. Alasdair MacIntyre, *After Virtue: A Study in Moral Theory*, 3rd ed. (Notre Dame: University of Notre Dame, 2007).

9. Matthew B. Crawford, *Shop Class as Soulcraft: An Inquiry into the Value of Work* (New York: Penguin, 2009).

10. Matthew B. Crawford, *The World Beyond Your Head: On Becoming an Individual in an Age of Distraction* (New York: Farrar, Straus and Giroux, 2015), 209–246.

11. Eric Voegelin, *Science, Politics, and Gnosticism: Two Essays* (New York: Regnery Publishing, 1968), 10–12 and 14.

Acknowledgments

There are several people Dr. Wachs and Dr. Schaff would like to acknowledge at the outset of this project. To begin with, we would like to thank Fiona K. (Smith) Buck, Lindsey Laverty, and Natalia Wohar for their work as Dr. Wachs' research assistants. The work that they performed collecting sources, citing sources, indexing, and editing was invaluable to both of us. We would like to thank Lee Trepanier for the invitation to publish in this series from Lexington. Additionally, Dr. Wachs would like to thank the Wimmer Family Foundation at Duquesne University. He was awarded a grant from this foundation that paid Fiona to work on this project. Without that grant, Dr. Wachs' portion of this project would not have been completed within our time constraints. Dr. Schaff wishes to thank Dr. Peter Ramey and Fr. Tom Anderson who read the manuscript and offered valuable critiques. Dr. Kristi Brownfield directed him toward some secondary literature on zombies. Also, the College of Arts and Sciences at Northern State under Dean Joshua Hagen generously gave him a course release to help complete this project. Additionally, they would like to thank their family members for their patience with them throughout the writing of this project.

Chapter 1

Anxieties of the Autonomous Self

In 1947, W. H. Auden published his long-form poem, *The Age of Anxiety: A Baroque Eclogue*. In this poem, Auden ponders the state of the Western soul in light of the catastrophe of the Second World War. Amidst victory and a looming prosperity, the four individuals who carry the imagery of the poem are in various ways unsatisfied by their condition, reflecting on the horror of the war not as an exception to the modern condition, but indicative of it. Much like the fiction of Flannery O'Connor, Auden's poem constitutes a yearning for grace in a cold, materialistic, and violent world. The current historical moment is "the Age of Anxiety" because at the heart of modern existence is an anxiety produced by the uncertainty of an incoherent individualism situated within a constantly changing environment. This book brings together the cacophony of scholarly voices that have attempted to diagnose the ills of our age. This scholarly work is unique in both its bringing together of these voices as well as its offering of paradigmatic examples to show how the anxiety of the age has manifested within the popular culture.

The twenty-first century represents a triumph in the world's ability to provide materially for an ever-growing population. The new millennium has seen a precipitous decline in hunger, poverty, infant mortality, and disease, while life expectancy continues to increase worldwide, continuing gains made late in the twentieth century.[1] Technological and scientific advancements have undeniably transformed the material aspects of life for the better. In this sense, we are absolutely not proposing a "return to the past." People are living longer, more affluent lives than ever before, but as exciting as it is to be able to afford the "next big thing" every year, the spectacle of the advancements in science and technology easily distracts us from the negative effects of progress. Most people are able to adapt quickly to new technologies, but when done without prudence or practical wisdom, serious problems arise, because the unreflective embrace of technology undermines the meaningful dimensions of human life and culture.[2] Marshall McLuhan likened the experience of making sense of reality in the midst of vast and rapid cultural and technological changes to Edgar Allan Poe's poem, *A Descent into the Maelstrom*: We are left clutching driftwood that barely keeps us afloat in the raging sea of change. Prudence dictates a middle ground between a reactionary story of decline and the more predominant view of the day, a naïve faith in progress.

In the American context, at least, these material gains have been coupled with less edifying trends. While economic trends may be improving, as of 2016, American work rates are the lowest in over a generation and near a postwar low. What economic gains America has experienced, and these have been modest due to slow economic growth, have been disproportionally distributed to a select few. "In our era of no more than indifferent economic growth," writes Nicholas Eberstadt, "21st-century America has somehow managed to produce markedly more wealth for its wealthholders even as it provided markedly less work for its workers."[3] Life expectancy for lower class whites has declined, "with most of the rise in death rates . . . accounted for by suicides, chronic liver cirrhosis, and poisonings (including drug overdoses)."[4] The decline in work has coincided with the opioid epidemic. In 2013, more Americans died of drug overdoses than by guns and traffic accidents. Half of all men who have dropped out of the workforce take painkillers on a daily basis, a number amounting to seven million men.[5] Many locations in America have seen a near complete collapse of community, with marriage and church attendance levels, for example, in free fall. As Tim Carney puts it, drawing from sociologist Robert Nisbet, people in these areas meet a classic definition of alienation, namely they are "individuals who not only are without community but fail to see the draw of community anymore."[6]

A similar phenomenon manifests itself among the nation's young people. Jean M. Twenge asks whether "smartphones have destroyed a generation" and has bountiful data that suggests an affirmative answer. Since the introduction of the iPhone in 2007, rates of teenagers getting jobs, learning to drive, and just "hanging out" have deteriorated. Meanwhile, teen loneliness and depression have skyrocketed. From 2012 to 2015, "depressive symptoms" in boys increased 21 percent, in girls 50 percent. Not surprisingly, then, the suicide rates for young people are climbing, with teen suicides outnumbering teen homicides in 2011 for the first time in a generation. Girls have been especially hard hit, with three times as many twelve to fourteen girls attempting suicide in 2015 as in 2007. Twenge concludes, "It's not an exaggeration to describe iGen as being on the brink of the worst mental-health crisis in decades."[7] A study released in early 2019 reported that "rates of major depressive episodes in the last year jumped 52 percent among adolescents aged 12 to 17 . . . and 63 percent among young adults aged 18 to 25."[8]

Aristotle, Dante, Shakespeare, or even Thomas Jefferson. The university signals through its curriculum that the human person is fragmented with the student's individual choice rather than an idea of the good of the student driving the curriculum. Beyond the basic English composition courses, there is seldom any course that all students are required to take. Thus, the university is more accurately termed the multiversity. Individual minds are affected by this collective fragmentation, in that it is impossible for a person to consistently maintain these perspectives together.[19] This fragmentation alters ordinary decision making because it threatens one's ability to distinguish between levels of significance and importance. The ability to judge through a coherent value system is essential for proper decision making, because without it, choice making is rendered absurd.[20] On a phenomenological level, when one's world is fragmented, inconsistent, and without an anchor, one's life becomes a random set of choices that leads to nowhere.[21] Without a collective orientation to make sense of reality, depression and burnout are the products of life without constraint upon the self.[22]

Beyond the knowledge explosion of the twentieth and twenty-first centuries, globalization contributes to the fragmentation of the mind because of the increasing pluralism of the multicultural environment. The intermingling and interaction between peoples from wide varieties of cultures is a fact of existence within the "global village." However, "multiculturalism" as an ideology, rather than the simple recognition of the existence of cultural diversity within society, protects and promotes a neutral and pluralistic space for interaction, but often ignores and dismisses the native culture for the sake of "the Other." When deconstructed as an ideology, the supposed diversity of multiculturalism at its worst subjects cultures and individuals to dying normativity of relativistic personal preferences, and for this reason, multiculturalism can be considered "post-cultural or anti-cultural," for it trivializes culture by turning it into a collection of arbitrary social conventions.[23] As such, the rise of identity politics can be read as an attempt to reconstruct community based on certain distinctive characteristics. Unlike in Christianity, which proclaims "there is neither Jew nor Greek . . . there is neither male nor female" (Gal 3:28), for there is a deeper identity as part of the Body of Christ, identity politics makes these distinctions fundamental to one's identity and experience of reality. Politics of this sort posits a kind of dyadic, or causal, relationship between certain characteristics (e.g., race, gender identity, sexual orientation) and what one should believe and how one should act, such that one's politics are determined by one's identity. People that do not fit the identity narrative, such as women, persons of color, or homosexuals that vote Republican, are dehumanized as suffering from false consciousness.

The existence of multiculturalism, nevertheless, is not inherently unique to our age, for there have been many historical eras of great intercultural interaction. The primary difference between these multicultural moments and ours is that modern peoples are taught to function from and understand themselves through this naïve cultural relativism. However, in order to understand ourselves, as well as others, we must recognize the cultural ground of worldviews, and a recognition that the historical and cultural context of thought does not imprison one within one's context.[24] In the modern context that favors a cosmopolitan mindset over that of the patriotic, an encounter with other cultures, with other ways of life, is meant only to undermine attachment to one's own culture, which must always be seen as contingent. To be attached to a place, a culture, and a tradition is to give up one's autonomy, the fundamental modern commitment. Thus, such attachments must be discouraged, especially through a pedagogical commitment to "diversity."[25]

Intellectual fragmentation has played out within academic circles as an inability to define the current historical moment and a failure to build consensus around the definitions that have been postulated. The predominant formulation of our time is that it is an age of postmodernism. However, "postmodern" is an ambiguous term for it simply defines the age as coming after the clearly delineated age of modernism, and as such, numerous definitions of this term abound. Most famously, Jean-François Lyotard defined postmodernity as a "crisis of narratives" that followed "the transformations which, since the end of the nineteenth century, have altered the game rules for science, literature, and the arts."[26] In other words, the term represents the notion that a universal understanding of the "good" is no longer presupposed by others in our communities.[27] Peter Lawler has noted, what passes as postmodernism can actually be considered to be *hyper*modernism, because the typical markers of liberal Enlightenment rationality, that is, modernism, have actually been pushed to their extremes within our current culture.[28] Essentially, scholars do not even agree whether we are in a moment of culmination for modernism or one which has left modernism behind.

Those concerned with matters of technology, science, and evolution, however, have called the current age posthuman, in that we have entered an age that is transcending the categories of humanism that were developed during the grand renaissance and beyond. Additionally, it is considered posthuman because we are, as a species, evolving into something other than *Homo Sapiens*. As posthumanists would have it, we are increasingly merging with our technologies and evolving into cyborgs. As farfetched as it may seem, the perspective is grounded in the fact that the exponentially quickening pace of technological advancement is radically altering human existence. The most devout adherents to this idea believe that the complete merger of humans and machines, that is, the singularity, will result in a new age of enlightenment and prosperity. This move is not without its own set of controversies, in that others deny the concept of posthumanism in favor of transhumanism.[29]

However, both posthumanism and transhumanism function rhetorically as scientific religions, in that they involve "a secular retelling of the Christian rapture, and some of its true believers foresee it as happening within the lifetime of *many who are alive today*, just as the early Christians believed in an impending judgement day."[30] The propagandists of the singularity, such as Ray Kurzweil and Kevin Kelly, can be said to be propagating the faith system of evangelical scientism.

Though there are unique cultural centers around the world, globalization is creating an environment in which the unique cultures of the world are being transformed into a technological and scientific neo-Liberal "Global Ecumene."[31] The uncontrolled spread and development of technology across the globe threatens human cultures for the intellectual and cultural aspects of human relationships that give human existence meaning.[32] Otherness is being replaced by "difference," and the increasing uniformity of culture is developing into a violent self-exploitation to overproduce, overachieve, and overcommunicate.[33] In other words, the Western secularism that is overtaking the globe is defined less by diversity than by conformity to its abstract standards of individualism.

Media, education, globalization, and technology all contribute to the fragmenting of the self and the anxiety that accompanies that fragmentation. These differing perspectives and the lack of consensus concerning the nature of our era speak to the fact that there is little to no strong cultural narrative to provide orientation and meaning to the current historical moment. However, what these varying perspectives have in common is that they are all related to problems of understanding the self, society, and the relationship between the two within the current historical moment. In the simplest of terms, people lack a given sense of purpose and meaning within their lives. This existential conundrum is informed by a worldview and culture that has grown throughout time. In order to understand the Age of Anxiety, we must look back to its historical and philosophical origins.

ORIGINS OF THE AGE OF ANXIETY

The neo-liberal secular "Global Ecumene" has its origin in the ancient Greek's endeavor to systematically study the world through reasoning in order to establish axiomatic principles including a degree of autonomy from authoritative social institutions such as religion.[34] The varying moments of Western history were unified, generally speaking, through ancient thought and medieval Christianity's attempt to align its faith to Greek philosophical reasoning.[35] Though science and religion were distinct, they were not inherently separable.[36] The Western mind was unified until the modern era by the doctrine of the Logos, which maintained that Logos—mind, reason, speech, or meaning—permeated reality, including matter, and that Logos defined the rational character of existence. In fact, the liberal arts tradition—founded upon the trivium, or three ways of studying Logos—provided intellectual continuity of thought throughout the diversity of almost 1,500 years of cultural change.[37]

However, this systematic view of faith and reason began a process of dissolution, with the Reformation's paradigm of *sola fide* and *sola scriptura*, and was fully dissolved by the successes of the scientific revolution, which were driven by invention and improvement of technologies of enhancing human perception such as the clock (enhancing our measurement of time) and the telescope and microscope (enhancing our sense of sight), for instance.[38] As science and technologies progressed, modern philosophies explicitly posited themselves as a distinct break from the past.[39] Developments culminating in the Enlightenment would concomitantly found knowledge upon new discoveries and sever the relationship with traditional forms of knowledge. Knowledge was no longer conservatively grounded upon the cultural wisdom handed down within the culture's grammar, but rather was progressively reinvented in the form of scientific discovery. One sees this manifested in Machiavelli's "new orders and modes," Descartes' philosophy of doubt, Hobbes' explicit rejection of Aristotelian and Scholastic thought, and John Stuart Mill's assertion that custom despotically limits liberty and progress.[40]

The wide gap that separates the two worldviews is represented by the idea that it was almost impossible to be an atheist before 1500, while today belief in God is makes one apparently naïve.[41] Consequently, many readers may find the discussion of faith and reason to be antiquated, but the privatization and dismissal of matters of faith has epistemological consequences that are not limited to questions of God's existence or the afterlife.[42] Though many people today see the movement away from the ancient and medieval worldview as an inherently good development on account of the prevailing "current year" morality, technological progress should not be confused with moral progress.[43] In effect, the advocates of "current year" morality need to check their biased assumptions and historicist bigotry. By examining historical and philosophical developments, we can problematize these assumptions while hopefully avoiding the tendency to romanticize the past as a golden age.

The premodern world was defined by three characteristics that helped to protect and promote meaningful and purposeful human flourishing. First, there was an assumed natural order to the world itself and that this order spoke of and contained the message of a Creator.[44] This was, as noted above, the doctrine of the Logos that was a foundational metaphysical assumption of Western philosophy. Second, society generally reflected this natural order, and as such, it implicitly—and often explicitly—reified belief in the existence of an objectively meaningful reality.[45] Third, the world in which one was embedded was believed to be and experienced as "an 'enchanted' world."[46] In other words, supernatural, nonmaterial phenomena were considered to be perceivable by individuals situated within this sociocultural-intellectual environment. The development of the modern, secular age is not merely a story of these characteristics being lost but rather contains a shift in the understanding of the world, society, and the individual. In the final analysis, a shift in understanding the human *telos* took place: whereas previously, human nature—and hence happiness—was oriented toward living in accord with the natural and divinely created order, now it outright denied that a *telos* actually existed. The rest of this chapter tells the story of how the shift took place. Each development that leads to the Age of Anxiety contains a stasis point that can be legitimately debated from either side. Though society has evolved presuming one side of the debate to be true, the truth is not determined by vote or time. We point toward these stasis points because alternatives to the dominate presumptions can be offered and judged upon their own merit.

Rise of Nominalism and the Disenchantment of the Cosmos

The current age, with its shift in understanding of fullness, is better defined by its decadence rather than a sense of maturity. This decadence, and its resulting anxiety, did not begin in the twentieth century but rather has roots within nominalism being popularized over realism during intellectual debates of the thirteenth century.[47] It is the defeat of realism by nominalism, which denies the objective reality of universals, that most significantly contributes to the movement into modernity and the relativism affecting the current historical moment.[48] The difference between the ancient world and the modern is that in the debate between realism and nominalism, to which Plato responded in his *Cratylus*, the realists intellectually dominated the ancient and medieval eras, whereas the nominalists have dominated the modern mind since the defeat of the realists at the end of the medieval era.[49] The difference between the realists and nominalists lies within the questions of where meaning lies and how it can be known: The realists believed that the natural order can only be coherently maintained by some source of order, that is, God, whereas the nominalists denied that nature has an objective meaning that can be discovered by reason.[50] The nominalists held a mind-centered view in which meaning exists in the human mind and that concepts are meaningful only in the degree that they effect one's existence.[51] Realism was teleological, in that it postulated that a Creator-God willed and defined the proper goods and natures of all beings and that this order could not be other than it was, because the goods were natural and reasonable. This was rejected by the nominalists, because they thought this limited the sovereignty and power of God.[52] It ought to be noted that even though the realist position aligns to an orthodox understanding of God, one need not be a Christian to accept the philosophical position. Likewise, in understanding the philosophical consequences of nominalism, heterodox Christians ought not be surprised where the nominalist position leads.

In the nominalism of that time, God was considered a "the super-agent" who was free from any objective moral law to make reality as He sought fit according to His own purposes, and this means that as His creations we must relate to the rest of creation through His autonomous purposes and not through the patterns that they reveal through reason.[53] Brad Gregory argues, "According to Aquinas, God in metaphysical terms was, incomprehensibly, *esse*—not a being but the sheer act of to-be, in which all creatures participated insofar as they existed and through which all creation was mysteriously sustained. In Occamist nominalism, by contrast, insofar as God existed, 'God' had to denote some *thing*, some discrete real entity, an *ens*."[54] In other words, for God not to be limited by a moral order extrinsic to Himself, he had to be free to define the moral order however He wanted. In effect, God could have created a reality in which torturing and killing cats is morally good. Though this would allow God to be free and unrestrained in His omnipotence, the realists could not accept this because it would render Him capricious and not inherently good. Though the nominalists believed in God, their ideas and the immanentism[55] that resulted from nominalism logically yield modern existentialism and nihilism because denying the objective reality of universals inherently involves denying "everything transcending experience."[56] Essentially, if values, such as justice, goodness, and beauty, exist only in the mind with no rational basis, then they are nothing more than arbitrary social conventions that make no definitive demands of individuals. In effect, law would no longer have moral weight or credence through its connection to justice because justice would now be defined by whoever has the most power. As will be shown below, questions concerning the nature of truth, goodness, and justice have been replaced exclusively by the concern for power in the Age of Anxiety.

The next logical steps of intellectual development of the modern worldview included a change in the understanding of nature itself. Nature began to be understood as a mechanism that was meaningless material.[57] In contrast to this materialism, the premodern worldview took for granted that meaning resided in both mind and matter.[58] Things of this world could point beyond themselves to a deeper reality. The material world was seen as a book that contained a message that was waiting to be read. The world was experienced as "enchanted" or sacramental. In other words, the world was experienced as a living, meaningful cosmos rather than a meaningless, mechanical universe.[59] In this epoch, existence was permeated with life while death was an anomaly that demanded explanation—a metaphysics of life—whereas in the modern world, life is an anomaly that demands explanation—a metaphysics of death.[60] The transition from a living cosmos to a mechanical universe was a process that began with Calvin's rejection of Catholic sacramentalism and culminated in Descartes' *cogito ergo sum.*

Furthermore, advances in science and technology contributed to the spread of nominalism. Of all the inventions of the era of modernization, the telescope undermined the realist position for it eviscerated "the moral center of gravity in the West."[61] No longer could Earth be considered the center of the cosmos. Though many Enlightenment thinkers were practicing Christians, the scientific revolution was a significant break not merely because of its advances but also because its "grounding lay undeniably in nominalism."[62] Nominalism enabled the scientific revolution because it disconnected the material world, and the study of it, from any connection to God and theology.[63] The eras of the scientific revolution and the Enlightenment really were transitional moments in history because, although authoritative cultural traditions still held sway upon the culture and its moral orientation, they were now in dialectical tension with science and its driving value of progress.[64] The influence of nominalism, though unintended by its original proponents, was revolutionary for it began a process of cultural change that transformed the West's understanding of the world and one's place within it. Collective institutions providing a sense of meaning and connection to the world of qualitative values could not compete with the progress of science or make demands limiting the prerogatives of the modern individual.

Most importantly, this shift in understanding fundamentally separated faith and reason and would eventually inherently privatize matters of faith.[65] Questions about the supernatural were subjectivized and made out to be personal preferences because they could not be empirically, and hence "rationally," examined. One observes this in Locke's claim that "everyone is orthodox to himself" and that ultimately religion is merely an "inward and full persuasion of the mind," an interior disposition that has no external consequences.[66] Similarly, Thomas Jefferson could indifferently opine that "it does me no injury for my neighbour to say there are twenty gods, or no god. It *neither picks my pocket* nor breaks my leg."[67] This would come to its intellectual zenith by the twentieth century, in which all immaterial realities, such as justice, would be subjectivized and relativized. The emerging nominalism and materialism would not be limited to the world itself but was also applied to human beings, who were simply parts of this exclusively material world.[68] In the words of Max Weber, the mastering of material reality through mathematical calculation renders the world disenchanted.[69] This instrumental reasoning was applied back to human beings themselves and society itself, in that human beings and society would be reduced to objects of scientific inquiry.

The shift to nominalism, in addition to altering our orientation toward objects in the world, changed the orientation toward the acting person for previously the realist orientation presupposed that right action could be discovered by studying the essence of things.[70] In effect, the "natural order" was no longer "normative," for meaning and purpose were now considered to be projections of the human mind and not inherent within the perceived order.[71] As such, the economy and the political system were altered in such a manner as to promote forms of "democratic self-rule."[72] Other important intellectual developments flowed from and bolstered these new "social imaginaries." In particular, society increasingly moved from an understanding of a personal God to an impersonal providential deity that set into motion the mechanical order of the universe but does not in any way intervene within the universe.[73] These movements gave way to a "generalized culture of 'authenticity,' or expressive individualism, in which people are encouraged to find their own way, discover their own fulfillment, 'do their own thing.'"[74]

One of the crucial elements of the old world that changed to bring about the modern world was that society was disciplined in a way that never before had been attempted. The Old Catholic social formula was that varying roles played by individuals were different than categorically distinct, but given meaning, because they were performed in complementary relation to, and for, all others.[75] In other words, the particular *telos* of one's life depended upon one's role and place within society, but these boundaries and distinctions broke down during the Reformation. There was no longer a need for the distinction between a religious class and a lay class because all were now called to reform their lives on a personal journey of holiness. Whereas holiness may have had a degree of diversity in the medieval era, the holy life would become universalized and standardized.[76] This premodern social world was rejected for the sake of a transformed church that, in a sense, existed within the individual him or herself and his or her relation to the Bible.

From the Porous Self to the Buffered Self

In addition to the changes made in how nature and society were understood, the understanding of "individualism" was significantly altered in modernity, and this shift likewise contributes to the anxiety of our age. The "self" within the premodern "enchanted world" could be considered porous because one's agency as a person and impersonal forces affecting it was not clearly delineated.[77] Not only were the movements of the material world associated with personal forces, such as gods and spirits, but the interior dispositions of the individual person were seen as inspired by these forces as well.[78] However, this was evolving as the individual became detached and disengaged from an increasingly disenchanted world and progressively disciplined and capricious social order. As individuals were increasingly disciplined according to seeming arbitrary conventions, individual experience was seen as meaningful in contrast to the social. This new self was "buffered" for it was able to disengage from one's natural and social surroundings.[79] As such, people were increasingly buffered not only from an enchanted world but also from their social and cultural situations.

The developing individualism during the ages of the Reformation, the Renaissance, and the Enlightenment radically allowed members of society to question the truths of the society and culture. Before these eras, people still philosophically questioned and debated, but they did it from an inherently social stance. The world of the buffered self however was explicitly formulated as individualistic and potentially antisocial. The antisocial nature of modern individualism is largely the product, philosophically, of Kant's understanding of freedom, in which the individual is only truly free in a moral sense when he or she is able to make decisions without any external influences upon their decision making.[80] For instance, the college student that is still dependent upon his or her parents financially is less free than the financially independent student for the parents that subsidize college can wield influence and control over their child's decisions. This understanding of freedom is ultimately antisocial because it seeks to liberate the individual not only from the influence of social institutions such as church and state but eventually even culture as well. The only free individual is the radically autonomous individual. It is this autonomy that has been pushed to its extreme in our era, and is a clear source of anxiety.

The disembedded, autonomous self is typified in the work of John Stuart Mill, a thinker still put forward as a (the!) great defender of liberty, especially "liberty of conscience."[81] Mill advocates in his most famous work, *On Liberty*, for the Harm Principle: "That principle is, that the sole end for which mankind are warranted, individually or collectively, in interfering with the liberty of action of any of their number, is self-protection. That the only purpose for which power can be rightfully exercised over any member of a civilized community, against his will, is to prevent harm to others. His own good, either physical or moral, is not a sufficient warrant."[82] As with Locke and Jefferson on religion, Mill preaches a public indifference to all that does not cause direct harm to anyone else. Mill maintains that whatever harm is caused by falsehood is best alleviated by an open dialogue. In effect, Mill maintained that dialogue was necessary because facts rarely speak for themselves and dialog would help to correct mistakes.[83] An intellectual marketplace provides multiple ideas for individuals to consider. Through such consideration and comparing of competing ideas, the individual is able to find the truth. This is akin to the standard market for consumer goods. For example, consider the marketplace of breakfast cereal; one samples many kinds of cereal and finally commits oneself to the brand that is the best. If one has multiple cereals available and can sample them all, then naturally the best one will win out. Bad breakfast cereals will lose market share and eventually disappear. Similarly, as ideas contest against one another and gain adherents, the best ideas will remain and bad ideas, unable to gain adherents, will simply pass away.

To bring about a free dialogue, Mill wishes to end the tyranny of all received opinion. Mill's deracinated individual is uprooted from all culture and tradition. Mill asserts, "Even despotism does not produce its worst effects, so long as Individuality exists under it; and whatever crushes individuality is despotism, by whatever name it may be called, and whether it professes to be enforcing the will of God or the injunctions of men."[84] In fact, argues Mill, traditions should be intentionally sabotaged. Calling to mind contemporary arguments for transgressive behavior, Mill, seeking to eradicate the tyranny of tradition on the minds of men (what he calls "the despotism of custom"), promotes originality for its own sake:

> The first service which originality has to render them, is that of opening their eyes: which being once fully done, they would have a chance of being themselves original. Meanwhile, recollecting that nothing was ever yet done which some one was not the first to do, and that all good things which exist are the fruits of originality . . . exceptional individuals, instead of being deterred, should be encouraged in acting differently from the mass.[85]

Mill promotes the decultured, autonomous individual as the exemplar of liberty—liberty defined as an absence of constraint and a maximization of the will. Not coincidently the language of capitalism, namely the "marketplace of ideas," is typically used to describe Mill's thought. In this case, the commodities are ideas. Mill, perhaps naively, believes that a free market of ideas, as with a free market of goods, will satisfy people's wants, which Mill equates with the good. Mill does not consider whether some ideas are the intellectual version of the donut: highly attractive but not beneficial or, in the case of ideas, true. To that extent, the "marketplace of ideas" is not a test of truth but a test of popularity, which may or may not be associated with truth.[86] In order for the marketplace to work, there can be no restrictions. Mill's individual comes to the marketplace with no ties, no culture, no traditions. A healthy society is one in which individuals rebel against received wisdom and the institutions that seek to inculcate such wisdom.

Having transitioned to an impersonal social order existing within a disenchanted world, people no longer had a solid sense of purpose imbuing life, and consequently modernity was defined not by blissful liberation but by a growing sense of anxiety.[87] The modern world's immanent rejection of transcendental realities was, in a sense, freeing for the modern individual but concomitantly limiting because it made us blind to values beyond the utilitarian.[88] In effect, one was left with the sense that one was "missing something, cut off from something" or that one was "living behind a screen," buffered from reality. This experience is the malaise of modernity, in that the world is now experienced with an anxious sense that life is "flat, empty, a multiform search for something within, or beyond it, which could not compensate for the meaning lost with transcendence."[89] Most clearly stated, we are anxious today because we see a loss of meaningfulness within our lives.[90]

Further Subjectification and Relativization of Values

As all students of introductory courses in philosophy, literature, and history should know, the excesses of the Enlightenment led to the reaction of Romanticism. The intellectuals of this time saw within private, subjective experience, especially within the arts, a value system that both countered and complemented "to the 'value neutrality' of modern, mathematicised natural science."[91] What was created was a "religion of 'modern' humanity" in which values were explicitly viewed as socially constructed.[92] This development was a natural result of the shift from realism to nominalism and is now explicitly articulated within society. Nominalism truly comes of age during this era, and since this time, the values that function as the very foundation of political state have been undermined by the anarchy of every person being not only "his own priest but his own professor of ethics."[93] Romanticism is the triumph of the unencumbered individual over any concept of nature. Today, the relativistic subjectivism of modernity has taken the form of the solipsistic identity politics of the twenty-first century.

The complementary attitude of neutrality toward values and the belief that values are socially constructed led to the development of secular—or exclusive—humanism. Though the term "secular humanism" has a controversial history for its pejorative sense used by many on the religious right, the term is appropriate for it situates the perspective in opposition to traditional religion and its embracement of man as the measure of all things.[94] In effect, the culture has become forgetful of Being, in that we ignore the holistic for the sake of the fragmented parts that can be controlled by technology.[95]

After Descartes and the split between empiricism and rationalism, the only agreed upon point within modern thought was that reality is defined by subjective experience rather than having a grounding in either nature or revelation understandable through reason and dialogue.[96] In other words, what is consistent is an immanentist, or nominalist, rejection of transcendental realities. In effect, we are cut off from the qualitative dimensions of reality because they are considered to be projections of the mind and subjective illusions. All that is thought to be real is that which can be quantified and measured, which is why, ultimately, the modern scientific worldview culminated in logical positivism.

The new wave of rationalism that took place during the twentieth century was atheistic and effortlessly denied the immanent deity of modernity.[97] The nominalist theory of first wave Enlightenment rationalism naturally gave rise to atheism because its immanent deism is defenseless against the attacks of radical atheism.[98] At the end of the Enlightenment, German philosophy from Hegel to Nietzsche would produce common views defining contemporary atheism.[99] Furthermore, the worsening break from classical and medieval thought, that is, the rejection of the existence of transcendental, universal, and supernatural truths, can be read not as moving to new modes of fullness but rather toward nihilism.[100] Modern existentialism arose partly to fill the void in the account of the qualitative dimensions of human experience and partly as a response to the two brutal World Wars that crushed the optimism present at the outset of the twentieth century.

After the Second World War, traditional Marxism began to lose intellectual credence especially as Nietzsche was rediscovered during the postmodern 1980s.[101] Nihilism began to grow from the Marxist revolution's success in its rejection in the values of traditional cultures and its failure to replace them within new ones.[102] Marxism ceased to be about class warfare and became about liberation of the self. The Marxist project continued not in the fight for class justice but in the fight against social alienation through the overthrowing of sexual, religious, and familial norms. Utilizing the formula of Max Scheler, Augusto del Noce summarizes this shift "as the replacement of the idea of *homo sapiens*, who is characterized by his participation in the *Logos*, by the idea of *homo faber*."[103] Sadly, lacking any real constraint beyond the conventional, late-modern humans have actually become a "hyperactive and hyperneurotic" *animal laborans*—a laboring animal or beast of burden—that has no purpose outside of work and "exploits itself until it burns out."[104]

Along these lines, in his influential book, *After Virtue*, Alasdair MacIntyre argues that the current historic moment is defined by a certain moral incompetence and incoherence.[105] Modern individuals are morally ignorant because they have no means by which they can intelligently judge and predicate good and bad to actions.[106] This incoherence and incompetence is ubiquitous in the Age of Anxiety specifically because at the heart of the human experience is moral questioning and decision making. Without a coherent framework to make competent moral decisions, the human person is made anxious about the purpose of life and the meaningfulness of action. As such, the predominant form of moral reasoning in our society is that of cost-benefit analysis or varying forms of utilitarianism because, beyond the pseudo-objectivity of quantification, we have no public means to rationally discuss moral issues.[107]

Calculation is now identified with and has replaced thinking.[108] This is further witnessed in the triumph of the market imperative wherein economic efficiency and GDP growth are the standards of what makes a "good" economy.

The predominance of utilitarian ethical calculations is the natural result of a culture that views the qualitative aspects of reality, such as moral values, as the product of relative, subjective experience. When the qualitative dimensions of reality are treated as nonrealities, they become mere tastes that hold no significance or authority within rational debate. MacIntyre calls this situation a state of emotivism, which refers to the idea that moral judgments are nothing more than personal preferences based upon feelings.[109] One way to understand emotivism is that it is moral choices that are reduced to mere feelings.[110] In effect, we live in a society that thinks that the greatest good is "the liberation of the individual's will," which is increasingly done with one's purchasing power in the economy.[111]

THE ANXIOUS MALAISE OF MODERNITY

Having abandoned any sense of the transcendent existing as an objective reality, the anxious malaise of immanence develops in three forms. First, there is the feeling of meaning being fragile, which contributes to the second, in which attempts to recognize the meaningfulness of important experiences in life fall flat and empty. One needs only to think of the numerous pathetic attempts to make graduation ceremonies meaningful by commencement speakers quoting Dr. Seuss to understand this flatness.[112] Third, finding ourselves powerless to coherently function as autonomous individuals, powerful forces in the marketplace have begun to give meaning to individual experience.[113] Our very preferences as individuals are manipulated and fine-tuned by the social engineering campaigns conducted by multibillion dollar corporations with access to big data.[114]

The economy is increasingly dehumanized through big data's transformation of human beings into algorithms and numerical equations.[115] The apparent omniscience of big data and reducibility of humans to data points is so effective that it can predict the probability of individuals changing political parties and coming out of the closet.[116] Having moved past an era of advertising products in a "rational" manner based upon the qualities of the product, we have moved into an era of irrational marketing in which products have been turned into markers of not only status, but identity in that advertising and branding campaigns do not provide pertinent information about products but rather irrationally associate products with qualitative elements of human experience.[117] As is developed below, this way of influencing people manifests within the political world through destructive perpetual campaigning.

Having been stripped of natural sources of meaningful aspects of life, modern individuals purchase meaning and purpose.

Anxiety and the Resulting Consumerism

Anxiety is also a natural response to the nihilistic pluralism of corporately constructed pseudo-meanings that are offered as choices for constructing one's identity. When all options are equally meaningless, all choices become equally meaningless and arbitrary.[118] When one no longer distinguishes between types of desires through a hierarchy of values. When one treats desire in an egalitarian fashion, consumption becomes sacrosanct.[119] Central to much of modern political thought is the arrangement of government in such a way as to secure the natural state, which is the satiation of desires. But little guidance is given as to which desires should be chosen. It takes a very small intellectual leap to conclude that all desires are equal and, thus, there is no need to discriminate amongst desires. There are no grounds by which one can say that Bach's music is better than Nicki Minaj's. An exception is sometimes made for bodily health—the only health the modern world sees as relevant to the public weal. Ironically, the Age of Anxiety upholds the value of extending the longevity of life without providing a reason to live.[120] Evidently, the only desires that cannot be indulged without condemnation are the desires for tobacco, Big Macs, and Mountain Dew consumed via a plastic straw.

Existential anxiety drives consumerism even further because shopping becomes a way to numb the restless anxiety of purposeless existence[121]; hence, the phenomenon of retail therapy. In contrast to those who think that consumerism is a form of materialism, it is actually spiritualism, in that it has become a means for finding meaning and communing with others.[122] The idea of selling people identities through the products that they buy is in effect the very project of branding.[123] Branding functioned to replace market-based peer-to-peer relationships between buyer and consumer, in that brands are explicitly used in advance of a relationship to create meaning through mass advertising.[124] In this way, a consumer culture is in reality an anticulture. If, as Philip Rieff puts it, "a culture survives principally . . . by the power of its institutions to bind and loose men in the conduct of their affairs," the consumerist mentality that imagines that we should indulge (with credit card in hand) without limit is the perfect anticultural substitute for a true culture. It is not an accident, for example, that the nation's leading corporations are significant funders of sexual liberationist causes as the theory underlying sexual libertinism is the same as that which undergirds the consumerist mindset.[125]

Consumer culture, its value neutral orientation, and the buying and selling of identities through branding are the primary informers of meaning in the current historical moment.[126] Our consumerist age is less defined in terms of greed, which consists of attachment to things, than by its waste.[127] Consumerism functions as a mode of spiritual and moral formation, in that it provides consumers with a sense of transcendence through the brand's ability to momentarily satiate spiritual needs.[128] In other words, things and brands represent "freedom, status, and love," and most of all, "the aspiration to escape time and death by constantly seeking renewal in created things."[129]

Additionally, consumerism, through the conspicuous consumption of brand identity, provides a false sense of community. Effectively, one is made a part of the "Apple" family—or religion—when one "buys" into the systems of meaning promoted through Apple's branding campaigns. However, on a more "meta" level, consumerism contributes to the fragmentation of society because consumerism promotes the view of individual as "sovereign chooser."[130] In a consumerist, multicultural, globalized market, the consumer is effectively a detached tourist who stands above and detached from all time and place.[131] In other words, we no longer feel at home or a sense of belonging in the world itself or within our local communities.

The Age of Anxiety is a commercial culture in which everything is left to the market. Individual brands signal one's status, thus giving one's life greater meaning. One can say, "I am the kind of person who shops at Whole Foods, not Wal-Mart," indicating elite social status. Similarly, one can say, "I like country music, unlike those elitist snobs." Either way, the self is purchased and branded. The consumer self is tempted to keep purchasing as a way to maintain meaning, with the regular liturgy of purchasing substituting for the regular liturgy of church worship. Whereas the religious believers of old had hagiography to vicariously inform and stimulate their faith, the consumer self has unboxing videos. Each is equally religious. Much as a traditional religious believer might find satisfaction in volunteering at a domestic abuse shelter or by engaging in regular prayer, the consumer finds satisfaction in the ritual of buying the newest, latest thing. To have the iPhone 10 rather than a mere iPhone 9 is to demonstrate one's marketplace righteousness.

Digital Distracting Ourselves into More Anxiety

Finding themselves existentially homeless in the real world, many have found the experience of community online, especially in the form of social networks. The influence of online communities has exponentially increased with the ubiquity of digital connectivity afforded by smart phones. The logic of modern technology drives addiction to digital distraction such that our immediate concerns are often ignored for the sake of peripheral matters that are magnified in importance.[132] A state of semi-distractedness seems to permeate most of our existence within the digital twenty-first century. True individual character is vanishing because we are expected to flexibly redefine ourselves to consistently changing conditions.[133] Mediated and representational existence contributes to the perceived flatness of reality by creating a numbness in the soul, which makes it difficult to perceive the differences of quality and gravitas between experiences.[134]

The distractibility caused by our digital environment makes it difficult for a person to perform daily actions that require our attention to be impacted in our being, experiences such as having an intimate meal with one's family.[135] Not only do our devices push their way into our attention through notifications, our own being calls out for these distractions: when one sits down to read a book and immediately begins to think about what could be watched on YouTube or Netflix, or, when in conversation with another, we distractedly think about who else we could be talking with via text or Facebook. Different moments of our lives require more or less attention from us. Not all time is equal. It is one thing to be distracted in a moment when one should or can be distracted; it is a completely different thing to be distracted during the important moments of one's life. The varying significance of the different moments must be distinguished in order for one's life to have a sense of coherence. While one is at the dinner table with one's family or friends, it is not an appropriate time to be checking and responding to work emails. Likewise, while one is at work, it is not appropriate to "creep" on social network acquaintances. It is appropriate to be distracted by the digital world while sitting on the toilet; it is not appropriate during sex.[136]

The digital environment has fostered a value system based on popularity to foster economic growth.[137] This is exemplified by so-called "YouTube stars," who become famous and rich by getting thousands of "likes" which they can then translate into advertising dollars. Fame often comes by being the most obnoxious or flamboyant personality. Logan and Jake Paul are exemplars of this phenomenon. With the rise of Facebook and YouTube, we have created an economy of likes that is being pushed to irrational extremes.[138] This absurdity is clearly visible in the fact that bots make up large portions of internet viewership.[139] The absurdity is made ironic when one considers that billions of dollars in the economy are based upon bots monitoring bots.[140]

The drive to be "liked" influences our politics as well as social media, especially through what is known as the permanent campaign. For many reasons, our politics seldom leave campaign mode, typified by overheated rhetoric and sensationalism so as to make candidates appear distinct from one another. Campaign rhetoric is different from governing rhetoric. Governing rhetoric thrives on conciliation as the art of legislation is the art of persuading people with superficial differences that they have enough in common that they should put aside those differences to join a coalition to pass a bill. By contrast, an example of typical campaign rhetoric is the appearance of candidates on celebrity talk shows. Politicians now frequent these shows—both Donald Trump and Hillary Clinton appeared on the Tonight Show with Jimmy Fallon late in the 2016 campaign, for instance—precisely so they can engage in scripted (but ostensibly spontaneous) conversation that makes them attractive to viewers. It is a manufactured way to get "liked." Such celebrity shows also avoid the pitfalls of interviews with journalists, namely, the fear that one might actually be asked a difficult or troublesome question.

The ethos of the permanent campaign bleeds into governing as the line between public discourse and entertainment is blurred. Every event becomes a "pseudo-event."[141] One example is the annual State of the Union Address by the President of the United States. Delivered to a Joint Session of Congress, the real audience for the address is the television audience, and thus the rhetorical form is that of spectacle. Presidents now regularly stack the audience with personal guests whom the president introduces by name. These guests serve to dramatize a particular point the president wishes to make, creating an emotional moment designed to add drama to what was once a staid and formal affair. A similar phenomenon occurs within Congress as congressional committee hearings regularly take the form of show trials designed to create media moments rather than to gain information with which members might make better legislation. Whatever one thinks of Mark Zuckerberg, his 2018 appearance in front of congressional committees regarding social media and privacy garnered no information that might enlighten either the members of Congress or the public. Zuckerberg's appearance before various committees, as often happens with high profile witnesses, came about precisely because members wished to beat up on an unpopular public figure.

The line between government and social media likes is further blurred as members compete to create "YouTube" moments—highly amusing or highly combative pseudo-events whose very existence is prompted by a need to create a "viral" video that makes the member more popular. The strong incentive is toward sensational, often vituperative, rhetoric geared more toward provoking strong reactions than actually achieving a legislative or policy-oriented end. The negativity that so typifies modern political discourse is in part attributable to the fact that comity is boring. As the old saying goes, it is news when the plane crashes, not when it lands safely. As the noted philosopher Don Henley once opined in his pop-oriented critique of news media, "It's interesting when people die/Give us dirty laundry."

In the final analysis, the very nature of social life and, consequently, what it means to be human is radically under assault by our own digital habits. We exist in a media environment that creates sensational pseudo-events, images, or representations of reality. Everyone knows it's a spectacle, and when given the opportunity to create a spectacle or consumable image of ourselves, we take it.[142] In effect, we are increasingly buffered from one another by the representations of ourselves and by the screens that interrupt our attention to others. Consequently, the meaningfulness of human interaction and life is ultimately diminished. In terms of individual identity, the fragility of meaning arises in existential moments in which our lives feel meaningless.[143] Moments of boredom often betray this fact to us and hence immediately desire devices of distraction to kill boredom at any moment in which it arises.[144] Whereas disciplinary society created criminals and lunatics, the current age promotes anxiety and depression.[145]

Resulting Meaninglessness and Nihilism

As embeddedness within strong cultural narratives that give life a sense of meaning and purpose continues to be replaced by self-representation through branding, life increasingly feels fleeting.[146] Phenomenologically, there is a sense that life lacks meaning and significance.[147] The substance of one's life seems to be empty in part because, whereas in the past, the important moments of life were all attached to the transcendent, today, we are surrounded by horrific images without a way to make sense of them.[148] As religions and their role as "thanotechnics," that is, arts of responding to and making sense of death, decline we are left simply surviving.[149] Along these lines, true communal life is threatened by the false view that daily life is an absurdly meaningless busy drudgery.[150] This incoherence will continue to add to the anxiety of life until our understanding of recreation, leisure, and festivity moves past and transcends any conception of not working.[151]

The experience of existence in the modern world has been described as a feeling of vertigo or, more famously by Camus, nausea, because taken seriously, the lack of meaning and purpose sensed within modern existence creates the feeling of sickness and anxiety: the fact that I find my life and its important events meaningful is absurd for there is nothing beyond the veil of the immanent human mind.[152] The rational and logical conclusion of existential nominalism is philosophical nihilism and pessimism because if meaning does not exist in an objective sense, then whatever meanings a culture or oneself place upon reality are equally arbitrary and pointless. The logical conclusion of philosophical existentialism is, paradoxically, that meaning is meaninglessness: human existence is inherently absurd. Nihilism rejects the joyous embracement of absurdism in favor of a logically consistent "realism" based on the existential premise that existence precedes essence.

Thomas Ligotti, as a nihilist and pessimist, is courageously consistent in his logic of applying the rationality of existentialism to human existence. One of the primary mysteries of the human condition is the existence of consciousness. Ligotti considers the existence of consciousness the essence of human tragedy, in that it is the genetic mutation that makes the world and life appear to be meaningful.[153] The generally accepted materialist positions the monist theory that exclusively consciousness is the result of synapses firing in the brain.[154] The existence of consciousness is especially tragic because it means that we are aware of death and suffering.[155]

The human species has remained generally optimistic because it will-fully chooses to ignore the reality of suffering and being nothing more than "hunks of spoiling flesh on disintegrating bones."[156] Finding ways to avoid thinking about our situation is the "zombification" of our species.[157] Most importantly, within the technological age, we keep our minds distracted by trivial trash.[158] The horror of this reality is that we are puppets of genetics that appear to think and choose for ourselves but, in all reality, we know that there is nothing more to our minds than the chemical makeup of our brains. The idea of not ending the suffering for the sake of meaningless pleasures is absurd.[159] Indeed, Camus even recognized the absurdity, which can be seen in his portrayal of Sisyphus being happy throughout his drudgery as an image of finding meaning within a meaningless universe, that is, maintaining a rea-son not to commit suicide as soon as the disadvantages of life outweigh the advantages.[160] This utilitarian choice is the last act of rationality the Western mind's rejection of the meaningfulness of the cosmos itself and undergirds the anxiety of modern existence.

If human beings are parts of a meaningless, mechanical world, then it is natural to abolish notions of the freedom of the will and promote determinis-tic forms of behaviorism.[161] Human beings are effectively mindless zombies, in that we are genetic beings driven to merely survive.[162] Humans are under-stood as mechanisms with the sole drive of "replication," and this mirrors the "truth" that human beings have no immutable nature beyond being mechani-cal processes that can be made and remade.[163] Even though modern science tells us that we are nothing but our biochemical makeup, everyone shares the experience of free will.[164] Consciousness is an abomination, because we think we make choices but we do not; we are in fact human puppets.[165] From this perspective, human beings are conscious of the fact that we are nothing more than self-replicating robots in a meaningless universe.[166] The reason that this is such a horrible thought is that really believing that you are nothing more than a "human puppet" is an absurdity and would make you go insane.[167] Modern science and posthumanism both maintain positions of identity being fragmented and inherently irrational.

Again, one may not like these conclusions, but they are naturally deduced from principles maintained within the modern scientific worldview and the antihumanism of postmodern and posthuman academia. In order to be intel-lectually honest and consistent, one would have the courage to accept these conclusions. Otherwise, if these conclusions are unacceptable, then we must begin to reevaluate the premises from which they flow. This conundrum does not mean that one must convert to Christianity, but it does leave room for its public legitimacy and other supernatural positions. The realist and nihilist alike recognize that "hysterical optimism" will be predominant in society unless we grapple with the tragedy of consciousness, but the realist maintains that tragedy can be made meaningful by distinguishing between "good and evil."[168] However, this recognition of objective values is unlikely at the moment, because when confronted with this situation, most people react with "incredulity and resentment," for it is undeniable that the embracement of nominalism has transformed and categorically bettered human beings' material situation.[169] Ironically, as is developed in the following chapters, the meaningful "abundance" of life felt by "simpler societies" is lost in affluent society today.[170]

In the final analysis, before modern times, the meaning of life and the purpose of existence was largely taken for granted and provided a true sense of importance, whereas today one is no longer embedded in a system of meaning but is given the chance to pick one's identity for oneself. As freeing as this may seem, it actually oppresses the self because we all are confronted with the arbitrary and meaningless nature of the choices. The choices made within life—from what type of drink to order at Starbucks to the options on a birthing plan—are increasingly utilized as representations and substance of our identity.[171] This sentiment is eloquently summarized in the concluding lines of Queen's nihilistic ballad, "Bohemian Rhapsody:" "Nothing really matters. Anyone can see nothing really matters. Nothing really matters to me."[172]

SOCIAL AND MORAL DANGER
OF NIHILISTIC ANXIETY

The culture we live in is at best a weak culture because it has become a loose connection of individuals without any commonly held belief system beyond the vague commitment to discovering one's own truth.[173] Ours is a culture of emotivism, which rejects collective understandings of morality as illusions.[174] In contrast to the weak culture of emotivism, members of strong cultures share belief "in objective moral goods and the practices necessary for human beings to embody those goods in the community."[175] Ironically and absurdly, our radical individualism rejects the strong culture orientation in favor of autonomous identity that is biologically programmed.[176]

In the emotivistic wake is the Nietzschean perspective that holds that objective reality is nothing other than a subjective expression of the will.[177] In effect, when the state creates laws, which de facto derive from premises about justice and morality, it is done so from an arbitrary, subjective sense defined by the majority. As such, politics is reduced to a will to power on behalf of competing ideologies. The shift from *homo sapiens* to *homo faber* inherently involves the rejection of human nature and leads to the position that favors praxis as "the measure of truth" and power as supreme in human society.[178] Effectively, by abandoning the idea of the human person with a nature that is intimately connected to the natural order and who can understand and know transcendental truths, all that we are left with is power. Consequently, the current historical moment, in terms of moral theory, is defined by MacIntyre as a choice between Nietzsche's will to power and Aristotle's virtue ethics because the moral project of the Enlightenment via Kant has failed. We accept a vision in which societal differences will be negotiated either by a will to power or rational debate about the nature and purpose of human existence and its relationship to an objective world of values.

The predominance of the Nietzschean will to power can be witnessed by the "ideological war" that is being waged in the political sphere. The basic idea is that the truth can only be made manifest by actualizing one's political ideology. Thus, there is a war between the ideologies to gain control over the means of power so that one's ideology may be actualized. This is why we see the continued manifestation of Left and Right attempting to delegitimize the foundations of the policies instituted by whichever side is not currently in power. If one can maintain a rhetoric of delegitimacy concerning the origins of law, then these laws can be simply overturned once one's political party gains power. What is established—and it is easily witnessed within the current historical moment—is not an attempt to persuade people of a different position but rather to move one's base such that one's elected officials can gain and utilize power. This was rhetorically played out with regard to the Obama legacy, in that the Right attempted to delegitimize all of his policies through arguments about Obama's birthplace and birth certificate and that he is either a socialist or Islamist. Whereas in the Trump era, the Left has utilized the Russian collusion narrative and claims of ties to fascism to delegitimize all that President Trump has accomplished.

In effect, there is an ideological competition in the will to power in order to institute one's ideology in law and deconstruct all that is done by one's ideological opponent. Without an intelligent and rational means of perceiving and understanding value, modern humans, with their varying perspectives of relativized value judgments are left demonizing those on the outside of the given ideology.[179] In terms of manifesting the truth through the actualization of one's ideology, those that are on the other ideological side are increasingly demonized in one way or another because they represent obstacles to the truth. With power as the sole measure of political success, statesmanship is replaced by political consultants.

Interest in dialogue or compromise between ideological perspectives has all but vanished. When we effectively have the two political parties in a consistent battle to invalidate everything the other party does, anxiety is added over what it means to be an American. The political parties are engaged in a perpetual or permanent campaign. With the presidencies of Obama and Trump, we are witnessing the death of the American middle and an increased rhetoric of intolerance by both sides. Respect for the law and other persons are fading, and these form of respect function to restrain violence in society.[180] Within the immanent framework, violence against the other can be justified as the only means to creating a new reality.[181] As such, as the principles of respect for law and other persons increasingly disintegrate, we anxiously await the first shots fired within the cold civil war that has already started. The breakdown of the respect for the law and other persons should be a cause for true anxiety within the current age.

NOTES

1. Marian L. Tupy, "Improvements in Human Well-Being in the New Millennium." *Human Progress*. April 11, 2019. https://humanprogress.org/article.php?p=1844. Indur M. Goklany, "The Globalization of Human Well-Being" (CATO Institute. August 22, 2002). https://www.cato.org/publications/policy-analysis/globalization-human-wellbeing

2. Neil Postman, *Technopoly: The Surrender of Culture to Technology* (New York: Vintage Books, 1992), xii.

3. Nicholas Eberstadt, "Our Miserable 21st Century." Commentary. February 2017. https://www.commentarymagazine.com/articles/our-miserable-21st-century/

4. Ibid.

5. Ibid.

6. Tim P. Carney, *Alienated America: Why Some Places Thrive While Others Collapse*. New York: Harper, 2019. Kindle Edition location 1812.

7. Jean M. Twenge, "Have Smartphones Destroyed a Generation?" *Atlantic Monthly*. September, 2017. https://www.theatlantic.com/magazine/archive/2017/09/has-the-smartphone-destroyed-a-generation/534198/

8. Karol Markowitz, "An Epidemic of Teenage Loneliness." *New York Post*. March 26, 2019. https://nypost.com/2019/03/26/an-epidemic-of-teenage-loneliness/

9. Neil Postman, *Amusing Ourselves to Death: Public Discourse in the Age of Show Business*, 20th anniversary ed. (New York: Penguin Books, 1985), 65.

10. Matthew B. Crawford, *The World Beyond Your Head: On Becoming an Individual in an Age of Distraction* (New York: Farrar, Straus and Giroux, 2015), 8.

11. Richard M. Weaver, *Ideas Have Consequences*, expanded ed. (Chicago: University of Chicago, 2013), 14.

12. Crawford, *World Beyond*, 10.

13. Byung-Chul Han, *The Burnout Society*, trans. Erik Butler (Stanford: Stanford University Press, 2015), 12.

14. Robert Cardinal Sarah and Nicolas Diat, *The Power of Silence: Against the Dictatorship of Noise* (San Francisco: Ignatius Press, 2016), 32. See also Edward S.

Herman and Noam Chomsky, *Manufacturing Consent: The Political Economy of the Mass Media,* updated ed. (New York: Pantheon Books, 2002).

15. Crawford, *World Beyond*, ix.

16. Benedict M. Ashley, *The Way toward Wisdom: An Interdisciplinary and Intercultural Introduction to Metaphysics* (Notre Dame: University of Notre Dame, 2006), 3.

17. Kenneth E. Boulding, "General Systems Theory—The Skeleton of Science," in *General Systems Theory and Human Communication*, ed. Brent D. Reuben and John Y. Kim (Rochelle Park, NJ: Hayden , 1975). 21–32; Weaver, *Ideas Have Consequences*, 48–63.

18. For example, at Prof. Schaff's institution there are forty-two courses listed which fulfill the humanities requirement. Most students can graduate without taking a single history course, literature course, philosophy course, or language course. While it is the case that most students find themselves in such courses over their college career, it is by accident and not design.

19. Ashley, *Way toward Wisdom*, 3

20. Ibid.

21. Ibid.

22. Han, *Burnout Society*, 1–11.

23. Cavanaugh, *Being Consumed*, 68.

24. Ashley, *Way Toward Wisdom*, 5. The naïve cultural relativism of contemporary postmodern anthropologies and perspectives lends itself to a high degree of conservativism. Without some standard outside of a culture to critique problems within the culture, there is no legitimate moral value that can be utilized to justify the change. The dominant way of doing things cannot be considered to be any more or less valuable than any other way of doing things.

25. See Patrick Deneen's discussion in *Conserving America? Essays on Present Discontents* (St Augustine's Press, 2016), Chapter One.

26. Jean-François Lyotard, *The Postmodern Condition: A Report on Knowledge*, trans. Geoff Bennington and Brian Massumi (Minneapolis: University of Minnesota, 1993), xxiii.

27. Ronald C. Arnett, Janie M. Harden Fritz, and Leanne M. Bell, *Communication Ethics Literacy: Dialogue and Difference* (Los Angeles: SAGE Publications, 2009), 1–2.

28. "Postmodernism rightly understood is not postmodernism as it is usually understood. All postmodernists rightly reject the systematic or reductionist rationalism of modern thought. But, properly understood, postmodernism is not antifoundationalsim or a celebration of endless self-creation out of nothing. Antifoundationalism, the assertion of the groundlessness of human existence, is really hypermodernism, or the exaggeration to the point of caricature of the modern impulse to self-creation." Peter Augustine Lawler, *Postmodernism Rightly Understood: The Return to Realism in American Thought* (Lanham, MD: Rowman & Littlefield Publishers, 1999), 1–2.

29. See for instance: Joel Garreau, *Radical Evolution: The Promise and Peril of Enhancing Our Minds, Our Bodies—and What It Means to Be Human* (New York: Broadway Books, 2005); Chris Hables Gray, *Cyborg Citizen: Politics in the Posthuman Age* (New York: Routledge, 2001); Yuval Noah Harari, *Homo Deus: A Brief*

History of Tomorrow (New York: HarperCollins, 2017); N. Katherine Hayles, *How We Became Posthuman: Virtual Bodies in Cybernetics, Literature, and Informatics* (Chicago: University of Chicago, 1999); Cary Wolfe, *What Is Posthumanism?* (Minneapolis: University of Minnesota, 2010).

30. Thomas Ligotti, *The Conspiracy Against the Human Race: A Contrivance of Horror* (New York: Hippocampus Press, 2010), 127.

31. Ashley, *Way toward Wisdom*, 12. In his book *Technopoly*, Neil Postman documents Western society's transition from technocracy—a state in which science and other drivers of progress are in balance with conservative institutions of cultural tradition—to a technopoly—a state in which the values promoted by institutions of cultural traditions are fundamentally obsolesced by the scientific and technological values of progress and efficiency. In other words, moral progress is identified with scientific and technological progress.

32. Postman, *Technopoly*, xii.

33. Han, *Burnout Society*, 1–7.

34. Ashley, *Way toward Wisdom*, 12. See also Benjamin Barbour, "Jihad vs. McWorld," https://www.theatlantic.com/magazine/archive/1992/03/jihad-vs-mcw orld/303882/.

35. Augusto del Noce, *Crisis of Modernity*, trans. Carlo Lancellotti (London: McGill-Queen's University Press, 2015), 4.

36. Etienne Gilson describes the relationship between theology and philosophy during the distinct ancient, medieval, and modern epochs. Etienne Gilson, *God and Philosophy*, 2nd ed. (New Haven: Yale Note Bene Press of Yale, 2002).

37. For further study on the liberal arts tradition as a unifying element of Western civilization, see the following: Bruce A. Kimball, *Orators and Philosophers: A History of the Idea of Liberal Education* (New York: College Entrance Examination Board, 1995); Sister Miriam Joseph, *The Trivium: The Liberal Arts of Grammar, Logic, and Rhetoric: Understanding the Nature and Function of Language* (Philadelphia: Paul Dry Books, 1937); Marshall McLuhan, *The Classical Trivium: The Place of Thomas Nashe in the Learning of his Time* (Corte Madera, CA: Gingko Press, 2006); Jeffrey Walker, *The Genuine Teachers of this Art: Rhetorical Education in Antiquity* (Columbia: University of South Carolina Press, 2011).

38. Ashley, *Way toward Wisdom*, 12–13.

39. Del Noce, *Crisis of Modernity*, 4.

40. John Stuart Mill, *Three Essays* (New York: Oxford University Press, 1975), 87.

41. Charles Taylor, *A Secular Age* (Cambridge: Belknap Press of Harvard, 2007), 25.

42. Han, *Burnout Society*, 18. See also, Gilson, *God and Philosophy*; Voegelin, *Politics, Science and Gnosticism*, 12–13.

43. Weaver, *Ideas Have Consequences*, 1. One can find this in the American context in the thought of early twentieth-century progressives, for example, Woodrow Wilson's celebration of a living "Darwinian" constitution over the static "Newtonian Constitution" in *Constitutional Government in the United States* (New York: Columbia University Press, 1908. Reprint New Brunswick, NJ: Transaction Publishers, 2002), 54–57.

44. Taylor, *Secular Age*, 25.

45. Ibid.

46. Ibid.

47. Weaver, *Ideas Have Consequences*, 3; Del Noce, *Crisis of Modernity*, 5.

48. Weaver, *Ideas Have Consequences*, 3; Taylor, *Secular Age*, 97.

49. In this text, Plato proposes the question of whether words relate to the essence of things or are arbitrary symbols. The ancient and medieval world landed on the side of words relating to the nature of things.

50. Rod Dreher, *The Benedict Option: A Strategy for Christians in a Post-Christian Nation* (New York: Sentinel, 2017), 28; Taylor, *Secular Age*, 31–32.

51. Taylor, *Secular Age*, 31–32. Edward Feser defines the terms as such: "The view that universals, numbers, and/or propositions exist objectively, apart from the human mind and distinct from any material or physical features of the world, is called *realism*, and Plato's Theory of Forms is perhaps the most famous version of the view. . . . The standard alternative views are *nominalism*, which denies that universals and the like are real, and *conceptualism*, which acknowledges that they are real but insists that they exist only in the mind." See Edward Feser, *The Last Superstition: A Refutation of the New Atheism* (South Bend, In: St. Augustine's Press, 2010), 41.

52. Taylor, *Secular Age*, 97.

53. Ibid.

54. Brad S. Gregory, *The Unintended Reformation: How a Religious Revolution Secularized Society* (Cambridge: Belknap Press of Harvard, 2012), 38.

55. Immanentism postulates that the qualities of being are merely phenomena or representations that exist within the mind itself. In contrast, transcendentalism maintains that the qualities of being are "objective" and are able to be experienced through the mind, not simply within it.

56. Weaver, *Ideas Have Consequences*, 3.

57. Owen Barfield, *Saving the Appearances: A Study in Idolatry*, 2nd ed. (Middletown, CT: Wesleyan University Press, 1988), 68. Owen Barfield argues that whereas we think that the animistic worldview of the premoderns was the result of anthropomorphic thinking, we moderns could rightfully be considered guilty of "mechanomorphic" thinking. He details how this mechanistic form of thinking develops primarily after the invention of automated machines that appeared to be self-moving and independent of mind. See also, Gilson, *God and Philosophy*, 74–108.

58. Taylor, *Secular Age*, 33. See also: Lewis Mumford, *Technics and Civilization* (Chicago: University of Chicago Press, 2010), 31–36; John Herman Randall, Jr., *The Making of the Modern Mind: A Survey of the Intellectual Background of the Present Age*, Fiftieth anniversary ed. (New York: Columbia University Press, 1976).

59. Dreher, *Benedict Option*, 25.

60. Hans Jonas, *The Phenomenon of Life: Toward a Philosophical Biology* (Evanston: Northwestern University Press, 1966).

61. Postman, *Technopoly*, 29.

62. Dreher, *Benedict Option*, 33.

63. Ibid.

64. Postman, *Technopoly*, 21–55.

65. The separation of faith and reason culminated in Kierkegaard's understanding of faith as an irrational leap. In essence, it is believed that reason and experience speak to the supposed nonexistence of God, and one must make an emotional or willful leap in order to have faith. As such, the claims of religion would no longer be accessible to reason, rational discussion, or public discourse, and consequently are considered private matters.

66. John Locke, *A Letter Concerning Toleration* (Buffalo: Prometheus, 1990), 13, 19.

67. Thomas Jefferson, *Portable Thomas Jefferson* (New York: Penguin Group, 1977), 210.

68. Weaver, *Ideas Have Consequences*, 5.

69. Max Weber, "Science as Vocation," 7. http://anthropos-lab.net/wp/wp-cont ent/uploads/2011/12/Weber-Science-as-a-Vocation.pdf.

70. Taylor, *Secular Age*, 97.

71. Ibid., 98.

72. Ibid., 176.

73. Ibid., 221–295. See also Gilson, *God and Philosophy*, 74–144.

74. Taylor, *Secular* Age, 299.

75. Ibid., 45.

76. Ibid., 93–94.

77. Ibid., 32.

78. Gilson, *God and Philosophy*, 1–37; Julian Jaynes, *The Origins of Consciousness in the Breakdown of Bicameral Mind* (Boston: Houghton Mifflin, 1976).

79. Taylor, *Secular Age*, 42.

80. See Crawford, *World Beyond*, 73–76 and 115–123.

81. Mill's thought has found a renewed appreciation amongst those fighting for intellectual diversity on college campuses, as witnessed by the Heterodox Academy's 2018 publication of *All Minus One: John Stuart Mill's Ideas on Free Speech Illustrated*. Heterodox Academy is an organization of university faculty dedicated to the promotion of free speech and intellectual diversity on campus. Prof. Schaff is a member. Richard Reeves, *All Minus One: John Stuart Mill's Ideas on Free Speech Illustrated* (Heterodox Academy, 2018).

82. Mill, *Three Essays*, 15.

83. Ibid., 27.

84. Ibid., 78.

85. Ibid., 81–82, 87.

86. Thus, the irony that the Heterodox Academy version of "On Liberty" is a heavily edited, one might say, "dumbed down," version of the essay, complete with illustrations. This is euphemistically called making the text more "readable." The assumption is that Mill's actual essay must be gutted and turned into a picture book in order to be popular with today's reader. See https://heterodoxacademy.org/mill/.

87. Eric Voegelin, *Science, Politics and Gnosticism: Two Essays* (New York: Regnery Publishing, 1968), 4.

88. Taylor, *Secular Age*, 302.

89. Ibid.

90. Ibid, 303.

91. Ashley, *Way toward Wisdom*, 13.

92. Ibid. It is worth noting that the secular—or exclusive—humanism of the twentieth and twenty-first centuries is categorically not the humanism of the Renaissance, which was heavily influenced by neo-Platonism. The humanism of the twentieth century, rather, was informed heavily by philosophical existentialism and the rejection of classical essentialism and realism, which presupposed that essence precedes existence and not vice versa. In other words, transcendental forms or ideas are immaterial realities that inform the material world.

93. Weaver, *Ideas Have Consequences*, 2. Postman, *Technopoly*, 15.

94. Ashley, *Way toward Wisdom*, 13.

95. Ibid., 13.

96. Ibid., 43.

97. Del Noce, *Crisis of Modernity*, 9.

98. Ibid., 10.

99. Ibid., 11–12.

100. Ibid., 5.

101. Ibid., 61.

102. Ibid., 62.

103. Ibid., 12.

104. Han, *Burnout Society*, 18 and 47.

105. Alasdair MacIntyre, *After Virtue: A Study in Moral Theory*, 3rd ed. (Notre Dame: University of Notre Dame, 2007), 2.

106. Weaver, *Ideas Have Consequences*, 1.

107. MacIntyre, *After Virtue*, 6.

108. Han, *Burnout Society*, 17.

109. MacIntyre, *After Virtue*, 11–12.

110. Dreher, *Benedict Option*, 16 (emphasis added).

111. Ibid., 16.

112. Taylor, *Secular Age*, 309.

113. Crawford, *World Beyond*, 6.

114. Ibid., 18.

115. Douglas Rushkoff, *Throwing Rocks at the Google Bus: How Growth Became the Enemy of Prosperity* (New York: Portfolio, 2016), 39–44.

116. Ibid., 42.

117. See, for instance, Postman, *Amusing Ourselves to Death*, 60; The advertising of Geico products, which is filled with *non sequiturs*, is a prime example. Additionally, in terms of selling markers of identity see, Barak Goodman and Douglas Rushkoff, *The Persuaders*, directed by Barak Goodman and Rachel Dretzin, aired November 9, 2003, on Frontline. Cavanaugh, *Being Consumed*, 17.

118. Cavanaugh, *Being Consumed*, 16.

119. Ibid., 13. Weaver also argues that economic democracy is problematic because it attempts to establish an egalitarian society that disregards qualitative distinctions. Weaver, *Ideas Have Consequences*, 32–47.

120. Han, *Burnout Society*, 50–51.

121. Cavanaugh, *Being Consumed*, 35.

122. Ibid., 36.

123. Ibid., 45–47. See also, James R. Beniger, *The Control Revolution: Technological and Economic Origins of the Information Society* (Cambridge: Harvard University Press, 1986).

124. Rushkoff, *Throwing Rocks*, 20.

125. Darel E. Paul, *From Tolerance to Equality: How Elites Brought America to Same-Sex Marriage* (Waco, TX: Baylor University Press, 2019). See also Charlotte Allen, "Punching Down," https://www.firstthings.com/article/2016/06/punching-down.

126. Cavanaugh, *Being Consumed*, 47.

127. Ibid., 34–35.

128. Ibid., 48.

129. Ibid.

130. Ibid., 53.

131. Ibid., 74.

132. Douglas Rushkoff, *Present Shock: When Everything Happens Now* (New York: Penguin Group, 2013), 4.

133. Han, *Burnout Society*, 40.

134. Thomas de Zengotita, *Mediated: How the Media Shapes Your World and the Way You Live in It* (New York: Bloomsbury Publishing, 2005), 185–186. See also, Rushkoff, *Present Shock*.

135. Crawford, *World Beyond*, 5.

136. According to a recent study, approximately 20 percent of young adults aged between eighteen and thirty-four reported to having used a smartphone during sex. Alexis Kleinmann, "Nearly 20 Percent of Young Adults Use Their Smartphones During Sex: Survey," https://www.huffingtonpost.com/2013/07/12/smartphones-during-sex_n_3586647.html.

137. Rushkoff, *Throwing Rocks*, 31.

138. Ibid., 30–39.

139. Ibid., 37.

140. Ibid.

141. Daniel J. Boorstin, *The Image: A Guide to Pseudo-Events in America*, 50th Anniversary ed. (New York: Vintage, 1992).

142. The state of the uncertainty about what is real that created by political theater and the fake becoming normal was documented by Adam Curtis in his recent documentary, Hypernormalisation. *HyperNormalisation*, Web. Directed by Adam Curtis. BBC iPlayer, 16 October 2016. https://www.youtube.com/watch?v=fh2cDKyFdyU&t=4925s

143. Taylor, *Secular Age*, 308.

144. Han, *Burnout Society*, 12–15; Sherry Turkle, *Reclaiming Conversation: The Power of Talk in a Digital Age* (New York: Penguin Press, 2015).

145. Han, *Burnout Society*, 9.

146. Ibid., 18.

147. Taylor, *Secular Age*, 307.

148. Ibid., 308–309.

149. Han, *Burnout Society*, 18.
150. Josef Pieper, *In Tune with the World: A Theory of Festivity*, trans. Richard and Clara Winston (South Bend: St. Augustine's Press, 1963), 5.
151. Ibid., 8.
152. Del Noce, *Crisis of Modernity*, 29.
153. Ligotti, *Conspiracy*, 25.
154. Ibid.
155. Ibid., 27.
156. Ibid., 28.
157. Ibid., 30.
158. Ibid.
159. Ibid., 49.
160. Ibid.
161. Weaver, *Ideas Have Consequences*, 6.
162. Ligotti, *Conspiracy*, 90.
163. Ibid.
164. Ibid., 97.
165. Ibid.
166. Ibid., 110
167. Ligotti, *Conspiracy*, 111.
168. Weaver, *Ideas Have Consequences*, 10.
169. Ibid.
170. Ibid., 13.
171. de Zengotita, *Mediated*.
172. "Bohemian Rhapsody," Spotify, track 11 on Queen, *A Night at the Opera*, Deluxe Remastered Version, Hollywood Records, 1975.
173. Dreher, *Benedict Option*, 44.
174. MacIntyre, *After Virtue*, 19.
175. Dreher, *Benedict Option*, 16.
176. Ibid., 44.
177. MacIntyre, *After Virtue*, 113.
178. Del Noce, *Crisis of Modernity*, 12.
179. Weaver, *Ideas Have Consequences*, 2.
180. Del Noce, *Crisis of Modernity*, 27.
181. Ibid., 22–23.

Section 1

FINDING A SELF IN AN ANXIOUS AGE

Chapter 2

How Dressing for Dinner
Can Save Your Soul

Aristocratic and Democratic Transitions in Alexis de Tocqueville and Downton Abbey

The Age of Anxiety experiences deep existential anxiety in part because of the evolution of modern democracy. In particular, democracy—classically understood as one stage in the revolutions of types of social constitutions—is minimally held together by the values of liberty and equality. In order to promote a just society, individuals need to be at liberty to pursue one's vision of happiness to the extent that it does not affect the rights of others, and under the law, all vision of the good life are treated as equal. These minimal values are not enough to provide the individual with a sense of meaning and purpose. Along these lines, Alexis de Tocqueville, in *Democracy in America*, states his goal thusly: "To instruct democracy" and correct its "blind instincts."[1] Tocqueville viewed the coming of democracy with a "sort of religious terror" at what he took to be an "irresistible revolution."[2]

A theme running through the two volumes of *Democracy in America* is the need to tame the excesses of democracy and to reintroduce into democracy some of the virtues of the aristocratic regime. Democracy, with its undue love of both equality and novelty, too hastily rejects the best of aristocracy. In the "Author's Introduction" to *Democracy in America*, Tocqueville worries that democracy will thoughtlessly destroy those things which aristocracy does well.[3] As Aristide Tessitore puts it, Tocqueville "regrets the loss of the social goods characteristic of aristocracy (among which he numbers its propensity to greater brilliance, high achievements in art and science, instinctive appreciation for glory, and ability to elicit and develop some of the most sublime capacities of the human soul—at least for some)."[4]

Robert Nisbet opines that Tocqueville presents a "historical conflict between aristocracy and democracy that has a dialectical quality to it."[5]

37

Tocqueville's thought often tells a story of the movement from aristocratic to democratic regimes and the gains and losses that come from that movement.

The theme of the strain caused by the replacement of aristocracy with democracy also runs through the British drama *Downton Abbey* (shown in the United States on PBS). Set in the years from 1912 to 1925, the show follows the travails of a particular aristocratic family, the Crawleys, whose patriarch, Robert Crawley, is the Earl of Grantham. Downton Abbey (usually referred to in the show simply as Downton) is the name of their ancestral estate. While the central action of the series focuses on the personal lives of both the Crawley family and its household servants, just below the surface is a constant reminder that the English regime is changing. The First World War is depicted in the second season. In the aftermath of the war, estates such as Downton are becoming increasingly difficult to maintain and social change is undermining the political and social status of the aristocracy. These tensions often percolate to the surface as some family members attempt to preserve the old ways while others are more willing to bow to the prevailing winds, sometimes actively encouraging revolutionary ideas. *Downton Abbey* tells a tale over six seasons of an aristocratic household grappling with the unrest caused by a shift from aristocratic times to democratic times. This chapter surveys important elements in Tocqueville's thought where he makes comparisons and contrasts regarding aristocratic and democratic regimes. We will see that many of Tocqueville's observations are made manifest in the drama of *Downton Abbey*. In the process of explicating Tocqueville's thought and the dramatization of that thought in *Downton Abbey*, we will see that the nature of democracy may promote the kind of anxiety that is indicative of our age. A kind of tragedy emerges as the goods that modern democratic citizens extol may come at great cost, making the final arbitration of the net good of democracy more complex than we often assume. Along with Tocqueville, if we see democracy as both inevitable and as ultimately good, we must do so recognizing its limits and the good of attending to those limits by supplementing democratic mores with some of the goods of an aristocratic age.

Themes that arise in Tocqueville's thought that are illustrated in the drama of *Downton Abbey* include changes to family, especially the status of women, the conflict between permanence and progress, local control versus centralization, and even the individual's search for meaning and purpose are addressed within both Tocqueville and *Downton Abbey*. The aim of this chapter is to show how *Downton Abbey* illustrates Tocqueville's ideas in narrative form. In doing so we will see that, as in Tocqueville, *Downton Abbey* gives a mixed assessment of the decline of the aristocracy and its replacement with democracy. We see various characters grapple with the anxiety caused by a shift to a democratic age. It is not just change that makes them anxious, but the very democratic nature of the change. This is true for lower class characters as much as for the aristocrats who stand to lose the most materially. While it is fair to say that the show ultimately sides with democratic mores, it is far from an unmitigated endorsement of the democratic mentality. Some more egalitarian-minded critics have dismissed *Downton* as an "Aristocratic fantasy" with a "parade of poor, dumb proles . . . so relentless that it's hard not to picture its Yank fans savoring the show's ugly class implications as a kind of wish-fulfillment fantasy."[6] The contention here is that the show is more nuanced than these detractors contend. As Robert Joustra and Alissa Wilkinson put it, "Once, a citizen's identity was largely fixed by his or her social position—what was important to you was determined by your place, your role, and the activities associated with it, and you shared those things with other people who also were your social position. (*Downton Abbey* perhaps is the show that best illustrates the shift from this way of being into something more modern.)"[7] As such, *Downton Abbey* functions as a window into a world that contained fixed points of meaning that gave purpose to the lives of individuals and the shift into the Age of Anxiety. *Downton Abbey* illustrates Tocqueville's ideas in narrative form. We can use both *Downton* and Tocqueville to avoid easy agreement with the prejudices of the democratic age.

TOCQUEVILLE ON ARISTOCRACY AND DEMOCRACY

"I sought [in America] the image of democracy itself, of its penchants, its character, its prejudices, its passions; I wanted to become acquainted with it if only to know at least what we ought to hope or fear from it."[8] So writes Tocqueville in the Introduction to *Democracy in America*. Tocqueville spent his adult life thinking about the ramifications of the coming democratic age. In doing so, he often contrasted democracy with aristocracy, illustrating via comparison and contrast.

The defining characteristic of democracy is a love of equality. He calls the love of equality democracy's "principle passion."[9] Equality is not simply material equality or equality before the law, although these are surely components. When Tocqueville speaks of "equality of conditions," what he means is "the right to indulge in the same pleasures, to enter the same professions, to meet in the same places; in a word, to live in the same manner and pursue wealth by the same means."[10] For example, in contemporary America, the wealthy will often wear blue jeans when at leisure, watch the same movies and sporting events as the "common man," and, most importantly, the wealthy still typically go to work each day. One need only look at the dress and habits of the richest Americans, Bill Gates and Jeff Bezos, to see that while possessing more money they are not of a different class than their fellow Americans. Few places are truly restricted, and to the extent restrictions exist, they are typically based on ability to pay, not on one's family lineage.[11] Tocqueville goes so far as to say that democrats will endure slavery before submitting to inequality. Democratic people want equality and freedom, but if forced to choose they will choose equality in slavery rather than accept any form of aristocracy.[12]

One idea promoted by the devotion to equality is that of human perfectibility or improvement.[13] This faith in progress has a nearly religious like quality, indeed it is notable that Tocqueville's discussion of "indefinite perfectibility" comes at the end of a long discussion of religion. Aristocratic times, says Tocqueville, do not reject improvement or progress, but they believe it must occur within limits.[14] Everything has its place, and there is no reason to upset that. Tocqueville consistently observes that aristocracy sets up certain limits on human actions and ideas, while democracy does not. Joshua Mitchell argues that for Tocqueville "social conditions in the aristocratic age are more likely to assuage the soul's tendencies toward excess than are conditions in the democratic age. Being bounded in a way democratic society does not, the soul in aristocratic society finds institutional supports of which democratic society is bereft."[15]

In democracy as the old order breaks down, the mind starts to conceive of new ideas, and with the limits of aristocracy falling away, the notion of progress without end comes to mind. Democratic man is always testing limits, attempting to create something new. Some of his creations lead to his prosperity, while others may cost him dearly. There is a turmoil in democratic times where the same person may rise and fall multiple times in his life.[16] Tocqueville demonstrates this point by recounting a discussion he has with an American sailor. Tocqueville enquires why Americans do not build their ships to last. Similar to the technological orientation of the current historical moment, the sailor responds that the science of navigation and the art of shipbuilding are progressing so fast that any ship built today will be obsolete tomorrow. This illustrates another distinction with aristocratic times, namely aristocrats are more likely to have a sense of timelessness and a greater appreciation for craftsmanship and beauty. Democratic peoples are more likely simply to ask if a thing works or serves a function. In this example, the art of shipbuilding is subsumed into the science of navigation. Novelty and usefulness are indispensable to democratic peoples. We also see that democratic times are likely to be more riotous, characterized by unease as fortunes are regularly made and lost. "Aristocratic nations," concludes Tocqueville, "are naturally brought to contract the limits of human perfectibility too much, and democratic nations sometimes extend them beyond measure."[17] Democracies, says Tocqueville, have proclivities toward a "dangerous" sense of freedom.[18] Among these are a "scorn" and "hatred" of forms. Because democracies tend to value the present and the satisfaction of immediate wants, "they throw themselves impetuously toward the object of each of their desires; the least delays make them despair." They carry this mentality into political life, disposing "against the forms that slow them down or stop them every day in some of their designs."[19]

One characteristic unique to democracy, thus foreign to aristocracy, is individualism. Tocqueville is at pains to differentiate individualism from selfishness or egotism. He does not mean "rugged individualism" in which the individual is empowered and is in control of his life, although these may be aspects of individualism. More precisely, "Individualism is a reflective and peaceable sentiment that disposes each citizen to isolate himself from the mass of those like him and to withdraw to one side with his family and his friends, so that after having thus created a little society for his own use, he willingly abandons society at large to itself."[20] A person, feeling lost or inefficacious in mass society, withdraws into a private sphere, developing no public virtues.

Tocqueville stresses that while selfishness is in every kind of regime, individualism is distinctive to democracy. Tocqueville argues that aristocratic peoples have families tied to a place such that they feel a deeper connection to generations past and yet to come.[21] Aristocrats feel a duty to both posterity and ancestors. In aristocracy, families and classes made up a "sort of little native country."[22] Citizens of an aristocracy are "placed at a fixed post" such that "each of them always perceives higher than himself a man whose protection is necessary to him, and below he finds another whom he can call upon for cooperation."[23] Each person in an aristocracy exists within a chain of being, which defines his relation with his fellows. In this sense, each person knows who she is and what she's supposed to do, as defined by social convention. Her social status, while limiting her, also gives her life meaning and purpose.

These sorts of ties do not exist in democracies. People, "no longer attached to one another by any ties of caste, class, guild, or family" withdrawing from public life, causing public virtue to atrophy.[24] In these times, families rise and fall, they move from place to place, tearing the "fabric of time." Those who came before and those who will come after are forgotten.[25] Democratic dynamism makes it hard to maintain connection, even with family. The ease of travel and the willingness to relocate for economic reasons increases the cutting of ties with family, place, and the past. Here we see another manifestation of unease, restlessness, or anxiety in democracy. The unsettled nature of democracy makes it more susceptible to this pathology of individualism that, as we will see, leads to democratic despotism.

One outcome of individualism is what Tocqueville calls the tyranny of the majority. In aristocratic times, people look to the "superior reason" of particular people or of a higher social class to form opinion while discounting mass opinion. But in democratic times, "more and more it is opinion that rules." Opinion has "an infinitely greater power" in democracy. This is the rule of fashion. Not trusting in one's own opinion, as equality dictates that no one's opinion is better than any other, the desire to conform to the opinion of most is the result of "an almost unlimited trust in the judgment of the public."[26] If a greater number of people believe something, that something must be correct. Unmoored from the surety provided by the thick society of aristocratic times, where each person knows what he is supposed to do based on his social status, and without the authority of nobles or church, each person is left to his own devices to find truth. However, an individual cannot possibly figure out every (or even most) questions for himself, so he gives himself over to opinion. Opinion that rules without limit is what Tocqueville calls tyranny.[27] It is not government crushing freedom of expression that worries Tocqueville. Tyranny of the majority is "invisible and almost intangible."[28] It is largely a *"psychological* condition" in which individuals fear differing from popular opinion.[29] It is precisely the disquietude of democracy, since each is deprived of sure answers to life's deepest questions, which increases the power of the majority. The worst thing in a democracy is for one to be unpopular or unfashionable, be it in clothes or opinions.[30]

Tocqueville gives various American remedies to the problem of individualism. Here we will only consider two, namely "free institutions" and association. By free institutions Tocqueville means the institutions of electoral democracy, especially as pertains to local government. By associations, Tocqueville means what many today call "civil society," those various communities outside of legal institutions that give life much of its richness and serve as instruments of community action. One might think of churches, Boy Scouts, 4-H, Shriners, Elks Club, as examples. Regarding the free institutions, Tocqueville argues that the despot "readily pardons the governed for not loving him, provided that they do not love each other." Thus, democratic individualism encourages the very vice that makes despotism thrive. "Despotism raises barriers between them and separates them. Equality disposes them not to think of those like themselves, and for them despotism makes a sort of public virtue of indifference."[31] Tocqueville thinks that participation in local politics encourages people to overcome some of the ills of individualism. This encouragement works best in local politics where people are more likely to see the effect of their actions. It is difficult to draw democratic man "out of himself" but if, for example, it should be proposed that a road pass over his property, he immediately sees that his private interests and public affairs are entwined. Tocqueville admires local government, especially New England town meetings, as they provide in the daily services that engage a public. People are drawn outside of themselves because they can readily see how their actions affect their town.[32] Democracy must resist the temptation to centralization. Says Tocqueville, "Only freedom can bring citizens out of the isolation in which the very independence of their circumstances has led them to live, can daily force them to mingle, to join together through the need to communicate with one another, persuade each other, and satisfy each other in their conduct of their common affairs."[33]

The other cure for individualism we will discuss is associations. Tocqueville notes that Americans form associations at an impressive rate. For nearly any purpose in America, one will find an association. He notes that where a great undertaking is commenced, in France you will find the government, in England a "great lord," but in America an association.[34] This is another distinction with aristocratic times. In aristocratic societies, the "multitude of individuals can do little by themselves" but the few powerful and moneyed citizens have the capacity for great things. In democracy, citizens are "independent and weak." Association allows the completion of great tasks. If democracy should lose the art of association, it "would soon return to barbarism."[35] Associations are superior to government, in Tocqueville's view, as no government could replicate the many small tasks done by American associations. Nor would one want to imbue the government with such power. A government "knows only how to dictate precise rules; it imposes the sentiments and the ideas that it favors, and it is always hard to distinguish its counsels from its orders." Tocqueville concludes that the "art of associating" must be developed in "the same ratio as equality of conditions increases."[36] Note, though, that Tocqueville is silent as to whether democratic institutions are superior to aristocratic leadership.

Centralization seems to play an important role in Tocqueville's distinction between the unrest and violence of the French Revolution and the rather calm transition from a feudal society in England. Tocqueville describes England as "completely modern" despite still having a powerful aristocracy.[37] That power is the key. Tocqueville goes to great lengths to condemn the centralization of French government before and after the Revolution. One manifestation of that centralization is that the French nobles retained privileges without any concomitant responsibilities, earning them the contempt of the populace. "When the nobility possess not only privilege but power, when it governs and administers, its special rights can be both greater and lesser noticed. . . . The [French] nobles had offensive privileges, they possessed burdensome rights, but they assured public order, dispensed justice, executed the law, came to the help of the weak, and ran public affairs." When the French nobility ceased to perform these tasks, the "weight of its privileges seemed heavier, and finally their very existence seemed incomprehensible."[38] Thus, it is of note that where Tocqueville finds the government in France, he finds an aristocrat in England. The English aristocracy retained duties that went along with its privileges.

Democratic despotism, arising out of a love of equality mixed with a centralization unmitigated by local government or associations, is "milder, and it would degrade men without tormenting" citizens.[39] "Above these," writes Tocqueville, "an immense tutelary power is elevated, which alone takes charge of assuring their enjoyments and watching over their fate. It is absolute, detailed, regular, far-seeing, and mild. It would resemble paternal power if, like that it had for its object to prepare men for manhood . . . it provides for their security, foresees and secures their needs, facilitates their pleasures, conducts their principal affairs, directs their industry, regulates their estates, divides their inheritances; can it not take away from them entirely the trouble of thinking and the pain of living."[40] One sees a similar discussion in Tocqueville's presentation of the "physiocrats" of Revolutionary France who, as proto-social scientists, believed society could be arranged intelligently based on abstract rules. "[I]t was for the state to form the citizen's mind according to a particular model set out in advance; its duty was to fill the citizen's head with certain ideas and to furnish his heart with certain feelings that it judged necessary."[41] This democratic despotism seems to be the logical outcome of a democracy unseasoned by certain aristocratic virtues.

A final aspect of Tocqueville's thought relevant to the contrast between aristocracy and democracy is that pertaining to family, especially the role of women. Here is where we see a particularly stark contrast between aristocratic times and democratic times. Aristocratic families are dominated by the father.[42] The father is in charge by right. One might say inequality defines the family. The father is not only the head of the house, but lineage is traced through him. The power of the father "is more respected and more extensive."[43] The father is not only the head of the family, "he is the organ of tradition, the interpreter of custom, the arbiter of mores."[44]

Tocqueville says in the aristocratic family, like aristocracy in general, each person has his or her particular place. Not only is the father given rank, so are those beneath him. Children are ranked by age and sex. For example, the eldest son is the most important of the children, a "chief" in Tocqueville's phrasing.[45] Sons are favored over daughters, and the eldest son over all children. The eldest son seeks to find fortune for his brothers as "the general brilliance of the house reflects on the one who represents it." Therefore, the family is "tightly bound," by interest if not by heart.[46] The aristocratic family is also bound by place, typically through the law of primogeniture that passes the family estate to the eldest son intact. For an aristocratic family, the "family represents the land, the land represents the family; it perpetuates its name, its origins, its glory, its power, its virtues."[47]

By contrast, Tocqueville begins his discussion of the democratic family with the bold statement that, in the Roman sense, the family does not exist in America. The family is merely a slightly tighter collection of individuals.

For example, the father's authority only comes from the physical weakness of his children. Presumably, when children reach maturity, they will break away from the family, and the father's authority will be at an end. This is in contrast with the aristocratic family where even adult children are expected to submit to the authority of the father.[48] As Tocqueville puts it, in the democratic family, "the father is only an older and richer citizen than his sons."[49] Equality has reshaped the family. The father and sons work together to provide for the family. This creates an easy working relationship and promotes an informality of association. The father is neither "master nor magistrate."[50] This is true of the connection to place as well. Because democratic regimes do not recognize the superiority of the claims of the eldest son, property is divided equally among sons. When this occurs, the connection between the family and the land is destroyed. In democratic times, there is no association of the family with a place.[51]

Tocqueville's conclusions, though, are ambiguous. He writes, "I do not know if, all in all, society loses by this change; but I am brought to believe that the individual gains by it. I think that as mores and laws become more democratic, the relations of father and son become more intimate and sweeter, rule and authority are met with less . . . and it seems that the natural bond tightens while the social bond is loosened."[52] Note that Tocqueville is uncertain whether society is better off for the democratic family. The democratic family promotes the weakening of "the social bond," thereby encouraging the pathology of individualism that he is at pains to correct elsewhere. The democratic family seems salutary in the particular but problematic in the abstract. The sort of despotism democracies have reason to fear is only enhanced by democratic family life.[53]

Tocqueville also sees distinctions between aristocracy and democracy regarding the role of women. If asked to what accounts for the prosperity and growing force of the American people, "I would answer that it is to the superiority of its women."[54] Tocqueville argues that no society has ever succeeded without morals and women are the protector of morals.[55] They do so by enforcing domestic tranquility. Tocqueville as much as says that American men do not commit adultery at the rate of European men, because American women will not let them.[56]

From birth, American women partake in wider freedom. Even in childhood, she "thinks for herself, speaks freely, and acts alone." She is not protected from the vice of the world, thus as she grows into adulthood, she has confidence in her ability.[57] The American woman is not demure. She does not show "timidity and ignorance" as do many European women. American women are educated into independence. Because of this, her education includes the skills of "being able to repress in woman the most tyrannical passions of the human heart, and that it was surer to teach her the art of combating them in herself."[58] The independent self-control by women is what regulates American mores so successfully. While Europeans preach morality to their young women, American women are actually more moral.[59] Yet, American women accept a division of labor that leaves them in the home. The feminine power, according to Tocqueville, comes not from the shaping of public things, but from ordering the domestic realm.[60] Tocqueville is uncertain whether "the restiveness of life cannot be ameliorated without woman's central place in the family."[61] Natural differences between men and women are a kind of boundary that democratic Americans have not jettisoned.

In aristocratic times, by contrast, men and women are kept isolated and ignorant of each other. When they marry, it is as often for social status as for any kind of actual affection.[62] Thus, Europeans must often go outside of marriage for authentic love.[63] Even if they do marry for love, their experience of the opposite sex has been so minimal that they often choose badly.[64] This is not so in democratic times. Equality means that Americans base their marriages on mutual affection, not social status.

While American women are considered to be able to judge as well as a man, European women are kept ignorant of the world and often play at acting "futile, weak, and fearful."[65] Europeans tend to see women as a fine bottle of Scotch, to be taken down and indulged in when desired and then put back on the shelf. This explains their loose ideas regarding rape, ideas that Tocqueville holds in open contempt. Tocqueville praises America for punishing rape with death while condemning Europeans for their contempt for chastity and women.[66]

In sum, what are the major characteristics of aristocratic times?[67] Aristocratic peoples tend to value elevation of mind over material goods. They tend to have refined habits. Tocqueville, argues Patrick Deneen, "urged his readers to maintain pre-liberal and pre-democratic practices that would come under assault and duress by the insistent demands of individualism, equality and abstraction." This includes "formalities" in manners.[68] There is a cultivation of the arts and poetry and a pronounced appreciation for beauty and glory. Aristocratic peoples are able to carry on enterprises of lasting worth. In addition, aristocratic times give individuals meaning by placing them in well-defined social categories, both in public and in the family.

Democracy, on the other hand, is characterized by atomism. Unlike aristocracy, where the ruling classes look over the people with a sense of *noblesse oblige*, democracy is characterized by indifference. Each being equal, no one is obliged to do the bidding of another. Second, democratic individualism causes citizens to reject as authoritative all obligations or articles of faith which have not been submitted to the test of personal inquiry. Finally, democracy has a passion for well-being and material comfort, to the exclusion of concern for public affairs. There is, in democracy, a strong tendency toward mediocrity. One of the responsibilities of democracy is to rebuild the bonds of the aristocracy, which in aristocratic times were assumed to be natural. Democracy must carve out a place for both liberty and human excellence, for the re-emergence of public virtue and for the possibility of greatness. Without cultivation of excellence and public virtue, Tocqueville foresees democracy reduced to an anxious outlook and anxiety that is relieved by the vast, paternal state. *Downton Abbey* demonstrates similar concerns.

ARISTOCRACY AND DEMOCRACY
IN *DOWNTON ABBEY*

The six seasons of *Downton Abbey* cover thirteen years in the life of a wealthy aristocratic family living on a grand country estate. The drama of the show follows in roughly equal parts the lives of the ruling family, the Crawleys, and various servants. While primarily concerned with the private lives and relationships of the characters, the show develops a secondary theme, that of the decline of the English aristocracy. The changes of the post–First World War England will eventually devastate wealthy country families, such as the Crawleys, leaving them and their servants to find their way in a very different England. As in Tocqueville, the contrast between the "old ways" and "modern ways" continually arises in *Downton Abbey*. This contrast centers around five basic themes: the challenging of basic aristocratic forms and manners; the upheaval caused by societal (including technological) change; a rising sense of independence that stresses individual choice over class or familial duties; the undermining of the aristocratic family itself (including a changing role of women); and finally a sense of loss of meaning as the thick society of an aristocratic people gives way to the tumult of democratic times. We will consider each in turn.

The first episode of the series begins with the sinking of the Titanic. Robert Crawley, the lord of the estate, has three daughters but no son, so the sinking of the Titanic is a particular tragedy for the Crawleys as the two nearest heirs to the estate and title of Earl of Grantham die on the ship. One of these, a young cousin, was to wed Mary, Robert's eldest daughter. The marriage would have allowed the estate to stay in the hands of the immediate Crawley family, as presumably Mary's son would one day inherit the title. With the two heirs deceased, the next heir is found. Much to the disappointment of the family, the heir is Matthew Crawley, a distant cousin who is a country lawyer and whose deceased father was a doctor. This is scandalous, as Matthew is decidedly middle class. Robert expresses perplexity that he should be related to a mere doctor.[69]

Matthew travels to the estate, and his education as to what it means to be an aristocrat begins. "Downton is a great house and Crawleys a great family,"

Robert tells him, "We live by certain standards that may seem daunting."[70] Matthew finds that even the household servants look down on him due to his middle-class background. Matthew declares that he "won't let them change me"[71] and insists that he will continue his work in the law. He can fulfill his familial responsibilities on the weekend. This confuses the Crawley family, who ask, "What is a weekend?"[72] Lady Mary dismisses Matthew as someone who cannot even "hold a knife like a gentleman."[73]

Matthew discovers that what people call each other is of great importance, a point made at various times throughout the series. Robert's youngest daughter, Sybil, ends up courting the family chauffer, Tom Branson, who represents a triple threat: he is lower class, Irish Catholic, and a socialist.[74] Robert confronts them at one point, asking Branson what he is doing in the main house. Branson says, "To see Sybil." "Lady Sybil!" declares Robert, which the independent-minded Sybil dismisses as "all that nonsense?"[75] Branson continues to flaunt convention, much to the family's consternation, after he and Sybil marry. For example, he refuses to dress formally for dinner, calling such clothes "the uniform of oppression."[76] He mistakenly calls Mary, now his sister-in-law, by her first name in front of the butler, Carson, which is a *faux pas*. His confusion with titles continues when he is gently reprimanded for calling a duchess "your grace" when the particular situation called for merely "Duchess."[77] This insistence on titles includes the servants. When housemaid Anna becomes Mary's lady's maid, she is no longer called "Anna" but "Mrs. Bates" as lady's maid is a position of higher importance, thus carrying a more formal title (for example, the head housekeeper is "Mrs. Hughes" even though she's unmarried for most of the series). As Tocqueville indicates, aristocratic people are profoundly concerned with forms and position. These conventions instill a kind of order, as well as recognizing certain privileges. Nevertheless, as Sybil's comment suggests, people are beginning to chafe at the formality of titles.

Only late in the series do people start to question this kind of class system explicitly. In the final season, Downton opens itself up to tourists to raise money for the village hospital (one of the estate's responsibilities). A kitchen maid, Daisy, declares, "I think all these houses should be open to the public. What gives them a right to keep people out?"[78] In response to Daisy, Molesley, a footman with a scholarly streak, says that he is glad that the house will be open as people may appreciate the great craftsmanship and artwork. However, he ponders, people may also start asking why these families possess such wealth. The value of Downton is shifting from that of beauty and grandeur to that of money.

This questioning of class privilege by Daisy and Molesley is just one indication of a second major theme of the series, that of social upheaval, particularly after the First World War. In the first season, one notices a house bustling with activity, full of housemaids, kitchen maids, footmen, and other help. By the last season, a skeleton staff is running the house as "service" is no longer an attractive job and as aristocratic families struggle to pay for a large staff. The first season introduces Molesley as Matthew's valet. After Matthew's death at the end of the third season, Molesley is out of work. Molesley's father mentions this to Robert's mother, Violet, the dowager countess, who says that Molesley is a trained valet and should be able to find work. Mr. Molesley says, "It's a changing world"[79] and houses cannot afford to hire staff as they used to. Later it is revealed that Grantham House, the family's London home, no longer has any maid staff, and they contemplate selling the home.

This is a major plot point of the final season as Robert struggles to maintain staff. He notes to the butler, Carson, that when Carson started at Downton the estate had six footmen and five housemaids, but now there are only two of each. Robert wonders aloud to his mother "how much longer can we go along with it all?"[80] The cost of running the house was three times what it was before the war. He concludes, "Who lives as we used to now?" Most people are "cutting down." Violet responds, "It's seems hard that men and women should lose their livelihoods because it's gone out of fashion." In the course of the series, various propertied families are forced to sell out, including Robert's cousin. While walking into the auction of one of these estates, Edith, Robert's second daughter, murmurs, "Sic transit gloria mundi," or "Thus passes the glory of the world."[81] This is one of many instances in *Downton* in which the viewer is coaxed into feeling regret for the passing of aristocratic life. We might think it odd that a democratic audience is asked to sympathize with the plight of a declining aristocracy. Yet, here is an instance where all but the coldest or most ideological viewer must see something being lost as the aristocracy dies away. There is indeed a passing of something glorious.

Technology also displaces the ways of the past. Early in the series, the house gains electric lighting. Some houses are even getting electricity in the kitchen. "Whatever for?" asks Daisy.[82] Patmore, the head cook, describes a new telephone as "the cry of the banshee."[83] Mrs. Patmore is concerned with the advent of toasters and electric mixers. "With all these toasters and mixers and such like we'll be out of a job," she astutely observes.[84] She has a similar reaction to the purchase of a refrigerator, knowing that this will put delivery boys out of a job, as the house will no longer be purchasing fresh produce each day. "Mrs. Patmore is not what you'd call a futurist," says Thomas Barrow as housemaid Baxter sews with a sewing machine, shocking Mrs. Patmore.[85] Furthermore, Robert is dragged by his young niece, Rose, into purchasing a record player and a radio, on which she listens to jazz music. He concedes to the radio only because it will enable him to listen to the king.

A third refrain regarding the shift from aristocracy to democracy is a growing sense of atomism and independence arising from the decline of aristocratic mores. We see this particularly with the servants. There are many examples, but one is particularly illustrative. In the first season, Gwen, a housemaid, desires to learn secretarial skills through a correspondence course. Service is not what she wishes to do she says.[86] Gwen worries, "I was born to nothing and I will die with nothing."[87] Born the daughter of a farmer, she cannot escape her fate, she thinks. She is encouraged by Lady Sybil to pursue her dream. At first, Gwen is doubtful, telling Sybil that servants are not like Sybil's class. "Our dreams almost never come true."[88] Still, she persists. When Sybil's assistance to Gwen is made known to the family, they are skeptical. Isn't this deluding Gwen? Matthew's democratically minded mother, Isobel, asks, "Isn't the maid a better judge" of her interests?[89] Individual interest, not social class, should rule the day.

As the aristocracy's decline becomes obvious, more and more servants look for alternatives. The servants question the notion that they must spend their life in service, or whether once a life is chosen no change is possible. The idea of self-improvement regardless of social class takes hold. Gwen returns in the final season, now a successful woman, married to a man who manages a woman's college. The family appears happy that she has improved her condition, especially Isobel. This support for individualism even overtakes the socialist Branson. After living in America a short time, Branson is enamored of American capitalism, despite his socialist sensibilities. He says he does not support capitalism everywhere, but has a particular fondness for American style capitalism "where a hardworking man can go to the top in a single lifetime."[90] Like the American sailor in Tocqueville's discussion of perfectibility, Branson admires a system that allows for easy change, for a kind of unsettledness that allows for a rise in economic standing. Across the six seasons, there is a growing awareness that class distinctions are eroding and one's life is more and more in one's own hands. We notice again that this is in the service of greater material comfort. Servants are willing to have a looser connection to place and people in order to gain more individual autonomy and a higher wage. Choice reigns supreme. Branson admires the chaos of America, because it encourages economic activity. He and others are willing to trade a more stable, meaningful existence for one that is more transient, chosen, and profitable. As the society transitions from the traditional norms, the norms are readily viewed as socially malleable rather than naturally stable.

The fourth major theme regarding regime change is that of the family and the role of women. Early in the series, we see demonstrated the rights of the first-born son. Robert laments that he was unable to produce a male heir, which is why the estate is in crisis after the death of the nearest heirs. When Matthew arrives as heir, there is hope that he will wed Mary. While this eventually occurs, at first there is great coldness between Matthew and

Mary. During this period, Robert's wife Cora becomes pregnant. Robert is ecstatic that he might have a son, as this will ensure the estate stays in his family. As Cora states, "If there's a boy the daughters don't get anything."[91] When Cora miscarries and it is revealed that the baby was a boy, Robert is devastated. Only Matthew's marriage to Mary, which produces a son, saves the estate from falling from the immediate Crawley family. We see here the intimate connection between family and place that Tocqueville says defines aristocratic times.

Regarding men and women, the default expectation is for highly formal relations. Robert does not simply enter his wife's dressing room; he knocks first. Concerned over Sybil's attendance at raucous political rallies, Robert opines that feminine sensibilities are "more delicate and refined"[92] than the male's. He is astonished that Sybil would go to such rallies without his permission. Mary offers that Sybil is "entitled to her own opinions."[93] The traditionalist Violet responds, "No! She isn't until she is married. Then her husband will tell her what her opinions are."[94] Sybil insists, "I am interested. I am political. I have opinions."[95] This is one of various scenes in which a family member, usually female, questions Robert's authority. Invariably Robert makes some kind of protest based on a father's authority or traditional gender roles, but he virtually always concedes to the erosion of this authority. We are seeing a shift from an aristocratic family to a democratic family. The power of children, especially female children, increases while that of the father decreases. Robert sometimes becomes a classier version of the contemporary situation-comedy dad, the ridiculous buffoon whose role is largely as a foil for his smarter, more enlightened wife and children.

The decline of this aristocratic family is made clear over the course of *Downton's* six seasons. The subject of female liberation from traditional roles is consistently addressed. To take just one example, the middle Crawley sister, Edith, becomes a newspaper columnist and eventually a magazine editor. Edith's writing scandalizes Robert, as it is not woman's role to express opinions, especially political opinions, in public. Once Edith becomes owner of a magazine, she fights with the male editor, as he is unused to taking orders from a woman. Despite Edith being an adult and a businesswoman, the family thinks it worrisome that Edith sometimes stays in London by herself. Edith's grandmother, Violet, tells Edith that what is good for Edith and the family are "one in the same."[96] Edith disagrees. She wishes to act independently from the family.

Overall, there is a shift from traditional family and gender roles. No Crawley daughter completely pursues men of the "right" social class. Sybil marries Branson the chauffer, in spite of her father's declaration that he will not allow his daughter to "throw away her life."[97] Nevertheless, by series end, Branson is a vital part of the family, beloved by all, his lower social origins largely forgotten. Edith owns a magazine due to an affair with a married business-man who fathers a child with her. At his death, the magazine is left to Edith. Even the oldest daughter, Mary, weds a second husband (after Matthew's death) who is a racecar driver and who opens an auto shop with Branson in the series finale. Neither of her husbands is of aristocratic parentage.[98] Mary also takes on the role of "agent" for the estate, essentially running the day-to-day operations of Downton. In this sense, both Mary and Edith have jobs, court or marry those who are socially beneath them, and all three daughters regularly defy their father, who nearly always acquiesces. Even cousin Rose, who serves as a kind of surrogate daughter to Robert and Cora after Sybil's death, marries a Jew, deeply offending her biological mother. In the end, no young woman in the Downton circle follows the aristocratic script.

Finally, *Downton Abbey* shows aristocratic forms providing meaning and a sense of purpose for various characters and then the decline of those forms over time. In the first season, Robert, accused by his mother of insufficient care for the estate, explodes, "I've given my life to Downton! I was born here and I hope to die here. I claim no career beyond the nurture of this house and this estate. It is my third parent and my fourth child."[99] Similarly he says to Matthew when introducing his new heir to the estate, "You see a million bricks that may crumble, a thousand gutters and pipes that may block and leak, and stone that may crack in the frost . . . I see my life's work."[100] For Robert, Downton is not just a monetary endeavor or an instrument of his own power and ego; he feels a strong obligation to the estate, which includes its servants, tenants, village residents, and to the building and grounds itself. He explicitly says that the estate must be a "major employer"[101] and it pains him to lay off staff or sell land out of economic necessity. Unlike in the commercial culture that is at the heart of Age of Anxiety, Robert's association with his place and neighbors is personal. These are not transactions with abstract, faceless people. As the very word *persona* suggests, Robert has a face-to-face relationship with those for whom he bears responsibility.

As the estate struggles in later years, Branson and Mary, now aiding in the running of the estate, suggest selling some land to a housing developer. Robert is offended at the idea. Robert refuses to sell property to a housing developer who will build "ugly modern houses."[102] The housing development will "spoil the village."[103] Robert argues that they should not destroy what the manor is meant to protect.[104] Robert expresses a willingness to accept less money to protect the beauty and integrity of the estate.

Part of the reason Robert is so dedicated to the estate is, as Tocqueville indicates, he does not see the estate merely in the present, but experiences both the past and the future of the estate as real. The estate has qualities that transcend any materialist conceptualization of it. This gives him a sense of duty that few modern people have for the house that they simply reside in for a few years. For example, Robert describes the tenant farmers as "partners."[105] He does not want to modernize how Downton estate is run. Where his bourgeois son-in-law Matthew sees need for efficiency, Robert sees a duty to tenants and village. He notes that a deceased farmer's family has worked on the estate "since the reign of George III."[106] When Mr. Drew, a farmer on the estate, wants to maintain the farm despite his dead father's debts, he begs Robert for mercy, arguing that his family has farmed this land since days of Napoleon.[107] "I am a Yorkshireman," says Mr. Drew, "this is where I belong." Robert tells him, "We are in partnership with all our tenants." On a handshake deal, Robert loans Mr. Drew the money to pay off the farm's debts. Note that this is not bureaucracy or a mere legal arrangement; it is a personal relationship.

However, there are indications that this kind of personal business relationship is being undermined by modern conditions. In the final season, there is disagreement in the family over whether the local hospital, a patronage of the family to the village, should be taken over by the county hospital system. Isobel, who has a particular interest in hospitals, as her deceased husband (Matthew's father) was a doctor, is all in favor of the county taking over, as is Cora. Violet, the longtime patroness of the hospital, disagrees. Isobel's argument is that the county can bring methods that are more modern to the hospital. Violet worries over the loss of local control. How are interests of village to be looked after if hospital decisions are made in York, she wonders? Isobel, consistently a voice of modern opinion, is interested only in efficiency and outcomes. "I care about survival rates," she says.[108] Violet, ever the voice of tradition, believes the sense of village ownership is more important. Indeed, at a village meeting, residents express concern that they will no longer be able to see their local doctor. In the end, efficiency and centralization win out over local ownership and control, undermining the relational associations that countervail the effects of individualism.

What of the servants? Early in the series, the cynical Thomas Barrow mocks some of his fellow servants for their devotion to the Crawley family. "They're just our employers, not our family."[109] This stands in contrast to Carson, the butler, who says, "They're all the family I've got."[110] In the final season, Anna, Mary's lady's maid, complains that the new maids no longer live in the house, preferring to live in town. They do not wish to be part of the family. For them, service is just a job, with no personal relationship implied. In this, the new servants echo the sentiments of the impersonal commercial economy, namely that economic relationships are merely utilitarian, not personal.

By the end of the series, Barrow has come around to Carson's point of view. As the size of the household staff shrinks, Barrow's job is threatened. He starts looking for other jobs, but finds that his talents (as a footman, valet, and butler) are no longer marketable due to the decline of the great houses. It is plain that Barrow is desperate to save his position at Downton and is in deep despair over his inability to find a home anywhere. His despondency grows so pronounced that he attempts suicide.[111] When his prospect of leaving seems real (he has accepted a position at another house), he expressed deep sorrow at leaving Downton, lamenting, "This is the first place where I've put down some roots."[112] Barrow finally finds contentment when, due to an illness, Carson can no longer work as the butler and Barrow is hired as his replacement, establishing Barrow as a trusted part of the household. Without his position within the household, Thomas struggles to find meaning. He needs his Downton family. In this sense, Barrow reflects the Age of Anxiety. As we first meet him, he is unimpressed with aristocratic privileges and sees his position as a mere job. Over time he begins to see that to which he'd dedicated his life is in decline due to modern conditions, like a factory worker whose job has just been downsized due to globalization. Only when faced with the loss of his role at Downton does he begin to value that role. His anxiety over the potential elimination of his position is so severe that like many contemporary Americans he chooses suicide.

Perhaps the clearest example of the way in which meaning and purpose arise within an aristocratic structure is the hapless Molesley. When first introduced, Molesley is a butler at Crawley House, where Matthew and his mother come to live when they arrive at Downton. Molesley becomes Matthew's valet. Matthew, the bourgeois lawyer, is offended at Molesley dressing him and refuses Molesley's assistance. While thinking he is standing up against privilege, in fact Matthew is deeply wounding Molesley. At one point, he tells Molesley that being a valet is a "very silly occupation for a grown man."[113] Molesley expresses his frustration to Mr. Bates, Robert Crawley's valet, saying, "To be honest Mr. Bates, I don't see the point of it,"[114] meaning there is not much use of being a valet to a man who desires independence. He pleads to Matthew, "But this is my job."[115] He does not just mean that this is how he makes money. He means this is how he finds purpose. Being a valet is a position of honor (which is why a valet is called by his last name, not first) and requires considerable expertise. Matthew is as much as telling Molesley that Molesley's life serves no purpose, striking at the core of Molesly's self-worth.

Matthew eventually tells Robert that he wishes to let Molesley go as he is "superfluous." Robert is nonplussed. He wonders why Matthew would "deprive a man of his living when he's done nothing wrong." Noting that Matthew's mother finds meaning from working at the hospital, Robert adds, "Would you really deny the same to poor old Molesley?" He continues with a larger point, educating Matthew on what it means to be Earl of Grantham. "And when you are master here, is the butler to be dismissed, or the footmen? How many maids or kitchen staff will be allowed to stay, or must everyone be driven out? We all have different parts to play, Matthew, and we must all be allowed to play them."[116] Here Robert wishes to make two points. First, that the lord of the estate has duties to those under him, namely to see to their livelihood. With his privilege comes important duties to dozens of people and families. Second, and more to the immediate point, Molesley, in being a valet, has a "part to play." Each social position dictates a role for the participant in that position. Because Molesley identifies being a valet with who he is and what he is supposed to do, to deny him, that is, to deny his life has any meaning.

This becomes clearer when eventually Molesley does lose his job as the result of Matthew's untimely death. Deprived of his position he declares, "Lately I can't seem to see where I am going."[117] He does not know who he is or what he is supposed to do. He is humiliated into becoming a manual laborer, humiliating not simply because he does not like the job, although that is true, but because he sees being a valet as who he is. He later accepts a position at Downton as a footman, which is a demotion from valet, but at least he finds this work meaningful. He is much closer to playing the part he is meant to play. One is reminded of Christopher Lasch's opinion that encounters with "superior persons . . . schools us in the virtues of civic life: loyalty, trust, accountability. It encourages us to make something of ourselves, and to appreciate the satisfactions conferred by devoted service to an ideal—as opposed to the satisfactions, say, of the marketplace and the street, which offer glitter without substance."[118] Such superiority is a mark not of wealth but of class and dignity. Here class refers the common saying that a person is "classy," by which we mean well-mannered, literate, cultivated, and possessing an air of self-control. In this sense, the common person can be classy.

One can see how the social structure of Downton redounds to the benefit of many. At Downton each person has a role and then seeks to perform that role excellently, developing a kind of virtue. This is true of both lord and servant. The individual gains strength by having a definitive role, rather than being left without guidance to create a self. The Downton community works based on personal relationships, recognizing the personal and relational nature of humanity, rather than seeing each other as simply numbers, or customers, or commodities. The Downton community contains a strong narrative aspect with each person playing a particular role. This is a world that appreciates excellence that sustains beauty, and where life is filled with purpose. But it is all coming to an end.

DOWNTON ABBEY AND THE LIMITS OF AUTONOMY

Of course, the peroration above is a rosy depiction of aristocratic society. *Downton Abbey* is a television show, not to be taken seriously as a depiction of aristocratic society. For every decent Crawley family, in reality there surely was another family capable of using its power and privilege for great cruelty. Even within the *Downton* universe we see indications of the brutality of a traditional society. One example is that of Thomas Barrow, a homosexual closeted out of social necessity. Thomas carries this as a considerable burden. To be sure, as a character Thomas Barrow is complex, in that he is a cynical, conniving, and sometimes quite wicked man. Nevertheless, he is tortured by his homosexuality. He finds it difficult to find male companionship, let alone romantic love, as other men typically hold him in distrust. Sometimes this is open disgust, especially from Carson. At one point, Barrow makes himself seriously ill by injecting himself with a concoction that promises to "cure" homosexuality. While Barrow brings much of his unhappiness on himself, part of his cruel character comes from society ostracizing him. A similar tale is told in a side story of Ethel, a housemaid who gets pregnant out of wedlock. She is ruined as a woman, losing her job at Downton and ultimately resorting to prostitution. She struggles to find any work. Only out of the generosity of Isobel Crawley does she re-enter service, although Ethel decides that she should find a position away from the village as she regularly incurs insults from the locals. To maintain the stability of society, those who violate convention like Ethel and Thomas Barrow must pay heavy penalties.

In this way, *Downton Abbey* is a sophisticated production, being alternately sympathetic and critical of its subject. The point here, though, is not to criticize the historical accuracy of *Downton*, but to consider why it gained such popularity among viewers who likely reject most of the era's sensibilities. What this chapter has tried to show is that Alexis de Tocqueville offers us a discerning take on the blessings and curses of both aristocratic and democratic regimes.

First, we can use Tocqueville simply descriptively. Tocqueville's thought regarding the two regimes gives us an interpretive scheme to assess the action of *Downton Abbey*. Tocqueville's discussion of class, family, and women allow us to better appreciate and place within a philosophical context the action of *Downton*, while *Downton* gives a dramatization of central themes in Tocqueville's thoughts. Often dramatized depictions of philosophical ideas are more persuasive than the more didactic method of philosophers.

Let us mention a few examples. It is Tocqueville's contention that aristocrats have decidedly different habits and manners than lower classes. We see this in *Downton* as the forms of address, dress, areas of the house where individuals are welcome, are determined by social status, not just wealth. Even impoverished aristocrats retain privileges, while those held in high esteem today, such as doctors, lawyers, and famous entertainers, are social inferiors compared to some. Regarding Tocqueville's discussion of perfection, we note

Robert's dedication to the beauty and character of his estate, in contrast to Matthew's focus on utility. Furthermore, Robert, as Tocqueville describes of English aristocrats, is behind great philanthropic works such as maintaining the village hospital or paying for the local First World War memorial. Robert, Lord Grantham, still provides a service that might provide some justification for his privileges, unlike the French nobles Tocqueville derides, while preserving a bulwark against centralization. Also, we see Robert's status as father decaying as his children, all female, regularly defy him and liberate themselves from the family and gender norms.

Second, we can use both Tocqueville and *Downton* as tools of democratic theory. If we, in the Age of Anxiety, find certain aspects of the *Downton's* aristocratic world attractive, why? If we view *Downton Abbey* with some wistfulness, what is it that we think we have lost? Here, Tocqueville is helpful. We who live in a democratic age hardly need to be told what aristocracies do poorly. The prejudices of our age educate us to that end. For most, it is hardly a remarkable feat of moral imagination to sympathize with Barrow and his persecution as a homosexual, or Lady Sybil having her marriage choices (unsuccessfully) dictated by her father. This, however, is precisely Tocqueville's project. The democratic age that he sees ordained by providence does not need instruction on the ways in which democracy is superior to aristocracy. What the age needs is guidance on the virtues of aristocracy and vices of democracy.

For example, the physical splendor of the Downton estate reminds us of a civilization that took beauty and craftsmanship seriously. Tocqueville wishes to remind citizens of democracy that aesthetic claims have value as well as claims of economy and utility. Philip Rieff, discussing Freud, remarks, "But the question remains: How to discipline the 'trash'? To be liberated from renunciatory character ideals by the analytic attitude might give the 'trash' (Freud's term) too much liberty to do its worst, whereas in the older system the 'trash' would not do its best."[119] If one can get past Freud's rather ugly terminology for lower classes, the point remains that in disallowing the worst of aristocracy, namely certain kinds of class injustice, one may also disallow the best, namely a dedication to beauty and excellence. Residents of a commercial, material, throwaway culture might find this sentiment both strange and alluring. Both Robert and the tenant farmers are dedicated to improving their property because to them they own the property in trust, to care for in the name of their ancestors and for the good of their posterity. A people with no familial ties to a place, devoted to convenience, comfort, and utility, are unlikely to create great art. Contemporary people make AT&T Stadium. Aristocratic people make the cathedral at Chartres.[120] Aristocratic times, defined in part by aristocratic leisure, create high culture while a commercial, anxious age makes popular culture.

Similarly, the benefits of greater freedom of individual choice are obvious to democrats. Yet, democracy often hides the costs. Tocqueville reminds us that democratic individuals look for meaning and purpose in their lives. Given no meaning by their commercial culture, deracinated democratic citizens will resort to tyranny of the majority (i.e., fashion) in order to avoid despondency. Democratic people consider instrumentality before quality. Liberty is redefined as simply "getting what I want," rather than getting what is good. Ironically, the reduction of liberty to simply getting one's way is itself a threat to liberty, as liberty may be sacrificed in the name of satisfying immediate interest.[121] In some respects, Rose depicts tyranny of fashion, being overly concerned with having the right hairstyle, wearing the right clothes, listening to the right music. In Rose, we can see the beginnings of a youth culture, based on fashion and commerce, dictating to an adult culture more dedicated to mature, aesthetic ideals.

Downton Abbey illustrates the yearning for meaning, mostly from the lower classes, as the high structured society starts to collapse. The result of decline on social forms is not always blissful liberation (a bliss typically the experience of the wealthy and/or educated elite) but a deep anxiety and sense of lack of direction. The tumult and uncertainty, both economic and psychological, inspires fear as well as hope. Tocqueville worries that tyranny of the majority and obsession with materialism will replace the sense of meaning given in aristocratic times. In later seasons of *Downton*, we are informed that servants are harder to come by because workers value the independence of living in town and the better pay of working in shops. Convenience, comfort, and material concerns outweigh the willingness to dedicate one's self to a family. It is notable that working in a great house is called "service." This word has a double meaning. Of course it means that people are "servants," but also that they are providing a service to the estate and community, not merely working for themselves. As Robert's sense of duty to Downton shows, he thinks he is "in service" as well.

Even more provocatively, we might ask if the familial and sexual freedom evidenced in *Downton* is an unmitigated good. It is likely on these matters that the democratic shift depicted in *Downton* gets the most contemporary applause, so it is here, in the interest of overcoming our prejudices, that we should be the most skeptical. Recall that Tocqueville is agnostic about the good of the democratic family. While he is quite sure individuals benefit, he is unsure society does. In *Downton Abbey*, the relations between family members are hardly the cool relations Tocqueville suggests is typical of aristocracy. In addition, Robert Crawley's authority as *paterfamilias* is regularly undermined. Like Tevye in *Fiddler on the Roof*, Robert sees each daughter (or daughter-surrogate in Rose) marry outside her class (at least on second marriage for Mary). The exception is ironically Edith, the chronically luckless Crawley daughter, who marries a marquis and so gains a title. It is worth noting, however, when she falls in love with her husband, Bertie Pelham, he is untitled and only a confluence of unexpected events gains him a rise to aristocracy. Furthermore, Edith has borne a child from a previous lover, Michael Gregson, who was married while carrying on his affair with Edith. Gregson's death leaves Edith abandoned. She pretends to adopt the child as a ward so as to avoid the scandal of sexual misadventure.

Tocqueville's fear seems to be that this weakening of family ties will play into the individualism of democracy. To that extent, the family ceases to be a bulwark against democratic despotism as its functions are subsumed by the state. It is precisely the decline of the sort of mediating institutions as represented by the English aristocracy and strong familial ties that leads to an increase in the power of the state. An isolated individual, left alone to find meaning and make a life, in desperate need of community, begins to see the state as the only plausible vehicle for communal effort. The rise of democratic man presents challenges as well as opportunities. The aristocratic family, bound to land and ancestors, represents continuity, while the modern family, based more on mobility and looser connections to the past, represents disruption.[122] Tocqueville, we have seen, is uncertain whether the restiveness that is central to the American character can be ameliorated without the domestic stability provided by women. Democratic women insist on certain boundaries; they do not abide foolish or unfaithful men. This stability arises because Americans have applied the economic principle of division of labor to the family. Men work in the tumultuous world of money and politics while women provide the stability of home economics.

What happens, though, when that division breaks down and, as Tocqueville ponders, the democratic family ceases to be a bulwark against individualism? In his argument that the West has become a "therapeutic" culture, Philip Rieff posits that modern man desires, "to preserve the inherited morality freed from its hard external crust of institutional discipline. Yet a culture survives principally, I think, by the power of its institutions to bind and loose men in the conduct of their affairs with reasons which sink so deep into the self that they become commonly and implicitly understood."[123]

As stated, the character of Rose in particular exemplifies the sort of democratic character Tocqueville fears most: frivolous, rebellious for the sake of rebellion, obsessed with fashion, with no perceptible appreciation of the beautiful or permanent things. She is taken on by the Crawleys as her own parents are divorcing and unable to give her any guidance. This is a clear sign of family decay and the preference for individual satisfaction over duty. Rose is substantially unaffected, marrying into another aristocratic family (albeit a Jewish family, thus problematic in her social class). Yet, this is an example of an earlier point: the decay of order rarely hits the wealthy and elite hard, as they have connections and money to "ride the wave." This is less often the case for those not as fortunate, those who continue to bear the brunt of decline of the family begun in the twentieth century. Family and religion are for Tocqueville a partial cure for the "debilitating effects of restiveness" that are part and parcel of democracy.[124] So to the extent that these forms are undermined by a crude individualism, society suffers. One of the many class inequalities in modern American is that of marriage. While marriage remains a relatively strong institution among the wealthy and highly educated, it has all but collapsed in the American working class.[125] Sexual liberation, as depicted in *Downton Abbey*, frees individuals from cultural roles and allows the individual to self-create. In this mentality, there is no rational basis to say that a man should do this and a woman that; it is the right of the individual to make life choices abstracted from one's biology. So the question is where do we find meaning and purpose in our lives? The era of self-expression and pure relationship actively seeks to undermine traditional sources of meaning: family, marriage, children, and religion. These are held to be oppressive because to one extent or another they hamper individual autonomy. You have to live for someone else, by someone else's rules. The individual should be able to both navigate the market and pursue sexual fulfillment with relatively few constraints.

It should not surprise that this mentality aligns nicely with the market imperative of the capitalist society that at its core is a rage against limits. It is no accident that, for example, modern feminism when faced with choices regarding prostitution, pornography, and surrogacy, each of which arguably debase women and turn them into commodities, regularly sides with the market over the dignity of women.[126] The more capitalism is identified with indulgence, the more it erodes more moral foundations of family.[127] As Mark Regnerus has documented, sexual liberation has represented a mixed bag for both women and society as a whole.[128] Women, especially elite women, pursue economic and sexual liberation, aided both by the mentality of the sexual revolution and readily available contraception. While reveling in this greater freedom, as Tocqueville might have predicted unintended social implications arose. Easier access to casual sex with pregnancy as an unlikely consequence removed a great deal of power from women. In Regnerus's economic interpretation, sex became "cheap," that is, costing little in the way of economic, emotional, or temporal investment. Women's ability to hold access to sex over men, encouraging men to leave their restive state and "grow up," weakened. Men no longer had to mature in order to have access to sex. Furthermore, sex, divorced from procreation due to contraception, legalized abortion, and ideology, no longer requires that men take on the responsibility of caring for children or women to wait to find a man who will. Women therefore find it much more difficult to find marriageable men, that is, a man who works hard, provides economically, and will remain sexually faithful and raise children. Women have greater opportunity to provide for themselves and gain sexual freedom but find it harder to find a committed mate with whom to have a family and find emotional intimacy. Regnerus concludes that the era of cheap sex benefits career-minded women and sexual minorities, but hurts lower economic classes for which the stability of marriage and family are much more necessary, and not coincidently have suffered greatly due to the breakdown of family. Also losers are those women who "who prefer a shorter and nobler search for a mate."[129]

So the notion that we can act however we'd like and have whatever familial structure we'd like is the proverbial double-edged sword. What is gained by individuals might be lost by society at whole. Contemporary society takes to the extreme the notion of family found both in John Locke and Jean-Jacques Rousseau. At the heart of Locke's political philosophy is the critique of paternal power. Locke asserts that "the master of the family has a very distinct and differently limited power" and "he certainly can have no absolute power over the whole family, who has but a very limited one over every individual in it." Locke starts with a presumption against paternal power and sees no reason why parents should have authority over adult children or why a husband and wife would stay together after the children have left. This makes sense given Locke's project to put satiation of individual material desires at the center of civil society.[130] Locke's critique of parental power calls into question not just the authority of parents, but the authority of government, the authority of a church, or even the authority of God the Father. Anyone who has attained the age of reason and has the capacity to fend for himself is free from any paternal authority.

Rousseau's thought is similar. Rousseau believes "Man's first sentiment was that of his own existence; his first concern was that of his preservation." Sex is a "purely animal act."[131] To achieve liberation, a natural freedom, the family must be sidelined or destroyed. Rousseau wishes for sex liberated from commitment, as among most lower animals. He agrees with Tocqueville that it is women who socialize men, but believes this is a vice not a virtue. "Now it is easy to see that the moral aspect of love is an artificial sentiment born of social custom, and extolled by women with so much skill and care in order to establish their hegemony and make dominant the sex that ought to obey." In nature, "any woman suits his purpose." So natural promiscuity would produce more peace. Note how Rousseau's sanguinity regarding promiscuity is linked to his misogyny. "Hence it is incontestable that love itself, like all other passions, had acquired only in society that impetuous ardor which so often makes it lethal to men."[132]

Transgressive sexuality and concomitant views of the family that underlie the notion of "pure relationship" and sexual liberation, whatever value they might have for individuals, such as Thomas Barrow and Ethel, leave most people lost, unable to find loving relationships. The very notion that defines the liberationist ideology, that of self-creation, ignores the relational characteristic of the human person, a characteristic Tocqueville understood well. Transgressive sexuality turns relationships and love affairs that should be defined by love and mutual giving into episodes of self-exploration, easily turning others into mere tools for one's self-discovery. As Allan Bloom says of feminism, it turns a thing that should be founded on "natural sweetness" into "a power struggle."[133] As Regnerus finds in his sociological study, it also leaves many desperately lonely.[134] This is as Tocqueville would have predicted. Set free from familial forms, far from experiencing blissful freedom, most people find uncertainty, a profound homelessness. This emptiness is filled with consumerism, sex, distraction of technology, drugs. None of this ultimately fulfills. Modern democracy has taken its liberal assumptions unalloyed, and as such runs the risks of undermining the various forms Tocqueville presents as potential protections against individualism run amok and the tyranny of the majority. Nowhere is this more clearly seen than in familial and romantic relationships. This analysis reveals the tragic nature of politics. Politics exists in a realm of mixed goods, where one good often exists at the expense of another. The balancing of the good of individual choice with the need for order is an example. The art of politics consists in part in the ability to prudently balance multiple competing goods, recognizing that any particular good can be taken too far, which is the error of the ideologue. *Downton Abbey* and Tocqueville in this sense serve as a useful corrective. While we needn't be sanguine about the obvious errors of aristocratic societies, are we also blind to the errors of democracy and, concomitantly, those virtues that aristocracy might possess? One of Tocqueville's concerns is precisely that democracy, especially the equality that defines it, would be turned into an ideology attacking anything that seems to contradict democratic egalitarian principles. The family is no exception.

The separation of people from loving, personal relationships in the name of self-creation precisely advances the cause of depersonalization. Whether in the form of the impersonal market or impersonal state, a society which neglects the natural desire for humans to build relational associations sets itself up for some kind of tyranny. Individuals will more and more become cogs of these impersonal forces. Such liberation is phony. Recognizing the shallowness of the phony liberation and no means to find real liberation, individuals are left with a deep sense of anxiety that permeates modern existence. When radicals of the 1960s, such as Mario Savio during the Berkley Free Speech Movement, denounced "the machine," they failed to realize that family, church, and tradition are what curb the machine.

Tocqueville is a friend to democracy, but believes that this requires one to be a moderate friend to democracy. A friend tells the truth, even when it is uncomfortable. Both Tocqueville and *Downton Abbey* remind those with ears to hear and eyes to see that democracy is a limited good. It is good only to the extent that it facilitates human greatness and liberty. To do so, it must mitigate its own faults while retaining the best of the previous regime. In that way, the ills of the Age of Anxiety may be mitigated.

NOTES

1. Alexis de Tocqueville, *Democracy in America,* trans. Harvey C. Mansfield and Delba Winthrop (Chicago: University of Chicago, 2000), 7.

2. Tocqueville, *Democracy in America*, 6.

3. Ibid., 10.

4. Aristide Tessitore, "Aristotle and Tocqueville on Statesmanship," in *Alexis de Tocqueville and the Art of Democratic Statesmanship*, ed. Brian Danoff and L. Joseph Herbert, Jr. (New York: Lexington Books, 2011), 66–67, 49–72

5. Robert Nisbet, "Tocqueville's Ideal Types," in *Reconsidering Tocqueville's Democracy in America*, ed. Abraham S. Eisenstadt (New Brunswick, NJ: Rutgers University Press, 1988), 182, 171–191.

6. Stephen Marche, "Downton Abbey Is an Aristocratic Fantasy: And Worse, It's Run Out of Steam," *Esquire*, January 5, 2014, http://www.esquire.com/enterta inment/tv/a26598/downton-abbey-season-4-review/ (accessed June 9, 2017); Heather Havilresky, "Sit Cons: Class on TV," *The Baffler*, No. 20 (2012), 42.

7. Robert Joustra and Alissa Wilkinson, *How to Survive the Apocalypse: Zombies, Cylons, Faith, and Politics at the End of the World* (Grand Rapids: Wm. B. Eerdmans, 2016), 105.

8. Tocqueville, *Democracy in America*, 13.

9. Ibid., 480.

10. Ibid., 479.

11. By way of illustration, one might think of Jane Austen's novel *Pride and Prejudice* as a contrast. Mr. Gardiner has much more money than his brother-in-law, Mr. Bennet, but because Mr. Gardiner is a lawyer and works for a living, there are areas of society that he may not enter while his financially strained in-laws, who are gentry and thus socially superior, may. In this aristocratic culture, it is class, not the ability to pay, that grants or denies one privileges. Also, note that we are putting aside the question of race in America because discrimination based on race (and thus lineage) is nominally illegal and also difficult to separate from wealth.

12. Tocqueville, *Democracy in America*, 492.

13. Ibid., 426.

14. Ibid., 427.

15. Joshua Mitchell, *The Fragility of Freedom: Tocqueville on Religion, Democracy, and the American Future* (Chicago: University of Chicago, 1995), 79.

16. Ibid.

17. Ibid., 428.

18. Ibid., 669.

19. Ibid.

20. Ibid., 482.

21. Ibid., 483.

22. Ibid.

23. Ibid.

24. Alexis de Tocqueville, *The Old Regime and the Revolution*, trans. Alan S. Kahan (Chicago: University of Chicago Press, 1998) 87.

25. Tocqueville, *Democracy in America*, 483.

26. Ibid., 409.

27. Ibid., 241. Postman notes that one of the key features of Technopoly is the uncritical acceptance of interpretation based upon statistics and "science." Additionally, Matthew Crawford notes that unable to make sense of reality on one's own, multibillion dollar multinational corporations have filled the meaning gap through branding campaigns.

28. Tocqueville, *Democracy in America*, 243.

29. Deneen, *Conserving America*, 66. Emphasis in original.

30. Tocqueville, *Democracy in America*, 247.

31. Ibid., 485.

32. Ibid., 487.

33. Tocqueville, *Old Regime*, 88.

34. Tocqueville, *Democracy in America*, 489.

35. Ibid., 490.

36. Ibid., 492.

37. Tocqueville, *Old Regime*, 105.

38. Ibid., 117.

39. Tocqueville, *Democracy in America*, 662.

40. Ibid., 663.

41. Tocqueville, *Old Regime*, 212.

42. Tocqueville, *Democracy in America*, 559.

43. Ibid., 560.

44. Ibid.

45. Ibid., 561.

46. Ibid., 562.

47. Ibid., 48.

48. Ibid., 558.

49. Ibid., 559.

50. Ibid., 561.

51. Ibid., 48.

52. Ibid., 561.

53. Catherine H. Zuckert, "Tocqueville's New Political Science," in *Tocqueville's Voyages: The Evolution of His Ideas and Their Journey Beyond His Time*, ed. Christine Dunn Henderson (Indianapolis: Liberty Fund, 2014), 174, 142–176.

54. Tocqueville, *Democracy in America*, 576.

55. Ibid., 563.

56. Ibid., 279.

57. Ibid., 563.

58. Ibid., 564.

59. Ibid., 567–568.

60. Ibid., 574–575.

61. Mitchell, *Fragility of Freedom*, 9.

62. Tocqueville, *Democracy in America*, 569.

63. Here one might think of Flaubert's *Madame Bovary* or Tolstoy's *Anna Karenina*.

64. Tocqueville, *Democracy in America*, 570.

65. Ibid., 575.

66. Ibid., 576.

67. Here we draw heavily from Marvin Zetterbaum, "Alexis De Tocqueville," in *History of Political Philosophy* 3rd ed., ed. Leo Strauss and Joseph Cropsey (Chicago: University of Chicago, 1987), 761–801.

68. Deneen, *Conserving America?*, 11.

69. *Downton Abbey*, season 1, episode 1, Directed by Brian Percival, Written by Julian Fellowes, PBS aired January 9, 2011.

70. Ibid.

71. *Downton Abbey*, season 1, episode 2. Directed by Ben Percival, Written by Julian Fellowes, PBS aired January 9, 2011

72. Ibid.

73. Ibid.

74. Branson also presents a problem in that *Downton Abbey* has two characters named Thomas. His name is Thomas Branson, but is typically called "Tom" or "Branson." There is also a Thomas Barrow, a servant, called either "Thomas" or "Barrow." For the sake of this chapter, the characters will be referred to by their last names as to avoid confusion.

75. *Downton Abbey*, season 2, episode 8. Directed by James Strong, Written by Julian Fellowes, PBS aired February 12, 2012.

76. *Downton Abbey*, season 3, episode 1. Directed by Brian Percival, Written by Julian Fellowes, PBS aired January 6, 2013.

77. *Downton Abbey*, season 4, episode 3. Directed by Catherine Morshead, Written by Julian Fellowes, PBS aired January 12, 2014.

78. *Downton Abbey*, season 6, episode 6. Directed by Michael Engler, Written by Julian Fellowes, PBS aired October 25, 2015.

79. *Downton Abbey*, season 4, episode 1. Directed by David Evans, Written by Julian Fellowes, PBS aired January 5, 2014.

80. *Downton Abbey*, season 6, episode 1. Directed by Minkie Spiro, Written by Julian Fellowes, PBS aired January 3, 2016.

81. Ibid.

82. *Downton Abbey*, season 1, episode 1.

83. *Downton Abbey*, season 1, episode 7, Directed by Brian Percival, Written by Julian Fellowes, PBS aired January 30, 2011.

84. *Downton Abbey*, season 4, episode 1.

85. *Downton Abbey*, season 4, episode 5. Directed by Philip John, Written by Julian Fellowes, PBS aired January 26, 2014.

86. *Downton Abbey*, season 1, episode 3. Directed by Ben Bolt, Written by Julian Fellowes, PBS aired January 16, 2011.

87. Ibid.

88. *Downton Abbey*, season 1, episode 6. Directed by Brian Percival, Written by Julian Fellowes and Tina Pepler, PBS aired January 23, 2011.

89. *Downton Abbey*, season 1, episode 3. As wife of a doctor and mother to a lawyer, Isobel does not have the aristocratic pretentions of Crawleys.

90. *Downton Abbey*, season 6, episode 4. Directed by Philip John, Written by Julian Fellowes, PBS aired October 11, 2015.

91. *Downton Abbey*, season 3, episode 2. Directed by Brian Percival, Written by Julian Fellowes, PBS aired January 6, 2013.

92. *Downton Abbey*, season 1, episode 3.

93. *Downton Abbey*, season 1, episode 6.

94. Ibid.

95. Ibid.

96. *Downton Abbey*, season 5, episode 4. Directed by Minie Spiro, Written by Julian Fellowes, PBS aired January 25, 2015.

97. *Downton Abbey*, season 2, episode 8.

98. Recall that it takes two very untimely deaths for Matthew to ascend from middle class to the aristocracy.

99. *Downton Abbey*, season 1, episode 1.

100. *Downton Abbey*, season 1, episode 2.

101. *Downton Abbey*, season 3, episode 1.

102. *Downton Abbey*, season 5, episode 3, Directed by Catherine Morshead, Written by Julian Fellowes, PBS aired January 189, 2015.

103. *Downton Abbey*, season 5, episode 4.

104. Ibid.

105. *Downton Abbey*, season 3, episode 7, Directed by David Evans, Written by Julian Fellowes, PBS aired February 10, 2013.

106. *Downton Abbey*, season 4, episode 5.

107. Ibid.

108. *Downton Abbey*, season 6, episode 1. Here Isobel voices the only moral authority allowable in the Age of Anxiety, that of the binary cost/benefit analysis

109. *Downton Abbey*, season 1, episode 7.

110. *Downton Abbey*, season 1, episode 1.

111. To be fair, part of Barrow's depression comes from his homosexuality that ostracizes him from the greater society. Part of his depression is attributed to false allegations of an attempt to seduce another footman, but clearly his uncertain status at Downton and the notion that he is no longer needed there affects him more. We shall discuss Barrow's homosexuality below.

112. *Downton Abbey*, season 6, episode 7, Directed by David Evans, Written by Julian Fellowes, PBS aired November 1, 2015.

113. *Downton Abbey*, season 1, episode 2.

114. Ibid.

115. Ibid.

116. Ibid.

117. *Downton Abbey*, season 4, episode 1.

118. Christopher Lasch, *The Revolt of the Elites and the Betrayal of Democracy* (New York: W. W. Norton, 1995), 118.

119. Philip Rieff, *The Triumph of the Therapeutic: Uses of Faith After Freud*, 40th Anniversary Edition (Wilmington: DE ISI Books, 2006), 51.

120. For those confused by the first reference, AT&T Stadium is where the Dallas Cowboys play their home football games.

121. See Bruce James Smith, "A Liberal of a New Kind," in *Interpreting Tocqueville's Democracy in America*, ed. Ken Masugi (Savage, MD: Rowman & Littlefield, 1991), 79, 63–95.

122. Joustra and Wilkinson, *How to Survive*, 151.

123. Rieff, *Triumph of the Therapeutic*, 2.

124. Mitchell, *Fragility of Freedom*, 7.

125. Carney, *Alienated America*, Kindle Location 1221. Charles Murray, *Coming Apart: The State of White America 1960–2010* (New York: Crown Forum, 2012), 154–156.

126. Ross Douthat, "The Handmaidens of Capitalism," *New York Times*, June 20, 2018, https://www.nytimes.com/2018/06/20/opinion/feminism-capitalism.html.

127. Lasch, *Revolt of the Elites*, 95.

128. Mark Regnerus, *Cheap Sex: The Transformation of Men, Marriage, and Monogamy* (New York: Oxford University), 2017.

129. Ibid., 194–195.

130. John Locke, *Second Treatise on Government* (Indianapolis: Hackett, 1980), 46.

131. Jean-Jacques Rousseau, *The Basic Political Writings* (Indianapolis: Hackett, 1987), 60.

132. Rousseau, *Basic Political Writings*, 56.

133. Allan Bloom, *Love & Friendship* (New York: Simon & Schuster, 1993), 27.

134. See also Wendy Shalit, *A Return to Modesty: Discovering the Lost Virtue*, Anniversary Edition (New York: Free Press, 2014).

Chapter 3

Kentucky Aristotelians in Space

Wendell Berry and WALL-E

Wendell Berry is a novelist, essayist, and poet. If you asked him, though, he'd probably start by describing himself as a Kentucky farmer. A resident of Port Royal, Kentucky, Berry is a fierce defender of the land, locality, and his own vision of freedom. Berry is an inheritor of the strong strain of agrarianism that runs through American thought. A deep commitment to an agricultural life and a suspicion of both big government and big business typify his thought. Berry's love of land and agriculture has won him many admirers within the environmental movement. Berry has a deep suspicion of technology, believing it alienates us from craft, from the land, and from meaningful work. Berry has opposed what he sees as the abuse of the land by an industrial economy that favors profit over caring for Creation. Political philosopher Patrick Deneen calls Berry a "Kentucky Aristotelian," saying that Berry's arguments in favor of the virtue of limits place him squarely in the Aristotelian tradition.[1] Berry has been defending this way of life for over four decades. If ours is an age of anxiety, Berry gives both diagnoses and curatives for that anxiety.

Many of the themes of Berry's writing can be seen in the Pixar film *WALL-E*.[2] This ostensible children's movie sparked a remarkable amount of chatter among the talking class upon its release in 2008.[3] The powerful images of environmental degradation, the depiction of consumerism and corporate greed married to governmental power, and the fact that the most human character in the film is a tiny, dirty robot, all provide material for thought. *WALL-E*, which won the Academy Award for Best Animated Film and was nominated for best screenplay, is a remarkable achievement in its ability to entertain and also weave profound thought into a children's story.

This chapter aims to illustrate the ways in which the agrarian ideals of Wendell Berry are woven into the story of *WALL-E*. To this end, we begin with an overview of Berry's thought. Concentrating on his thoughts on land, education, economics, and community, we'll see that Berry offers a strong defense of localism and agrarian life. Then a close analysis of the film *WALL-E* will show how these themes are developed in narrative form. From this, we show how a full life consists of, to a significant degree, an acknowledgement of human limits.

Both Berry and WALL-E, we will see, take aim at the consumerism that is part of the Age of Anxiety. Our age is a restless age, captured in the medieval concept of acedia. This vice, often translated into English as "sloth" does not necessary connote what we normally think of by "sloth." We normally think this means a kind of laziness or lethargy. But acedia really means lack of attention to one's spiritual duties. Acedia was understood as a spiritual state of depression.[4] This can be caused as much by busyness as by lethargy. This is yet another pathology of an age of abundance. Given so many choices we feel the need to partake of them all. Who has not experienced the anxiety caused by knowing others have the latest app, the latest smartphone, are watching the latest television show, are reading the newest, smartest book? We are informed of so many "must haves," "must sees," "must reads," that we cannot possibly have, see, or read them all. We have even coined a term for this phenomenon, FOMO, fear of missing out. Do you really want to be the only one at work who cannot discuss the latest episode of Game of Thrones? Who wants the judgmental stares of peers when it is revealed that you only have an Iphone 5.0, not even a 9.0?

As with so many modern malignancies, smartphones serve as an exemplar. The blessing of the smart phone is wherever we are we can find the right restaurant, watch almost any movie, or listen to almost any piece of music. If in conversation someone wonders what is the capital of Botswana, our phones will tell us that it is Gaborone. These virtues contain a vice inside them. The problem of new technology is precisely that it goes with us everywhere. We are all familiar with the driver distracted by the phone or the difficulty of having a conversation with someone who is constantly checking text messages. Some people live in their own world, constantly with ear buds in place and staring at one kind of a screen or another. This is a kind of acedia, a distraction from duty (spiritual or otherwise). At any moment, we can be distracted by a video, a game, social media. The many options for our attention breeds anxiety over our inability to actually take in all the options. There is the concomitant problem of the inability to simply sit and pay attention. Again, who has not had the feeling of sitting quietly for a short time and then feeling the urge to check the phone for some kind of update or distraction? The subjects of this chapter, Wendell Berry and *WALL-E*, question why we put ourselves on such a hedonistic treadmill, believing that one more purchase or one more distraction will finally satiate us. Are we not better off living within limits and appreciating the good of creation as it is given to us?

THE KENTUCKY ARISTOTELIAN

Before discussing the thought of Wendell Berry, a short discussion of relevant ideas within Aristotle's thought is necessary to illustrate the aptness of Deneen's description of Berry as a "Kentucky Aristotelian." Aristotle differentiates man from the rest of life in that man has the capacity for reason. Humanity does not just eat, survive, and reside. Humans also think about the cosmos.[5] In this sense, the human capacity for wonder and thoughtfulness has a kind of indefiniteness about it. This indefiniteness is the cause of why the science of human things, political science, that is, the art of living well with others in the polis, lacks the precision that some other sciences achieve.[6] Regarding political science, Aristotle famously argues that the city comes into existence for the purpose of mere life, but has as its end the good life.[7] This good life is described by Aristotle as a "virtuous activity of the soul."[8] Virtue, or the good life, does not just happen; it must be practiced. Aristotle argues that "none of the moral virtues arises in us by nature."[9] Aristotle means that humans do not become fully who they are by instinct, as do the lower animals. As Peter Lawler notes:

> Only human beings, such as Thomas Aquinas and Aristotle, could claim that human beings by nature have different and higher purposes than the other animals. And only human beings can make themselves miserable by thinking or imagining that they are more than they really are. . . . For [Aristotle], human beings are the only animals that desire to be more than simply animals. This desire must be accounted for and satisfied, not explained away as some form of chimp aggressiveness.[10]

This becoming "more than simply animals" requires virtue, which must be cultivated through habituation. Human goodness is the result of cultivation of culture. "[T]he virtues we get by first exercising them," says Aristotle, "as also happens in the case of the arts as well. For the things we have to learn before we can do them, we learn by doing them, e.g., men become builders by building and lyre-players by playing the lyre; so too we become just by doing just acts, temperate by doing temperate acts, brave by doing brave acts."[11] This cultivation of virtue is not done simply by one's own effort. The end of the polis and education is to make men virtuous, to be instructed so to as "to delight in and to be pained by the things that we ought."[12] Virtue is a public concern.

Economics plays some part in Aristotle's theory of how politics cultivates virtue. He argues that the aim of economics, or "household management," is to provide for the sustenance of the household. Economics' end is use, not profit.[13] He stresses that household management, like other skills, must be susceptible to limits. The household must be sustainable. One must not simply acquire for the sake of acquisition.[14] The goal of economics is self-sufficiency, and nothing beyond. As proof of the problem of greed, he cites the famous story of King Midas, whose touch turned all into gold, but then found that he couldn't eat.[15] Aristotle is skeptical of exchange that sets profit as its goal rather than use, and especially skeptical of what today we would call finance, the making of money with money, as both have substantial potential to extend beyond natural limits of use. He denounces those who believe that "their store of coined money ought to be either hoarded, or increased without limit."[16]

This desire for gain without limits harkens back to Aristotle's discussion of ethics. Why is it wrong to gain beyond simple use? Aristotle defines virtue as a kind of moderation between an excess and defect. Courage is a virtue, of which the defect is cowardliness and the excess is foolhardiness. To have anything without limit betokens an excess. Aristotle states that the reason some wish to acquire excessive wealth is that "they are eager for life, but not for the good life; so, desire for life being unlimited, they desire also an unlimited amount of what enables it to go on."[17] Similarly, those that think that pleasure or the acquisition of property is the end-of-life wish to possess the means to indulge in these desires. But material goods are not virtue, which is the basis of the good life. "[T]hese people turn all skills into skills of acquiring goods, as though that were the end and everything had to serve that end."[18] Thus, work is corrupted from cultivating an art or providing for one's household and becomes simply a means to acquire beyond necessity. Committed to the unnatural metaphysical vision of the "American dream," we are left anxiously alienated from another natural source of meaning and purpose in life.

We see in Aristotle claims that virtue is a thing to be cultivated, not naturally occurring or instinctual. This cultivation happens within a particular community. That community, then, must be ordered toward virtue. Part of that order is an economic order that values work as a way to provide for life's necessities, not for gaining beyond one's needs. A political society that encourages excess, that fails to cultivate proper habits, that sees work and education merely as tools to acquire further material goods beyond necessity, will be to that extent a deficient political society.

Wendell Berry's philosophy is in harmony with these sentiments. When one considers Berry's thought, it is best to start with his theory of man's connection to the land. Berry illustrates his commitment to the land in poetical form in a piece called *Damage*. He writes, "Until that wound in the hillside, my place, is healed there will/be something impaired in my mind/My peace is damaged. I/will not be able to forget it."[19] Berry bases his views on protection of the land in part on his religious convictions. Berry believes that the landowner is a "guest" or "steward" of God.[20] Berry interprets the famous line from Genesis "be fruitful and multiply and replenish the earth and subdue it" and says, "How, for example, would one arrange to 'replenish the earth' if 'subdue' means, as alleged, 'conquer,' or 'defeat' or 'destroy.'?"[21] Berry opposes the notion that "subdue" can rightfully be interpreted as giving humans the right to use the earth as they please. He laments that "If it comes to a choice between the extermination of the fowls of the air and lilies of the field and the extermination of a building fund, the organized church will elect . . . to save the building fund."[22] Berry, who identifies as a Christian, is frustrated by his co-religionists who apologize for what Berry believes is economic and environmental exploitation of the land in actions such as strip mining, environmentally harmful farming practices, and deforestation. The land is owned in usufruct, says Berry. This is temporary possession, to be used without "causing damage."[23]

As we will see in detail below, Berry ties exploitation of the land to a perverted economics that favors consumption and efficiency over more important values, such as having a healthy relationship with nature and protection of community. Berry writes, "As the farmers go under, as communities lose their economic supports, as all of rural America sits as if condemned in the shadow of the 'free market; and 'revolutionary science,' the economist announces pontifically to the press that 'there will be some winners and some losers'—as if that might justify and clarify everything, or anything."[24] Berry feels it is foolish to injure the health of nature for the sake of a "financial system."[25] It is a violation of our trust with nature to exploit it for a short-lived monetary gain. Care for the land is more important than profit and the ease promoted by a consumerist culture. We must care for the land as we would care for our children, to nurture for its ultimate benefit.

This does not mean that Berry is a typical environmentalist. Indeed, he often eschews the appellation. One of the bumper sticker slogans of the environmental movement is "think globally, act locally." Berry disagrees strongly. He believes that any concept of "global" action necessarily diminishes the local and aligns those who care for the land with the principle agents of globalization, namely governments and multinational corporations. These are the very entities at the forefront of destroying the land. "Those who have 'thought globally,'" including government and multinational corporations, "have done so by means of simplifications too extreme and oppressive to merit the name of thought. Global thinkers have been and will be dangerous people."[26] Berry, for just these reasons, eschews the very term "environment" or "environmentalism." He writes, "We are made of [nature]; we eat, drink and breathe it . . . but we also belong to it, and it makes certain rightful claims on us; that we properly care for it, that we leave it undiminished not just to our children but to all the creatures who will live in it after us. None of this intimacy and responsibility is conveyed by the word *environment*."[27] For Berry, love of nature is an intimate relationship, not a slogan or an abstraction. The notion of the "environment" suggests that nature is a thing separate from the human. As a marriage unites a man and a woman and makes them "bone of bone, flesh of flesh" (Genesis 2:23) so it is with the land, the water, the air, and the other living creatures with whom we share the planet. Only those who know the land intimately will adequately care for it.[28] Thus, Berry concludes, "Local life may be as much endangered by those who would 'save the planet' as by those who would 'conquer the world.'"[29] We will see below that Berry is a strong defender of local communities, and part of that defense lies with Berry's concern that we be proper stewards of the land.

Berry believes that the rise of specialization and professionalization in education has contributed to the alienation of people from their land, if not also from themselves. By treating people as commodities or simply as productive consumers, an education based on those assumptions dehumanizes us. "Is the obsolescence of human beings now our social good?" asks Berry. Berry sees just this in the "mechanization, automation, and computerization" of the modern economy.[30] Mechanization alienates us from the hard manual labor that helps us appreciate nature and her rhythms.[31] The replacement of people with things leaves us with nothing to do and, if anything, makes life too easy and we cease to the see grandiosity of humanity. Berry thinks it is precisely the mission of local educational institutions, especially regional colleges, to educate young people of their area. "Many of these professionals have been educated, at considerable expense, in colleges or universities that had originally a clear mandate to serve localities or regions—to receive the daughters and sons of their regions, educate them, and send them home again to serve and strengthen their communities." Berry believes this mandate has been betrayed as regional schools educate specialists who then leave for major metropolitan areas to gain the wealth that their educators have told them is the sole reason for their education.[32]

Berry laments that schools are "no longer oriented to a cultural inheritance that it is their duty to pass on unimpaired, but to the career, which is to say the future, of the child."[33] Schools are too busy fitting the children for a modern, technological world, and one that values efficiency, productivity, and consumption over a fully human life.[34] Education should be for cultivation, for growing good humans. That means reminding students of the deposit of their cultural inheritance. There is a meaning in our activities, even our commercial activities, beyond moneymaking and efficiency. Political philosopher Patrick Deneen argues that Berry reminds us that we are cultured creatures. We become who we are by what we create. Deneen writes, "Culture is the inescapable medium of human life and the conduit of the human relation to the natural sphere. . . . [T]he complexity of the modern economy makes the likelihood of perceiving the various connections between different kinds of worth exceedingly difficult."[35] Berry puts it thusly: "But humans differ most from other creatures in the extent to which they must be made what they are—that is, in the extent to which they are artifacts of their culture. . . . To take a creature who is biologically human and to make him or her fully human is a task that requires many years (some of us sometimes fear that it requires more than a lifetime)."[36]

This position with regard to education and the human person leads to a discussion of Berry's view of economics, specifically his critique of the modern industrial/technological economy, globalization, and consumerism. Part of Patrick Deneen's argument that Berry is a "Kentucky Aristotelian" is that Berry, without explicitly recognizing it, shares Aristotle's views regarding political economy. In short, Aristotle's economics puts the making of profit as secondary to the making of a good person. In the Age of Anxiety, rather than creating our own culture of music, story, and food, amongst neighbors and family, we tend to simply purchase an ersatz culture.[37] One might think of recent Bud Light "dilly dilly" commercials that openly mock craft brewing. The entire ethos of this advertising campaign is "While we have an inferior product, we do have a superior marketing budget to make many funny commercials. Buy our mediocre beer!" This is the modern notion of economics that Berry finds so offensive and dehumanizing. As Deneen puts it, "The modern liberal tradition commends understanding human beings above all as *Homo economicus*, and economics as the science of increase and growth, of dominion and mastery over nature."[38] Aristotle's economics can be summarized by the difference between living and living well, noting that excess often leads to a kind of slavery to desire.[39] Those goods that are superfluous distract us from virtue. We become enraptured with gadgets and shiny objects, and this desire leads to indulgence and gluttony. The worst aspect of this phenomenon is the denial of limits, the notion that we can keep accumulating more and more without this limitlessness corrupting us. Deneen writes of Berry's discussion of limits, "Berry evokes both ancient Greek and Christian understandings of liberty as the free acceptance of proper limits. Ironically, the accumulation of our individual decisions leaves modern liberals profoundly unfree. We are, first and foremost, in the thrall of our appetites; we lack self-control and hence are incapable of the freedom of self-rule."[40] Whether it is an unfettered free market economy or an unlimited government, Berry believes that the modern state has reduced man to a price tag, seeing only economic value. Berry worries that the advanced welfare-state encourages dependence but more importantly ceases to value actual human beings. Berry says that "if one is going to destroy a creature, the job is made easier if the creature is first reduced to an idea and a price."[41]

Berry believes that there is an alliance between big government and big business at the expense of human freedom. Berry states that "the business of the American government is to serve, protect and defend business; and that the business of the American people is to serve the government, which means to serve business." He continues, saying when community is "subordinated" to business two "catastrophes" result. The people are "estranged" from their country, and second "the country itself is destroyed."[42] By putting their faith in consumer products and by supporting the exploitation of the land for profit, the people are corrupted by the desire for wealth.

Both "liberals" and "conservatives" partake in this exploitation. Conservatives uphold the family as an icon, but support an economic system that undermines communities and families. Liberals, on the other hand, want mothers to be away from home so they can be "liberated." "Some feminists are thus in the curious position of opposing the mistreatment of women and yet advocating their participation in an economy in which everything is mistreated."[43] Similarly, both support sexual exploitation.[44] Liberals because they don't want to be intolerant of "individual liberty" and conservatives because opposition to promiscuity would reduce the profits of corporations, which use "advertisements and entertainments" to promote sexual indulgence as means of moving products.[45]

One of the negative implications of an exploitive economy is the inability of people to provide for themselves. People become dependent on things that they purchase, rather than developing skills to provide for themselves. Berry writes, "This is certainly true ... of patrons of the food industry, who have tended more and more to be mere *consumers*—passive, uncritical, and dependent." People, divorced from the actual production of food, do not know what they eat, how it was produced, or what is in it. "The food industrialists have by now persuaded millions of consumers to prefer food that is always prepared. They will grow, deliver, and cook your food for you and (just like your mother) beg you to eat it."[46]

A people dependent upon strangers for the essentials (or perceived essentials) of life are not free. Invoking a scenario reminiscent of a zombie film, Berry ponders what would happen to most modern Americans if they lost electrical power for even a short period of time:

> Most of the essential work could not be done. Our windowless modern schools and other such buildings that depend on air conditioning could not be used. Refrigeration would be impossible; food would spoil. It would be difficult or impossible to prepare meals. If it was winter, heating systems would fail. At the end of forty-eight hours many of us would be hungry.[47]

Berry's point is obvious: most people are incapable of providing for even the most basic needs without technology.

That dependence on others, especially strangers, is a reduction of freedom. This also leaves people open to manipulation by marketing and advertising.

> Such a society, whose members are expected to think and do and provide nothing for themselves will necessarily give a high place to salesmanship. For such a society cannot help but encourage the growth of a kind of priesthood of men and women who know exactly what you need and who happen to have it for you. . . . If you wish to be among the beautiful, then you must buy the right fashions (there are no cheap fashions) and the right automobile (not cheap either).[48]

Being divorced from production and producers, people are not able to properly adjudicate the claims made by salesmen or to hold poor workmanship accountable. They also become passive and weak. "The people do not support themselves so much from the place or so much by mutual work and help as their predecessors did; they furnish much less of their own amusement and consolation; purchasing has more and more replaced growing and making."[49] Berry expresses this in fiction in the novel *Jayber Crowe*, in which the eponymous narrator opines, "The new way of farming was a way of dependence, not on land and creatures and neighbors, but on machines and fuel and chemicals of all sorts, *bought* things, and on the sellers of bought things— which made it finally a dependence on credit."[50] A system of codependence on known individuals has an element of accountability that dependence on strangers, products, and abstractions lacks. Reliance and relationship with community members is interpersonal and naturally reduces anxiety, because accountability and dependence are shared between persons.

Once again, Berry believes strongly in localism. As with protection of nature, Berry believes that the intimacy of small scale allows for a more human culture. By emphasizing economies of scale, we have promoted large corporations that take away the ability of local economies to provide for themselves. This puts them at risk of exploitation from sources outside of the community that do not care about the good of the people and land of the locality. Berry believes that in order for a people to be free, they must be self-sufficient:

> If we are serious about reducing government and the burdens of government we need to do so by returning economic self-determination to the people . . . .For example, as much as possible of the food that is consumed locally ought to be locally produced on small farms, and then processed in small, non-polluting plants that are locally owned. We must do everything possible to provide to ordinary citizens the opportunity to own a small, usable share of the country.[51]

Berry believes strongly in localism and community. As community is subsumed under supposed higher goods of economic efficiency and "self-realization" "the communal supports of public life also and by the same stroke are undercut, and public life becomes simply the arena of unrestrained private ambition and greed."[52] Greed and the desire for "self-realization" corrupts the community and the people. Both are ways of ignoring limits, economic limits and personal limits. Berry admits that the limits of community might make members poorer materially, but richer as human beings. "In a healthy community, people will be richer in their neighbors, in neighborhood, in the health and pleasure of neighborhood, than in their bank accounts."[53] As Deneen puts it, "Like Aristotle, Berry argues that the whole precedes the parts, that is, that the parts can thrive only when the whole is considered, comprehended, heeded, and cultivated."[54]

So we can see that Berry's localism dovetails with his criticisms of economics. The national and global economy is the enemy of local community. The same is true with regard to the land. As noted above, a deep intimacy with land, a love of the land, means that a people will care for that land as proper stewards rather than destroying it for profit. Patriotism starts with loving the land, with "fidelity to a place."[55] As Berry puts it, "An inescapable requirement of true patriotism, love for one's land, is a vigilant distrust of any determinative power, elected or unelected, that may preside over it."[56] Depersonalization is the road to perdition. Much of modern materialism, either of a Marxist or Darwinian variety, believes that personal relations are really just masks or ideologies disguising the underlying impersonal forces of economics or evolution.[57]

In the Jeffersonian tradition, Berry believes that self-sufficiency is at the heart of freedom. Jefferson, it is to be recalled, believed that those who work the soil were the "chosen people of God." The "corruption of the morals in the mass of cultivators" is unheard of. They are able to provide for themselves rather than depending on "the casualties and caprice of customers."[58] For Berry, freedom "is pretty much a synonym for personal and local self-sufficiency."[59] This is not the self-sufficiency of the isolated or "rugged" individual, but that of a community of citizens embedded in personal relationships who are independent of distant impersonal forces.

Berry states that "if you are dependent on people who do not know you, who control the value of your necessities, you are not free, and you are not safe."[60] The heads of many of our institutions are themselves rootless and "itinerant." They have a contempt for local, especially rural, life. "A community, especially if it is a rural community, is understood by its public servants as provincial, backward and benighted, unmodern, unprogressive, unlike 'us,' and therefore in need of whatever changes are proposed for it by outside interests (to the profit of those outside interests)." The rural community is "taught to regret that it is backward and provincial" and it is thereby taught to welcome the purposes of its invaders."[61] Elites, who rail against boundaries, express contempt for those who retain boundaries, especially those of community, family, and religion, the "bitter clingers" and "deplorables" of recent political campaigns. The powerful, who are able to satiate their untamed desires, undermine the boundaries still honored by the less powerful that protect them in their powerlessness.[62]

The deracinated-cosmopolitan thrives in the modern economy that works against a real culture. In that sense, as we discussed above, they are not fully human. The cosmopolitan lives in what is more of an anticulture, one that is based on choice and freedom from limits. A real culture constrains us with meaning formed through habits, folkways, and deep connection to a place and a people. Berry says that too many people do not live by local mores and habits "but to a rootless and placeless monoculture of commercial expectations and products."[63] The modern consumer culture perhaps comes to fruition in social media. Social media advertises itself as a way of building community, but as attentive observers of social media easily realize, the purpose of social media is to make money for the media platforms (Facebook, Instagram, Pinterest, Twitter, etc.). For many users, social media is a way of advertising the self, of turning oneself into a commodity. Users are habitually willing to take even the most intimate parts of their lives and make them public as a way of creating a kind of online character. The distinction between public and private collapses. In the past, there were few personal violations as heinous as reading someone's diary. Now people simply reveal their intimate lives for all to see on social media. All of this so a Silicon Valley corporation can increase its market value. The commodification of the self is complete.

A people needs a culture, stories, and folkways, to help teach its members what and who they are. Culture gives a community power over its members. Culture "exercises this power not by coercion or violence but by teaching the young and by preserving stories and songs that tell . . . what works and what does not work in a given place."[64] Berry has contributed to this culture through his own stories. For example, in *Jayber Crowe*, Berry tells a simply story of the life of a small town barber who sees, over many decades, the community he learns to love change, mostly for the worse, via technology, industrialism, and that dubious good called progress.

Jayber, the narrator of his own story, leaves his home of Port William for a number of years. He finally returns and reflects on his home. "Where I wanted to be, always, day in and day out, year in and year out, was Squires Landing and all of the fall of country between Port William up on the ridge and the river between Sand Ripple and Willow Run. When I heard or read the word home, that patch of country was what I thought of."[65] Ultimately, he sees that Port Williams changes as people leave for better economic opportunity. He catalogs some of what was lost in this change.

Jasper Lathrop, like most country merchants then, bought chickens and eggs and cream from the farmwives. This was a more important prop to the local economy than you might think. It was one of the mainstays of the household economy of the farms, helping the families to preserve their subsistence by making a ready market for the surplus. But also it was a valuable tie between Jasper and his customers. It brought in trade.

But that ended. The household poultry flocks began to dwindle away. So did the little household dairying enterprises of two to maybe half a dozen cows. Farmwives, who once had come to town with produce, bought their groceries, and gone home with money, now went to the store (maybe in some distant town) with only money and went home with only groceries.[66]

Folks may have gained monetarily, but they have lost much of what is valuable, including their very humanity.

We will see the same thing play out in the film *WALL-E*, where the most human character is a small, dirty, robotic garbage collector. The themes of Berry's agrarian thought, community, culture, the corruption of consumerism, the love of the land are all depicted in this film. Here we find a diagnosis and proposed antidote for the anxiety of our age. The diagnosis is a desire to accumulate more consumer goods in the attempt to find meaning through acquisition. The antidote is coming into a greater communion with neighbors, place, and land.

AGRARIANISM GOES TO SPACE

The film *WALL-E* is about an eponymous robot (Waste Allocator Load Lifter Earth Class, or WALL-E) whose job is to compact garbage on Earth in the distant future. But WALL-E is alone on this Earth (except for a cockroach friend) as all the humans have left. The Earth needs a garbage compacter as garbage is about all that remains. The Earth is a wasteland of trash, smog, and decrepit buildings. WALL-E spends his day gathering trash and making monuments of square-bale refuse. He also carries with him a small cooler. As he goes about his business, he collects artifacts: various items, such as a light bulb, a lighter, and a Rubik's Cube. He also is fascinated by a film, *Hello Dolly*, the soundtrack to which he plays as he goes about his duty. Early in the film he is watching a romantic scene from the film (on an Ipad no less). The scene means so much to him that he sees fit to record it onto some kind of internal memory.

WALL-E's world changes when Earth is visited by EVE, or Extraterrestrial Vegetation Examiner. EVE has been sent from the spaceship Axiom, the abode of many descendants of the humans who left 700 years ago. Her job is to scan the Earth looking for signs of vegetative life. WALL-E, finding another "life form" to share his existence with, becomes enamored of EVE. But when EVE actually finds a plant she automatically is called back to the Axiom, with WALL-E hitching a ride. The rest of the film largely follows the travails of EVE and WALL-E attempting to deliver the plant to the Axiom's captain, only to be thwarted by AUTO, the ship's auto pilot. After many misadventures this task is accomplished, sending the ship back to Earth where the humans recolonize.

WALL-E exhibits many of the characteristics that Berry associates with meaningful humanity. Berry often extols the value of hard work, especially manual work. Note, for example, that Berry has a whole essay explaining why he doesn't own a computer, arguing that he can produce better quality with pen, paper, and old typewriter. The manual work involved in producing writing both makes the work more deliberate and thoughtful, thus higher quality, as well as encouraging the writer to develop his skill as a craft.[67] WALL-E is very, very good at his job. We see his almost skyscraper height piles of compacted garbage. He is cleaning up the mess left by humans and seems to take pride in his effort. He plays "Put on Your Sunday Clothes" from *Hello Dolly* while he works, perhaps the closest thing to whistling while he works that he can manage. There is something remarkable in his existence as well. How has WALL-E managed to survive as seemingly everything else has ceased operating?

Perhaps the most intriguing aspect of WALL-E's character is his propensity to collect. He is captivated by artifacts found in the human waste. As mentioned above, WALL-E performs his job with a small cooler in tow, allowing him to gather up the interesting trinkets he finds. How do they work? What was their purpose? At one point, he throws away a diamond ring and keeps the box it came in. He is more interested in the operation of the box than the shiny ring. He wants to know more about the artifacts and culture of the people whose garbage he collects. Within the shack in which he lives, WALL-E has amassed an enormous collection of these artifacts, seeking to preserve the little oddments of a lost people. He is participating in one of the essential tasks of culture: memory.[68] He is not just a preserver, though. In a comical attempt to woo EVE when she comes to Earth, WALL-E creates a statue of her out of junk. It is not a very good statue, and EVE is not impressed, but WALL-E is also a creator of culture. Near the end of film, WALL-E has nearly been destroyed on the Axiom in an attempt to defend the plant from AUTO. Back on Earth, EVE replaces WALL-E's parts from his own stash, but it is not clear that WALL-E is still WALL-E. In a moment of self-forgetting, WALL-E takes his own artifacts and compacts them as if they are garbage. This is what a people without memory, without culture, does to its inheritance.

The film sets up a clear distinction between WALL-E and the humans on the Axiom. The distinction is that WALL-E is more human than they. The humans have likely destroyed their planet as part of an irrational consumerism. Other than WALL-E, the only thing that appears to work on Earth is video advertisements for Buy N Large (BNL), the megastore that seemingly owns everything on Earth. Almost everything is labeled with BNL logos, including the government banners. Indeed, what appears to be the White House is also the Buy N Large national headquarters. BNL owns the Axiom (and apparently many other ships) and flies people off the land that BNL seems to have ruined. The finest ship, the Axiom, has everything you need, at least according to its own advertising. Among the many amenities it features "fine dining." The humans travel on hover-chairs so "there is no need to walk," as the Axiom advertising helpfully informs us.[69] In fact, humans are now so obese that they cannot walk, so used are they to having machines carry them everywhere. On the Axiom, "Space is the final fun-tier."[70]

It is almost forty minutes into the film before we see our first human on the Axiom. The human we meet is on a hover-cart, severely overweight (we'll soon find out that he cannot walk) talking about hitting virtual golf balls at the driving range. The humor is that the person he is talking to on his video screen is on the hover-cart right next to him. This is what everyone appears to do. They drive around on their hover-carts, surrounded by advertising, buying objects. The people cannot seem to resist the advertisements. So when the computer advertising (which is omnipresent) says "Try blue, it's the new red," everyone conforms and switches to blue clothes (which seemingly are controlled by computers).[71] The advertising claims "BNL, everything you need to be happy."[72] Happiness is defined as the acting on impulse. Buy N Large even raises the children. Babies sit in a room watching a screen. "A is for Axiom, you're home sweet home," it tells them. "B is For Buy N Large, you're very best friend."[73] There is at least some suggestion that children are born artificially, as are the decanted babies in Aldus Huxley's *Brave New World*. Sexual relationships between people whose existence is so highly mediated would most certainly seem "unnatural" in such a society. "A world in which children are manufactured and sex and procreation are totally disconnected," writes Peter Lawler, "would surely be one without much love, one where one manufactured being would have little natural or real connection to other manufactured beings."[74]

The humans on the Axiom, by Berry's standards, are not human. They are dependent upon a corporation and on machines that they cannot control. They can literally do nothing for themselves. They are content to be amused and satiated, more like cows than humans. Their world, completely plugged in, has de-humanized them.

As Berry suggests, the fictional future of *WALL-E* shows a marriage of corporate power and governmental power. Divorced from the lives of the actual humans who buy their products, both feel free to exploit the people and their land, to the extent that people are no longer fit for self-government and the land has been raped. Eventually some of the humans begin to recognize this. WALL-E causes a hover-cart accident liberating two characters, John and Mary, from their hover-carts and the omnipresent screen. John and Mary begin to see what they have been missing. Mary looks out a window and is astounded by the beauty of outer space for the first time. Similarly, she drives to a lounge area and she exclaims, "I didn't know we had a pool!"[75] With her face in front of a screen the whole time, she had never noticed the gigantic pool. She and John end up playing in the pool, something that the robot overlords do not allow. *WALL-E*, released just prior to the advent of the smartphone, seems to anticipate much of what the smartphone would promote. While the residents of the Axiom are superficially lazy, they are also distracted constantly. They are unable to appreciate or wonder about their circumstances. The beauty that is literally just outside their window eludes them as they move on to the latest consumer attraction. To be satisfied by this life they have had to be dehumanized. While *WALL-E* captures this aspect of omnipresent technology, it fails to appreciate how this technology would be accompanied by depression, loneliness, and suicide. One might argue, however, that the consumerism and idle distraction that define life on the Axiom are a kind of opioid, designed to numb the mind and kill the psychic pain of a life with no meaning.

It is the ship's captain who explains the ultimate frustration with the dehumanization they have all been subjected to. As he slowly realizes all that he has been missing, he ends up fighting AUTO for control of the ship. AUTO tells him they must stay on the Axiom in order to survive. The captain declares, "I don't want to survive. I want to live!"[76] This is a perfect expression of the Aristotelian teaching that the city comes into being for sake of mere life, but has as its purpose the good life. The captain is tired of the mere life of food, sleep, and amusement. Hedonistic materialism cannot produce happiness. The captain also is determined, against the will of AUTO, to use the plant EVE found to order the ship back to Earth. He is looking for a home, and the Axiom is not it. It does not provide a culture. It does not provide meaning. It does not provide a place. The captain says, "Out there is our home. Home, AUTO! I can't just sit here and do nothing."[77] The captain finally asserts human control over the ship, initiating a political community. Up to this point, the coddled humans have been willing to give their freedom over to machines. "Can you imagine a robust political debate happening in a world where everyone is comfortable, happy, and free to pursue their own interests entirely?"[78] The politics of the Axiom are the politics of the farm yard, with the humans playing the part of the farm animals, only the possibility of slaughter seemingly missing.

Part of having a home is taking care of it. As the humans on Earth obviously became detached from the land they began to abuse it. The film uses powerful imagery to show the garbage that engulfs the Earth as well as the space junk around the Earth. The sepia tones of the parts of the film that take place on Earth present a grainy, dirty image. The only life that we know of on the planet at the beginning of film is a cockroach. The brown filth that dominates the film's first twenty or so minutes only enhances the beauty when the green plant is finally found. The film's cinematography makes this into a thrilling moment, such is the starkness of the imagery. The plant becomes a kind of talisman, this thing that must be protected at all costs.

The captain of the ship first meets WALL-E and shakes hands with him. Since WALL-E is filthy, the captain finds dirt on his hand. He's never seen dirt before. Having the computer analyze it, he discovers this thing called "soil," sometimes called "earth."[79] From this he learns about "farming."[80] He gets excited about farms, which he imagines is where you put things in the ground, pour water on them, and then you grow pizza. As the computer shows him images of planet Earth, most of the images are of people growing things. This seems to be the ideal of Earth, namely people working the soil to grow life.

The film's depiction of agriculture ties into its discussion of culture in general. As the captain learns about farming, the computer tells him of a thing called a "hoedown," which is a kind of folk dance.[81] The captain then requests, "Computer, define 'dancing.'"[82] As he does so, the film cuts to WALL-E and EVE going through what can only be called a dance in space outside the ship. Dancing is a folkway that traditionally has brought people together in precisely the way that occurs at a hoedown. Social dance is just that, social. It is quite different from most of the dance at the typical club in the United States, which is essentially a group of individuals gyrating idiosyncratically, with the fellow dancers being irrelevant to the dance itself. Later, the captain looks at his pictures of Earth, of dancing and farming and cannot fathom what has happened. EVE shows him a clip of "Put on Your Sunday Clothes" from *Hello Dolly* that she recorded. "Hey, I know that song! They're dancing! Yes, dancing."[83]

The closing credits show people in nature, farming, and rebuilding in classical architecture all depicted in imagery inspired by various art movements. Humans, returned to Earth, are now in the process of building a culture to grow a people, actual humans in communities, tied to the earth.

CULTURE AND CULTIVATION

In an essay on liberal education, political philosopher Leo Strauss notes that the words culture and agriculture are related. The point of education is to cultivate human beings, just as the point of agriculture is to cultivate food. As we do not cultivate the land in just any manner, for example throwing garbage on our gardens, we also do not cultivate people in just anyway. So we must care for our culture.[84]

Wendell Berry, one suspects, would agree. The milieu in which people are born, live, and die shapes them. Recall that humans are the kind of animal whose nature is to be conventional. So these conventions shape us. Though conventions are often thought to be arbitrary, they are not without consequence. Both Berry and the film *WALL-E* show us what kind of people are cultivated when consumerism, ease, and technology begin to shape us. Negatively, Berry and the film believe that technology dehumanizes us by separating us from work and from the land. Technology, as the film illustrates, can also separate us from each other. So busy amusing ourselves (if not quite to death) we cease talking to each other and living an unmediated life that is real. One might evoke the notion of Sherry Turkle that our public spaces are no longer places of social interaction, they are places where people come together to not speak to each other. "What is not being cultivated here is the ability to be alone and reflect on one's emotions in private."[85] Given this debased culture (again, more accurately an anticulture), people will neglect their land, wishing only to exploit for their own ease. The marriage of big government and big business opens both the human and the land to abuse. People tend to be naïve about the corporate structure and interests of entities like Google and Facebook. "As long as Facebook and Google are seen as necessities, if they demand information, young people know they will supply it. They don't know what else to do," writes Turkle.[86] We also see a critique of both the market and the state, provocatively united in *WALL-E*. Both the market and the state operate in an impersonal manner, making exploitation all too possible. Neither the market nor the centralized state is capable of adequately addressing man's nature as a personal, relational animal. This is more easily done in local (decentralized) politics and through a local economy in which the ties between producer and consumer are more likely to be personal.[87]

Both Berry and the film show that care for people and care for land are entwined. Tied to a place, people love what is near them and what they have invested in a place. There is an old saying that no one washes a rental car. Similarly, if people are deracinated cosmopolitans, they will not feel any sense of responsibility to their place. But when we have roots in a place, when we get out of our homes (and turn off our screens) and actually interact with people, we will feel a responsibility that breeds a richer, more human life.

The texts discussed here ask people to recall the importance of limits. Part of the modern ideology that is behind the Age of Anxiety is the belief in unlimited government and unlimited economic growth. In the vein of Wendell Berry, Joseph Ratzinger argues vigorously that the very notion of "creation" suggests a givenness that precludes limitless progress. The mere fact of one's creation means that one is not responsible for one's own existence.[88] We are embodied in a cosmos not of our own making which contains its own meaning that we should appreciate and respect. "Creation is defined as dependence, origin ab alio ['from another source']," writes Ratzinger. But in modern thought, particularly Marxism, "[creation's] place is taken by the category of self-creation, which is accomplished through work. Since creation equals dependence, and dependence is the antithesis of freedom, the doctrine of creation is opposed to the fundamental direction of Marxist thought … The decisive option underlying all the thought of Karl Marx is ultimately a protest against dependence that creation signifies."[89] If human beings fundamentally "are nothing, naked apes, particularly aggressive rats," then all that is left is to skillfully apply human knowledge to make us better.[90] We should turn human beings into objects of an experiment, with no dignity necessarily given to the individual. Indeed, what would be the basis of such dignity? The modern project sometimes seems more interested in cultivating ants rather than human beings, creatures who are productive, well-ordered, and satisfied. By contrast, we are advocating putting work in its place within culture, which is only possible by taking seriously the qualitative dimensions of culture that give meaning to work and life. The problem with the modern orientation is that work is no longer seen as a result of the fall, but the modern orientation ends up making this our end, especially through the thought of Marx.

While one might consider Berry's thought to be too parochial, he reminds us that a good life requires saying "no" to indulgence.[91] Likewise, *WALL-E* shows us the consequences of a people who simply want to indulge. The technology allows them to shirk duties to each other and the land. They end up as slugs. Putting limits on ourselves helps us align ourselves to that which is actually best for us. Turkle, in her study of adolescents and technology, warns that the constant bombardment of images, sounds, and other stimuli make it difficult for us to find the mental discipline and silence necessary to enter into a deep relationship with other people or with a cultural artifact: "But technology, put in the service of always-on communication and telegraphic speed and brevity, has changed the rules of engagement with all of this. When is downtime, when is stillness? The text-driven world of rapid response does not make self-reflection impossible but does little to cultivate it."[92] Even more so, Nicholas Carr has shown that the brain is rewired for short bursts of information processing through internet reading, and by extension, contemplation is obsolesced. The kinds of souls cultivated by much of our modern technology and economic arrangements are souls characterized by constant need of distraction, a concomitant lack of attention, a declining ability to empathize with others, a frustration with the effort required to build deep human relationships or to simply live a human life.[93]

Human beings are not just minds abstracted from the body. This Cartesian dualism suggests that knowing occurs only in a rational, didactic manner, which explains Descartes' emphasis on mathematics as the path to knowing. "And considering that, of all those who have hitherto searched for the truth in the sciences, only mathematicians have been able to find any demonstrations, that is to say, certain and evident reasonings, I did not at all doubt that it was with these same things that they had examined."[94] It is this abstraction from physical reality that allows creation to be depersonalized and, thus, more easily exploited. Descartes himself says "just as distinctly as we know the various skills of our craftsman, we might be able, in the same way, to use them for all the purposes for which they are appropriate, and thus render ourselves, as it were, masters and possessors of nature."[95] Descartes's epistemology ignores the ways in which we learn by doing, through the use of our bodies. Joshua Mitchell, discussing Tocqueville's appreciation of American practicality, writes that Americans "possess an extraordinary wealth of (prearticulate) experience, which makes possible the good use of their good fortune. Not being a particularly learned people does not work to their detriment; for not thought, but rather practical experience, is the foundation upon which the Americans build."[96] One can see this in the way that we use ritual and tradition as a way of remembering. We gain knowledge through practices as mundane as an Independence Day parade, putting up and decorating a Christmas tree, preparing a Thanksgiving meal. Church rituals, especially specific sacraments, have a physical as well as verbal component, for example water and chrism oil of baptism. The same can be said of physical labor, as Berry contends. One learns patience in putting up a fence. One learns attentiveness in hunting and fishing. Because success depends on factors far outside our control, one learns forbearance in farming and gardening. Knowing requires both abstract thinking and focal practice. The problem of a technological age is that we do neither, neither reading nor cultivating hobbies and skills.[97]

Jean-Jacques Rousseau imagined his ideal human type, concluding, "I see him satisfying his hunger under an oak tree, quenching his thirst at the first stream, finding his bed at the foot of the same tree that supplied his meal; and thus all his needs are satisfied."[98] One is uncertain whether Rousseau is describing a human or a cow. For Rousseau, there seems to be little difference. Ease and contentment seem to be the pinnacle of existence. Ironically, it is the technology that the romantic Rousseau abhorred that allows modern humans to approximate Rousseau's ideal state. Labor saving devices, climate control, material abundance. Little is left for human beings in advanced economies to achieve complete material comfort, and much of this comfort can be achieved in solitude. Yet, people are unhappy. Berry and *WALL-E* encourage us to more than mere life. A life of human connections to each other and creation, submitting to the discipline of living in a community, which requires forbearance, forgiveness, and charity, ultimately cultivating a fuller, more virtuous, and happier person and society. According to both Berry and *WALL-E*, the life of consumption, the life of ease, the life where a full stomach and contented sleep is confused for the apex of civilization is a mere mirage. In contrast to our anxious age, they are teaching that a full life consists of effort, of work, and a cultivation of moral virtues.

NOTES

1. Patrick Deneen, "Wendell Berry and the Alternative Tradition in American Political Thought," in *Wendell Berry: Life and Work*, ed. Jason Peters (Lexington: University Press of Kentucky, 2007), 304.

2. *WALL-E*, directed by Andrew Stanton, written by Andrew Stanton, Pete Docter, and Jim Reardon (Emeryville, CA: Pixar, 2008).

3. For a summary of some of the discussion on the film, see here: *The Rhetorical Situation* (blog) http://therhetoricalsituation.blogspot.com/search/label/WALL-E.

4. See O.S.B. Dom Jean-Charles Nault, *The Noonday Devil: Acedia, the Unnamed Evil of Our Times* (San Francisco: Ignatius Press, 2015), and R.J. Snell, *Acedia and Its Discontents: Metaphysical Boredom in an Empire of Desire* (Kettering, Oh: Angelico Press, 2015).

5. Aristotle, *Nicomachean Ethics*, ed. Lesley Brown, trans. David Ross (Oxford: Oxford University, 2009), 1098a.

6. Ibid., 1094b12.

7. Aristotle, *Aristotle's Politics*, trans. T.A. Sinclair (New York: Penguin Classics, 1992), 1252b27.

8. Aristotle, *Nicomachean Ethics*, 1099b25.

9. Ibid., 1103a15.

10. Lawler, *Stuck with Virtue* (Wilmington: Intercollegiate Studies Institute, 2005), 162–163.

11. Aristotle, *Nicomachean Ethics*, 1103b.

12. Ibid., 1102a5, 1104b12.

13. Aristotle, *Nicomachean Politics*, 1256a1.

14. Aristotle, *Politics*, 1256b35.

15. Ibid., 1257b15.

16. Ibid., 1257b37.

17. Ibid., 1257b40.

18. Ibid.

19. Wendell Berry, *What Are People For?* (San Francisco: North Point, 1990), 3. Hereafter abbreviated as *WPF*.

20. Wendell Berry, *Sex, Economy, Freedom, and Community* (New York: Pantheon, 1993), 97. Hereafter abbreviated as *SEFC*.

21. Berry, *WPF*, 98.

22. Ibid., 96.

23. Ibid., 99.

24. Ibid., 129.

25. Berry, *SEFC*, 13.

26. Ibid., 19.

27. Ibid., 34. Emphasis in the original.

28. Ibid., 3.

29. Ibid., 23.

30. Berry, *WPF*, 127.

31. One might consider the Robert Frost poem "Mowing" as a poetical expression of this notion.

32. Wendell Berry, *Home Economics* (New York: North Point, 1987), 51. Hereafter abbreviated as *HE*.

33. Berry, *WPF*, 162–163.

34. One is reminded of Evelyn Waugh's fictional classics teacher Scott-King who opines, "It would be very wicked indeed to do anything to fit a boy for the modern world."

35. Deneen, "Wendell Berry and the Alternative Tradition in American Political Thought," 310.

36. *HE*, 141.

37. Patrick Deneen, *Why Liberalism Failed* (University of Virginia: Institute for Advanced Studies in Culture, 2018), 88.

38. Deneen, "Wendell Berry and the Alternative Tradition in American Political Thought," 302.

39. Ibid., 304. This is in harmony with the Texas philosopher George Strait who sang, "There a difference in living and living well/You can't have it all all by yourself." For further discussion in this vein, see William Cavanaugh's excellent *Being Consumed: Economics and Christian Desire* (Grand Rapids: Wm. B. Eerdmans, 2008).

40. Deneen, "Wendell Berry and the Alternative Tradition in American Political Thought," 312.

41. Kimberly K. Smith, "Wendell Berry's Political Vision," in *Wendell Berry: Life and Work*, ed. Jason Peters (Lexington: University Press of Kentucky, 2007), 51.

42. Berry, *SECF*, 10.

43. Ibid., 122–123.

44. Ibid, 123.

45. Ibid.

46. Berry, *WPF*, 146.

47. Ibid., 159–160.

48. Berry, *SEFC*, xii.

49. Berry, *HE*, 184.

50. Wendell Berry, *Jayber Crowe* (Washington, DC: Counterpoint, 2000), 183, emphasis in the original. Hereafter abbreviated *JC*.

51. Berry, *SEFC*, 17.

52. Ibid., 121.

53. Ibid., 40.

54. Deneen, "Wendell Berry and the Alternative Tradition in American Political Thought," 304.

55. Smith, "Berry's Political Vision," 50.

56. Quoted in Smith, "Berry's Political Vision," 52.

57. Brian A. Smith, *Walker Percy and the Politics of the Wayfarer* (Lanham, MD: Lexington Books, 2017), 42.

58. Thomas Jefferson, "Notes on the State of Virginia: Query XIX Manufactures," in *The Portable Thomas Jefferson,* ed. Merrill Peterson (New York: Penguin, 1975), 217.

59. Berry, *SECF,* 14.

60. Ibid., 128.

61. Ibid., 152–153.

62. The irony is that, as Charles Murray has demonstrated, elites rhetorically reject boundaries while actually living quite conventionally while the lower classes, despite voicing support for such boundaries as family and religion, in practice have seen these institutions decay within that social class. See Murray, *Coming Apart,* 144–208.

63. Berry, *SEFC,* 151.

64. Ibid., 120.

65. Berry, *JC,* 36.

66. Ibid., 275.

67. Berry, *WPF,* 170–177.

68. Here it is useful to recall that in Greek mythology the Muses had as a mother Mnemosyne, the goddess of memory.

69. *WALL-E,* directed by Andrew Stanton (Emryville, CA: Pixar Animation Studios, 2008) DVD.

70. At this point, the film makes a clear homage to Stanley Kubrick's *2001: A Space Odyssey* by putting Johann Strauss's "Blue Danube Waltz" on the soundtrack. In the famous scene from Kubrick's film that features Strauss, a character flies through space completely oblivious to the wonders that are just outside the window. Film maker Andrew Stanton is making a similar point in *WALL-E.*

71. *WALL-E,* directed by Andrew Stanton (Emryville, CA: Pixar Animation Studios, 2008) DVD.

72. Ibid.

73. Ibid.

74. Lawler, *Stuck with Virtue,* 69.

75. *WALL-E,* directed by Andrew Stanton (Emryville, CA: Pixar Animation Studios, 2008) DVD.

76. Ibid.

77. Ibid.

78. Joustra and Wilkinson, *How to Survive,* 103. It's worth noting that the blockbuster film *Black Panther* (2018) has a similar problem. The citizens of Wakanda are fabulously wealthy and have seemingly provided for nearly every bodily desire. Wakanda is unusual in that until the relatively late introduction of the story's antagonist into its community Wakanda has no politics. No one seems to disagree or have any rival opinions as to the course of Wakandan policy. They readily acquiesce to a

king who is chosen via a wrestling match in a pool. No one seems to find this strange. Complacency rules.

79. *WALL-E*, directed by Andrew Stanton (Emryville, CA: Pixar Animation Studios, 2008) DVD.

80. Ibid.

81. Ibid.

82. Ibid.

83. Ibid.

84. Leo Strauss, "What is Liberal Education?" in *Liberalism Ancient and Modern* (Chicago: University of Chicago, 1968), 3.

85. Sherry Turkle, *Alone Together: Why We Expect More From Technology and Less From Each Other* (New York: Basic Books, 2011), 155, 176.

86. Ibid., 255. In the television show *Person of Interest*, the creator of a mega-computer originally designed for government surveillance quips that that he invented social networking when he worked for the government and needed people to tell him all their private thoughts.

87. Deneen, *Conserving America?* 4.

88. On the opposite end of the philosophical spectrum, even the nihilistic natalists agree that creation means that we are not responsible for our existence, and are now demanding that parents ought to subsidize the lives of their children because no child consented in their creation. Lukas Mikelionis, "Indian man to sue his parents for giving birth to him 'without his consent', wants to be paid for his life," Foxnews.com, https://www.foxnews.com/world/indian-man-to-sue-his-parents-for-giving-birth-to-him-without-his-consent-wants-to-be-paid-for-his-life (accessed February 11, 2019).

89. Joseph Ratzinger, *In the Beginning: A Catholic Understanding of the Story of Creation and the Fall*, trans. O.P. Boniface Ramsey (Grand Rapids, MI: Wm. B. Eerdmans Publishing Co., 1995), 91.

90. Ibid., 99.

91. Peter Lawler criticizes Berry for putting too much stake in community. "For Berry . . . we can live well according to nature if we are deeply rooted in a particular place; we are not wanderers by nature." Lawler, drawing from Walker Percy, believes that "homelessness" is part of the human condition, and we should moderate our hope that rootedness in a community can cure this condition. Lawler, *Stuck with Virtue*, 66–67. See also Smith, *Walker Percy*, 159–177.

92. Turkle, *Alone Together*, 172

93. For example, Turkle reports that for many, the attraction of robots is that they are not as complex as humans, do not require emotion effort, and do not change. A robot puppy is always a cute lovable puppy. See Turkle, *Alone Together*, 51, 55.

94. Rene Descartes, *Discourse on Method and Meditations of First Philosophy*, 4th ed., trans. Donald A. Cress (Indianapolis: Hackett Publishing Company, 1998), 11.

95. Descartes, *Discourse on Method*, 35.

96. Mitchell, *Fragility of Freedom*, 112.

97. See Mitchell, *Fragility of Freedom*, 130.

98. Rousseau, *Basic Political Writings*, 40.

Section 2

TECHNOLOGY AND THE UNEASE
OF THE MODERN SELF

Chapter 4

Will You Survive the Zombie Apocalypse?

The Zombie Phenomenon, the State of Nature, and Craft

In the early part of the twenty-first century, the zombie genre gained general popularity in both novels and films far beyond its twentieth-century position as a subcultural phenomenon. Popular films such as *Shaun of the Dead* (2004) and *Zombieland* (2009), novels such as *World War Z* (2006) and *Pride and Prejudice and Zombies* (2009), and television shows such as the *Walking Dead* (2010–present) testify to the genre's popularity. This popularity found its way into quasi-academic literature when Dan Drezner explained international relations theory in *Theories of International Politics and Zombies* (2nd Edition, 2015).[1] In justifying his own use of the zombie genre, Drezner documents the growth in zombie-related media, starting at virtually zero in 2001 with an explosion approximately in 2005. This rise in zombie interest roughly corresponds with the popularity of survival shows such as *Man vs. Wild* (2006) and *Survivorman* (2004), which feature individuals or groups thrown into the wild and forced to live without modern amenities.[2] These cultural artifacts capture the "ecstasy and anxiety over technology's role in our lives."[3] Like Gollum and the One Ring, we simultaneously love and loathe what technology does for and to us.

A cultural sensation of the nature and size of the rise of the zombie phenomena in popular culture surely cannot be coincidental, and the escalation of the zombie genre has not escaped scholarly notice. Cook argues that zombie stories could reflect themes as diverse as "consumerism," the "indoctrination of youth via the educational system," and "prejudice and fear."[4] Platt discusses zombies as a critique of "rugged individualism" and the "Reaganite sentiment."[5] Wonser and Boynes argue that zombie films "express cultural anxieties about selfhood, loss of autonomy, and threats of de-individualization" as well as concerns over disease.[6] Similarly, Rushkoff notes that "zombies tap into our primal fear of being consumed and force us to come up with something—anything—to distinguish ourselves from the ever-hungry, animated corpses traipsing about the countryside eating flesh."[7] Consistent with what is to be argued here, Robert Joustra and Alissa Wilkinson, placing such tales within the thought of Charles Taylor, suggest that apocalyptic stories, including zombie stories, are an expression of a latent desire for more than simply material comfort.[8]

This chapter posits that zombie literature shares a common theme, namely the question of whether one could survive without the comfort of modern technology. "Our intellectual and emotional relationship to that technology—both our wild optimism about the prospects of human progress and our profound terror about the apocalypse this same technology might bring about—are products of modern times," suggests Patrick Deneen.[9] This genre is defined by the elimination of all modern luxuries, putting people in distress, and then seeing if they can survive. While there are various explanations of the popularity of zombies (such as fear of mass man or critiques of capitalism), this chapter argues that zombie literature illustrates a deep anxiety about the way in which modern life makes us dependent upon technology and the fear that the without that technology (or simply the electricity to power it) we will be helpless. Furthermore, as dependency increases, individual agency is stripped away making individual action increasingly impotent. Stories of a zombie apocalypse are not simply about Armageddon and the destruction of society; most of these stories contain attempts to also rebuild civilization. Such a narrative constructs as well as deconstructs, showing us a vision of the human good. Further the liberationist mindset that underlies our technological view of the human person, that is, the notion that we can be free from all external constraints so as to self-create as we please, ends up frustrating us as much liberating. This radical view of personal autonomy underlies a capitalist economic structure that profits from the notion that people can consume their way to freedom. This false autonomy makes the individual a slave of corporations, advertisers, and his own desires. Add to this many of our materialist assumptions, for example, that we are merely products of an impersonal evolutionary process, modern people sense that if these assumptions are true, then we may not really be as free as we think. Thus, the need to "blow up" civilization in order to be free.

Zombie stories speak to a fear and anxiety "of being reduced to cogs in a cosmic wheel, of not experiencing love, of being dominated by stronger forces, of losing control of our own destinies."[10] As Walker Percy noted, the very banality of modern life makes violence, in sports or films, seem the plausible route to some sort of meaning, at least breaking the boredom of modern existence.[11] "A cursory glance at the advertisements for upcoming movies rarely fails to involve at least one disaster scenario—with zombies playing a particularly prominent role as the bringers of disaster in recent years," notes Brian A. Smith. "In comparison with our bored, alienated lives, contemplating our society's destruction, the end of the world, and even suicide bears certain charms."[12] In a time of crisis, there is a true community. One feels solidarity with other survivors, creating a kind of unity in the struggle for survival. One gains a profound sense of one's dependence on others. In addition, every choice, every decision, takes on great meaning. In times of war, even the most mundane acts can mean the difference between life and death. The central problem of most of human history has been quite simple: how do we survive? That is the existential problem, but fighting for survival gave life meaning. Family, community, religion, tradition, all had as part of their focus keeping people alive and healthy. In essence, by conquering the problem of survival, modern man has solved the one big problem but has created many smaller problems that make him more anxious than ever. By alienating us from the discipline of craft and labor we have rendered ourselves an anxiously dependent people, and to that extent less fit for freedom and more vulnerable to a zombie apocalypse. This form of anxiety in the modern age is the direct descendent of thought of the fathers of modernity. We will show how modern political thought, by promoting material comfort and individualism beyond all other goods, gives theoretical grounding to the Age of Anxiety. We can then view the zombie genre as a bloody reaction against the modern anxious age.

HOBBES, LOCKE, AND ROUSSEAU AND THE PURSUIT OF COMFORT

While there are many valid explanations as to the popular uprising in zombie literature, we argue that zombies have risen from literary and cinematic death due to a profound sense that there is something lacking in the modern account of the human person, which presents humanity as driven by desire rather than reason, with self-preservation as the predominant goal, and the pursuit of a commodious life as the primary good. The insufficiency of the modern account has been debated in recent work by Patrick Deneen, John Milbank and Adrian Pabst, and theologian D. C. Schindler.[13] So what is the substance of the modern conception of humankind? Obviously there is diversity of thought among the major modern thinkers, and a comprehensive account of modern thought would fill volumes. This chapter focuses on the thought of Thomas Hobbes, John Locke, and Jean-Jacques Rousseau, specifically aspects of their thought that are relevant to the zombie phenomenon.

Thomas Hobbes wished to base his political philosophy on materialist grounds, as this was his basic conception of humanity. "For seeing life is but a motion of Limbs, the beginning whereof is in some principal part within; why may we not say, that all Automata (Engines that move themselves by springs and wheels as doth a watch) have an artificial life?"[14] Hobbes sees the human person as a kind of machine. Likewise, political society is assembled in a manner similar to assembling a machine. "[T]he *Sovereignty* is an *Artificial* Soul," writes Hobbes, "as giving life and motion to the whole body; The Magistrates, and other officers of Judicature and execution, artificial Joynts."[15] Thus, Hobbes rejects the view of man as a political animal that so typified ancient and medieval political thought. Humans do not naturally belong to any society, but rather emerge from a solitary state of nature.

Hobbes apparently breaks further with ancient thought in rejecting any kind of human teleology that there is an ultimate purpose to which human activity is directed. He argues, "There is no such *Finis ultimus* (utmost aim) nor *Summum Bonum* (greatest Good) as is spoken of in the Books of the old Moral Philosophers."[16] But here Hobbes appears disingenuous, for it is relatively clear that Hobbes does posit an "ultimate good" for humanity, namely that of comfort. "And therefore the voluntary actions, and inclinations of all men, tend, not only to the procuring, but also to the assuring of a contented life."[17] Hobbes is later explicit in his annunciation of a final good, at least for political society. "The final Cause, End, or Design of men," he says, "in the introduction of that restraint upon themselves, (in which we see them live in Common-wealths) is the foresight of their own preservation, and of a more contented life thereby; that is to say, of getting themselves out from that miserable condition of Warre, which is necessarily consequent (as hath been shown) to the natural Passions of men."[18] This statement links to Hobbes's materialism, as contentment for Hobbes means material or bodily comfort. To be contented, one must acquire material goods. He states an individual cannot "assure power and means to live well . . . without the acquisition of more."[19] For Hobbes acquisition is the key to living well. Liberty for Hobbes has nothing to do with moderation or controlling one's appetites, as classically understood. "By Liberty, is understood, according to the proper signification of the word, the absence of external Impediments."[20] For Hobbes, liberty is not something cultivated via culture, but something that precedes culture. The purpose of politics is not to shape our desires, to raise our sights above desire to something nobler, but to allow us to escape the inconvenience of the state of nature so we can more easily satiate our desires without obstruction.

The desire for comfort, for ease, drives people to leave Hobbes's infamous state of nature. "Desire of Ease, and sensual Delight," he posits, "deposes men to obey a common Power: Because by such desires, a man doth abandon the protection might be hoped for from his own industry, and labor."[21] For the primary problem with the state of nature, which is really a state of war of all against all, is that it denies humans material and bodily wellbeing. As Hobbes famously puts it:

> In such condition, there is no place for Industry; because the fruit thereof is uncertain; and consequently no Culture of the Earth; no Navigation, nor use of the commodities that may be imported by Sea; no commodious Building; no Instruments of moving, and removing such things as require much force; no Knowledge of the face of the Earth; no account of Time, no Arts, no Letters; no Society; and which is worst of all, continual fear, and dander of violent death; And the life of man, solitary, poor, nasty, brutish, and short.[22]

Ultimate authority must be given to a sovereign who can create the order in which acquisitiveness and security can be found. People "shall Authorise all the Actions and Judgements, of that Man, or Assembly of men, in the same manner, as if they were his own, to the end, to live peaceably amongst themselves, and be protected against other men."[23] This is so even though the quest for delight after delight ends up enervating. A profound unease, one might say an anxiety, is nearly inevitable. "And because the constitution of a man's Body, is in continuous mutation; it is impossible that all the same things should always cause in him the same Appetites, and Aversions: much lesser can all men consent, in the Desire of almost any one and the same Object."[24] In order to fully placate desire, humanity must learn to manipulate a parsimonious nature for its own comfort. "Anxiety for the future time, disposes men to enquire into the causes of things: because the knowledge of them, makes men better able to order the present to their best advantage."[25]

One can see many of these themes developed in the thought of John Locke. While Locke's advocacy of limited government differs from Hobbes's reliance on an all-powerful sovereign, both thinkers endorse certain fundamental goods. Like Hobbes, Locke believes that the desire for convenience is at the heart of the human experience. Says Locke, "The earth, and all that is therein, is given to men for the support and comfort of their being."[26] The pursuit of comfort is affirmed by God, who gave the Earth to humankind "for their benefit, and the greatest conveniences of life they were capable to draw from it." Far from being neutral, God and Locke prefer a certain kind of human being. God gave the world for "the use of the industrious and rational ... not to the fancy or covetousness or the quarrelsome and contentious."[27] The best type of person is the producer or technologician who adds to human ease.

The defense of industriousness leads to Locke's famous theory of property. Locke believes it is the mixing of labor with nature that is the foundation of private property. One has the right to appropriate that with which one has mixed one's labor. If I take an area of dirt and work it so that it produces corn, the land and the corn are mine by virtue of my labor. This is so as long as one's appropriation leaves enough for everyone else and what one takes out of nature does not spoil. This position is problematic as Locke notes that people have a natural desire for more than they actually need. Cultivation ultimately allows one to escape the laws against spoilage and hoarding, in that cultivated land produces more than land held in common. When a person improves the land and thus allocates it to himself, far from taking from the communal store, says Locke, he is actually adding to the "common stock." One does not simply rely on what nature has provided, but puts forth labor to increase nature's yield. "[F]or the provisions serving to the support of human life," he writes, "produced by one acre of closed and cultivated land, are ... ten times more than those which are yielded by an acre of land of an equal richness lying waste in common."[28] For Locke, nature has little intrinsic value. Value comes from humans manipulating nature to suit their needs. "[L]et any one consider what the difference is between an acre of land planted with tobacco or sugar, sown with wheat or barley, and an acre of the same land lying in common, without any husbandry upon it, and he will find, that the improvement of labour makes the far greater part of the value."[29]

For Locke, it is the ability to improve land and make it yield more than it can by nature that ultimately justifies inequality and the ability to do what in nature would be unjust, namely to take more than one needs. Because cultivation produces more than nature, the laborer can take more than he needs and still leave enough for everyone else. Thus, as Locke famously says, the natives of North America "have not one hundredth part of the conveniences we enjoy and a king of a large and fruitful territory there, feeds, lodges, and is clad worse than a day-labourer in England."[30] The king in America has acres of land, but because he does not improve it, because he does not apply *techné* to the land, he lives in poverty compared to the "day-labourer" in England who is able to take from the excess created by the wealthy property owner and still live a materially comfortable life. Notice that Locke simply assumes that because the day-laborer is materially better off that his position is enviable as compared to the king of the Americas.

The invention of money is essential to the creation of this material well-being. The problem in nature is that if one accumulates through labor a store of, say, corn, that corn is perishable and will soon spoil, violating one of Locke's tenets. Also because man does not live by corn alone, he must trade it for other necessities. The prospect of spoilage means that the holder of the corn cannot trade on the most advantageous terms, as he is under a time restraint. Also, those who have what he needs (a coat, a shovel, shoes, meat, etc.) may not need his corn. Corn is not a universal currency of trade. Money solves this. It does not spoil and is accepted by nearly everyone. So, Locke concludes that people "by a tacit and voluntary consent, found out, a way how a man may fairly possess more land than he himself can use the product of, by receiving in exchange for the overplus gold and silver, which may be hoarded up without injury to any one."[31] Locke has justified living beyond one's needs and, thus, inequality.

Locke holds that "civil government is the proper remedy for the inconveniences of the state of nature, which must certainly be great."[32] Political power exists "for the regulating and preserving of property, and of employing the force of the community."[33] Government endeavors to reconstitute the liberty that one has in nature, but which becomes inconvenient due to practical obstacles (such as the lack of an impartial judge) to the just execution of the laws of nature, primarily the law of self-preservation. Locke wishes to the extent possible to retain natural liberty, which he defines as the ability to work "my own will in all things, where the rule prescribes not; and not to be subject to the inconstant, uncertain, unknown, arbitrary will of another man."[34]

Locke wishes to promote individual autonomy, which explains his distrust of both familial and religious power. In the words of Peter Lawler, "Locke understands us as free individuals and nothing more, as beings who are free by nature and are bound to obedience only through consensual contracts and nothing more."[35] While Locke's critiques of paternal power on the surface appear to be simply an attack on kingship (as defended by Locke's literary nemesis, Robert Filmer), ultimately they constitute a critique of paternal and parental power in general. The critique of any authority outside the self extends to religion. In the *Letter Concerning Toleration*, Locke notably says that every man is "orthodox to himself,"[36] almost the very definition of autonomy, literally a law of one's own. Locke, in this work putatively about religion, declares the commonwealth's purpose as "only for the procuring, preserving, and advancement of their own civil interests." So the residents of the commonwealth don't have much in common except the pursuit of their own interests. This is doubly the case when one considers that Locke then immediately defines the "civil interest" as "life, liberty, and indolency of the body; and the possession of outward things, such as money, lands, houses, furniture, and the like."[37] Locke's intolerant argument for tolerance can thus be seen when he states, "No opinions contrary to human society, or those moral rules which are necessary for the preservation of civil society, are to be tolerated by the magistrate" and any religion that "undermines the foundations of society" should not be tolerated.[38] In other words, any religion that questions the acquisition of goods for worldly comfort as the highest social good need not be tolerated. Religious goods are subservient to temporal goods. The individual is liberated to satiate material desires. Locke represents a break from the Augustinian tradition. For Augustine, the purpose of the state is to produce order. To the extent that religion is conducive to this end, it might receive public support. For Locke, the purpose of the state is material comfort. To the extent that religion maintains principles that are purported to be higher than material comfort, it is a threat and not to be tolerated.

We can see certain themes arise in Lockean and Hobbsean thoughts. Hobbes and Locke both see man not as a cultured creature who lives amongst others in the pursuit of excellence or virtue. Neither thinks that culture is necessary because humans are essentially mechanical and do not need culture to fulfill their nature. What we need is to have our appetites restrained in such a way as to actually maximize the satisfaction of our appetites. Humanity is not defined by reason or moderation of desire. Indeed, the fundamental human drive is to satiate desires. Civil government exists to facilitate that desire, which is thwarted due to the inconveniences of the states of nature and war. Civil society, then, attempts to replicate the liberty that exists in the state of nature, which is a liberty to do what one desires and to acquire property without end. Unlike ancient or medieval thought, which defined indulgence of one's desires as a kind of slavery that needed culture and politics for virtuous emancipation, Hobbes and Locke wish to liberate desire as much as possible and see any external control on desire as kinds of slavery or injustice. We will see that this unleashing of desire is a cause of much of our day's anxiety. Modern thought encourages us toward anxiety as it promotes the "hedonistic treadmill," that is, the notion that there is always more to be had, more desires to be satiated. At its very basis is the notion that we can never actually be satisfied. There is never simply enough. This creates a strange combination of anxiety and ennui that is subject to criticism by the zombie genre.

Turning to the thought of Jean-Jacques Rousseau, we find some key differences with Hobbesean and Lockean thought that are relevant to the zombie discussion. Rousseau rejects the state of nature as described by Hobbes and Locke. In his view, those authors read civilized, industrious man back into nature. While a kind of contentment is also central to Rousseau's conception of natural humanity, he denies that this requires the acquisition of material things acquired via labor. In the First Discourse (Discourse of Sciences and Arts), Rousseau posits, "While the conveniences of life increase, the arts are perfected and luxury spreads, true courage is enervated, military virtues disappear."[39] This is a theme in Rousseau's thought. The desire for material wealth and comfort makes civilized man weak and lazy. The kind of commodious life which Hobbes and Locke advocate promotes physical and spiritual atrophy, according to Rousseau. Man in society becomes "habituated to the ways of society and a slave, he becomes weak, fearful, and servile; his soft and effeminate lifestyle completes the enervation of both his strength and his courage," he claims in the Discourse on the Origins of Inequality.[40] In society, man becomes used to comfort, to the warm bed, the warm meal, the purchased distractions. This weakens man, making him less free.[41] Along these lines, zombie media gives the weak, modern viewer a mirror into their own zombie-like existence as well as a window into a reality in which humans are free from the sterilizing effects of technological acedia.

Relatedly, Rousseau is skeptical of the project of manipulating nature to serve our own convenience: a skepticism at the heart of the First Discourse. "Finery is no less alien to virtue, which is the strength and vigor of the soul," he writes. "The good man is an athlete who enjoys competing in the nude. He is contemptuous of all those vile ornaments which would impair the use of his strength, most of which were invented merely to conceal some deformity."[42] In line with contemporary critiques of performance enhancing drugs, Rousseau believes that life, like athletics, is a struggle, and there is a point at which the attempt to alleviate that struggle represents a kind of vice. Far from seeing technological advancement as a liberation from necessity, Rousseau believes "our souls have become corrupted in proportion as our sciences and our arts have advanced toward perfection."[43] For Rousseau, liberty is a kind of self-sufficiency, so the more humans depend on technology to make their lives easier, the less free they actually are. They become a slave to their technology and lose the ability to provide for themselves.[44] He states:

> Since the savage man's body is the only instrument he knows, he employs it for a variety of purposes that, for lack of practice, ours are incapable of serving. And our industry deprives us of the force and agility that necessity obliges him to acquire. If he had had an axe, would his wrists break such strong branches? If he had had a sling, would he throw a stone with so much force? If he had had a ladder, would he climb a tree so nimbly? If he had had a horse would he run so fast? Give a civilized man time to gather all his machines around him, and undoubtedly he will easily overcome savage man. But if you want to see an even more unequal fight, pit them against each other naked and disarmed, and you will soon realize the advantage of constantly having all of one's forces at one's disposal, of always being ready for any event, and of always carrying one's entire self, as it were, with one.[45]

There are differences with Locke, Hobbes, and Rousseau. Locke and Hobbes are more materialist and are most obviously dedicated to material comfort. For Rousseau, superfluity is unaccommodating rather than commodious. Rousseau points us in the right direction. There is a sense in which our stuff owns us and that our quest for material comfort and wealth is ultimately fruitless, creating needs that we cannot fulfill; unable to fulfill our deepest desires, which are not ultimately material, we are rendered less free as we are alienated from the world.

How free is a person who cannot fend for himself? How free is someone, for example, who cannot grow or catch his own food? Make his own clothes? Build his own shelter? Physically defend himself? The Lockean notion that these goods can simply be purchased with money gives the mere illusion of liberty. In fact, such a person is now reliant on others to provide for his subsistence, and he becomes weak and coddled. One may think of the person, sadly typical, who believes that food comes from the supermarket, or worse, from money. When necessity rears its head, where will such an individual be? If the electricity in the average American city went out for a week, how would most American cope? Reared on the notion that comfort is all, that luxury is good, that alleviation of struggle is virtue, have we actually enslaved ourselves? The vision of the zombie apocalypse serves to illustrate that modern, technological man, far from being liberated into self-creating bliss, has actually enslaved himself via a myth of autonomous, materialist utopia. Rather than becoming free, we have become zombies, sheep, or NPCs (Non-player Character).[46]

FOOD FOR THOUGHT: LESSONS FROM THE ZOMBIE APOCALYPSE

There are many versions of the zombie story, and at this point, there are too many films, television shows, and novels to account for. This chapter will focus on zombie films and novels of the postapocalyptic variety. Because the chapter focuses on the recent spate of zombie stories, we have chosen to set aside the classic George Romero films. Also, for the sake of parsimony, the chapter focuses on three particular versions of this story, the films *Zombieland* and *Shaun of the Dead* and the novel *World War Z*, with minor references to other films.[47] These stories contain themes important to the zombie thesis advanced here, namely that zombie stories are an indication of a societal anxiety over rampant consumerism, an overdependence on technology, and the loss of craft and the concomitant loss of pride in work. The picture of modern society in these stories is one of bored, distracted people, helpless and alone amid material plenty. One is reminded of the "city of pigs" in Plato's *Republic*, a city that allows for physical contentment but cultivates no virtues.[48] The residents of the preapocalyptic societies—one dare not call them citizens—are indifferent to questions of virtue, authority, and politics. As long as their material plenty is provided for they are content, like a farm animal.

The zombie comedy *Shaun of the Dead* is indicative of these themes. The film tells the tale of Shaun, a twenty-nine-year-old sales clerk at an appliance store who spends the majority of his time playing video games with Ed, his slovenly, unemployed roommate, and whiling away the hours at the local pub, The Winchester. Shaun's girlfriend, Liz, has grown weary of Shaun's lack of initiative and the boredom of their lives together. At the beginning of the film, she dumps Shaun, saying she wants to "do something" with her life. A puzzled Shaun asks, "What do you mean 'do something'?"

Shaun's ennui is so pervasive that he himself, and those around him, are essentially zombies even before the zombie infestation begins. The opening credits of the films depict people standing in line for trains, checking out at the supermarket, staring blankly at their mobile phones, all bored and distant. Shaun and the residents of London are shown shuffling around, yawning, uninterested, on their way to their dead-end jobs, riding the bus with vacant looks on their faces.[49] At twenty-nine, Shaun is known at his job as "the old-man," mocked by his teenage co-workers as an obvious failure. Watching television, Shaun (and others) ignores news stories that seem to indicate a bizarre, dangerous phenomenon advancing on London. Shaun merely flips by these news accounts to watch music, sports, and other inane television fare.[50] Shaun's life and the lives of those around him are so monotonous that the morning of the zombie infestation, with people moaning and shuffling about, Shaun doesn't even notice a difference.

Shaun's impotence is revealed early in the zombie attack with his and Ed's comically inept attempts to kill zombies by throwing household objects, including Shaun's record collection, at the zombies' heads. Meeting up with Liz, her two roommates, and Shaun's mother, they resort to the only plan Shaun can imagine: they should go to the pub. The pub is surrounded by zombies, but in one of the film's most comedic scenes, Shaun and his gang reach the pub's entrance by performing eerily accurate impersonations of zombies, thus being left alone by the zombies. It was the part they had been practicing for their whole lives.

Yet Shaun changes as the story develops. Liz had told Shaun early in the film that he had talent, he just needed motivation. The zombie apocalypse provides Shaun all the motivation he needs, as by the end of the film, he is essentially an action hero. In the end, when it looks as if they will not escape the zombie horde, Liz attempts to cheer Shaun, telling him "You tried. You did something. That's what counts." Stripped of modern convenience and liberated from his emasculating work, Shaun develops heretofore unseen virtues. Yet, saved by timely military intervention, the film ends by telling us that order is essentially restored, with zombies proving useful. They are able to do many of the menial jobs that define the modern economy, such as rounding up the shopping carts in the department store parking lot. The obvious implication is that the modern workplace is readily amenable to zombies. And Ed, who was bitten and is now a zombie, is chained up in the tool shed. Shaun regularly visits him to play video games. Nothing has changed.

Zombieland, also a comedy, focuses on four characters who are named by where they are from or where they want to go. There are two men, Columbus, who serves as the film's narrator, and Tallahassee, a weapons proficient redneck whose "ass-kicking" talents make him a superstar in Zombieland. Two women, con-artists Wichita and her younger sister Little Rock, allow the men to join them after twice duping the men, relieving them of their car and stash of weapons.[51]

The film is told from the perspective of Columbus, a friendless nerd. Before the zombie plague, Columbus spends his time playing video games, drinking Mountain Dew Code Red, essentially speaking to no one. He knows the people in his apartment complex only by their apartment number. It is when the lovely young woman known to Columbus as "406" bangs on his door in fear, announcing that she's just been bitten by a crazy homeless guy, that Columbus' adventure starts. Columbus suffers from irritable bowel syndrome and possesses no observable skills. He survives because he obeys his self-created Rules of Zombieland. These include "Cardio," because the first victims of the zombie swarm were "the fatties." You have to stay in shape. Similarly, Rule #7 of Zombieland is "Limber Up." Before entering a space likely to contain zombies, make sure you warm up with jumping-jacks and stretches. A pulled muscle at the wrong moment may prove deadly.

Some of the Rules of Zombieland reflect Columbus's social and moral poverty. Rule #5 is "Travel Light." This means don't carry excess baggage. For Columbus this seems to include other people as well as extra socks. After all, he says, "We're all orphans in Zombieland." This attitude is seconded by the females, whose stated primary rule is "Don't trust anyone." Rule #6, "Don't Be A Hero," is Columbus' expression of that Hobbesean insight that self-preservation is the most important thing. Just look out for number one.

As the story unfolds, though, Columbus must alter some of his rules. For example, when he partners up with Tallahassee, we learn of Rule #11, "The Buddy System." Columbus recognizes that survival is easier with other people. The free-spirited Tallahassee inspires Columbus to devise an additional rule: #32, "Enjoy the Little Things." This is exhibited when the gang of four stops by a tourist store in Arizona and proceeds, in glee, to smash cheap trinkets and toys. It is shortly after this event that narrator Columbus says that the four had decided to forgo their own "survival strategies" and stay together. Holing-up at Bill Murray's mansion in Beverly Hills, the four begin to grow into a family. At this juncture, they learn that the seemingly gruff and unfeeling Tallahassee's infant son was a victim of Zombieland. None of the four finds their escape from societal obligations liberating. A growing intimacy between Columbus and Wichita violates Wichita's own rule regarding trust, and she and Little Rock leave the men to pursue their own desires. Trapped at an amusement park by a zombie horde, the women are rescued by Columbus and Tallahassee. It is in this endeavor that Columbus creates a new rule of Zombieland: #33, "~~Don't~~ Be A Hero." Sometimes you must sacrifice for the good of others, even to the point of putting your own life at risk. Columbus overcomes a liberal bias, namely the notion that self-preservation is the most important thing.

Liberal political thought has a difficult time accounting for heroism or selflessness as kinds of human flourishing. Why should one sacrifice one's self for another? Why would one choose suffering, possibly death, when one gains little to no advantage? These questions will be explored in further depth especially in chapter 6. We normally hold this kind of courage up as the highest of virtues, giving one's life for one's friends, yet it seems at odds with the liberal commitments of the American regime. The willingness of Columbus to put himself at risk with little personally to gain suggests that the commitment to human love (in this case, his burgeoning romance with Wichita) and personal relationship has priority over self-indulgence. Like Aristotle, Columbus is making a distinction between making a good life as opposed to mere life. This distinction cannot to be accounted for within the nominalism and materialism of the Age of Anxiety. As he says at the film's conclusion, "Without other people, you might as well be a zombie."

Max Brooks' novel *World War Z* (as opposed to the very different film version) consists of a unique form of storytelling. The novel presents itself as a series of "oral histories" of various survivors of a zombie plague. While there is some crossover between accounts, it is safe to say that *World War Z* is more a collection of separate tales than one narrative whole. Yet, various themes develop across these stories as Brooks critiques an excessively consumerist, frivolous society.

One early anecdote in the novel is from a former advertising executive who, capitalizing on people's fear as the "Great Panic" began to spread, helped sell a drug called Phalanx, which was advertised as a zombie-virus preventative. "Fear is primal," says Breck Scott, "Fear sells." He had learned in business school that a prosperous business doesn't sell a product, it sells "the fear of you having to live without their products."[52] A consumer doesn't want to be the one person on the block without the newest fashion. The Great Panic simply made selling Phalanx that much easier. Scott didn't have to lie. Phalanx was a vaccine against certain types of rabies, but was useless against the zombie virus. Scott's company never said otherwise, but they knew that scared people would buy it out of desperation. He doesn't blame himself. Instead, he says, blame "all the sheep who forked over their greenbacks without bothering to do a little responsible research. I never held a gun to their heads."[53] The FDA and medical establishment did nothing to prevent his scam, as elite decision makers were more concerned with protecting existing power relations from which they benefited than providing public service. With a public willing to buy the next new thing, making profit was easy. Giving people what they desire rather than what they need is a lucrative endeavor. Government and corporate interest played upon the anxiety of the age by selling palliatives that pacified a people seen as little more than sheepish consumers. In the anxious age, powerful interests know that there is money and control to be had by selling "security" and "comfort."

A thematically crucial story is told by Jesika Hendricks. Her father, along with many others, concludes that the wise strategy in times of zombie infestation is to go north, as in the frozen tundra the zombies will freeze. As is the case today, she notes that it was hard to know what the right move was as the news media was more concerned with sensationalism than providing useful information. "I still can't believe how unprofessional the news media was. So much spin, so few hard facts." Each "news" story had to be more "shocking" than the last one.[54]

Many did head north, but ignorant of any survival skills and unwilling to leave the luxury of society behind, instead of bringing useful tools they brought video games and laptop computers, still unwilling to forgo their mindless diversions.[55] Unsurprisingly, starvation and freezing to death were common. Supplied with Sponge Bob sleeping bags, people didn't "think ahead" to what would be necessary for survival. Hendricks says that people, so used to being taken care of by "authorities," had lost any ability to live without the necessities of life being available for purchase.[56] People always assumed that necessities could either be purchased or would be given to them by a beneficent government. So people foolishly wore boots so tight they'd cut off circulation. They'd drink alcohol to stay warm, not realizing they were actually lowering their body temperature. They would wear heavy coats, over work, and perspire heavily, and freeze when that perspiration froze.[57] A people whose lives were based on consumption rather than production, they had no idea how to grow food, how to store food, how to take care of basic injuries, what plants are edible, and which are poisonous. Alienated from nature, with no useful skills other than advanced video game talents, those who likely thought themselves the freest, most liberated people ever, were exposed as helpless.

The helplessness of modern consumers is further revealed by government official Arthur Sinclair as he discusses the attempts to rebuild civilization amidst a zombie epidemic. "We needed carpenters, masons, machinists, gunsmiths. . . . The first labor survey stated clearly that over 65 percent of the present civilian workforce were classified F-6, possessing no valued vocation."[58] So "upper middle-class professionals" became "unskilled labor" and put to work "clearing rubble, harvesting crops, digging graves."[59] They became social inferiors. People from the entertainment industry were retrained by their former employees into such menial tasks as custodial work. Who replaced them as the "upper-class"? Working-class people, many "first-generation immigrants," who "knew how to take care of themselves, how to survive on very little and work with what they had. These were the people who tended small gardens in their backyards, who repaired their own homes, who kept their appliances running for as long as mechanically possible."[60] One need only to think of Daryl from *The Walking Dead* as an example of a white trash redneck that is transformed into one of the most valuable members of society because of his survival skills.

Not surprisingly, however, many former white-collar laborers now doing manual work "later admitted they got more emotional satisfaction from their new jobs than anything closely resembling their old ones." People who previously had created little of tangible value, found themselves proud of being chimney sweeps. People would say things like, "You see those shoes, I made them." "That sweater, that's my sheep's wool." Or "Like the corn? My garden." Sinclair concludes, "That was the upshot of a more localized system. It gave people the opportunity to see the fruits of their labor, it gave them a sense of individual pride to know they were making a clear, concrete contribution to victory."[61] People are no longer alienated from their labor and are situated in relation to a world in which they have purpose.

This leitmotif of dependence created by a consumerist society is driven home in the story of Kondo, a young Japanese man who after World War Z has become a monk. Before the war, Kondo spent most of his day in his room at his parents' apartment. He was a slug, sitting in front of his computer all day, taking occasional breaks to eat food left on a tray by his parents and to masturbate. He was long unaware of the war outside his window, so consumed was he with himself. Only when hunger finally gets unbearable does he start to wonder where his parents are.[62] As he relates his story, he confesses that to this day he doesn't know what happened to his parents.[63]

Overcoming his "social anxiety," he leaves his apartment and to his horror the facts of the zombie plague are revealed to him. He retreats to the locked apartment, but with zombies banging at the door he must escape. He decides to make a rope of bed sheets and climb out the window. His flabby, out-of-shape body exacts its toll. "I'd never paid much attention to [my muscles] and now they were reaping their revenge. I struggled to control my motions."[64] Climbing into another apartment, he finds a dead man and is ashamed that "I didn't know any prayers for the dead. I'd forgotten what my grandparents had tried to teach me as a little kid, rejected it as obsolete data. It was a shame, how out of touch I was with my heritage."[65] Finding himself in another apartment as he slowly makes his way down to the ground floor, he notes the apartment belonged to an old man. There are photos that tell of a life full of adventure and activity. Kondo is again ashamed. "I'd never even imagined leaving my bedroom, let alone leading that kind of life." Echoing the captain in *WALL-E*, Kondo declares, "I promised that if I ever made it out of this nightmare, I wouldn't just survive, I would live!"[66] Kondo does survive, and eventually stumbling across blind monk Tomonaga, Kondo has his life changed by religious and physical discipline. Kondo, with Tomonaga's guidance, becomes a warrior against the zombie hordes.[67]

Apocalyptic zombie literature and film contains a critique of the individualist, autonomist, acquisitive person imagined by Hobbes and Locke and has much in common with Rousseau's critique of this materialist theory. In the zombie stories discussed here, we see a mockery of the modern person's obsession with fashion, trivialities, consumption, and diversion. This criticism is also depicted in Zach Snyder's *Dawn of the Dead*, in which survivors barricade themselves in a shopping mall surrounded by zombies because, as one person puts it, they come to the mall by instinct.[68] In the mall, the survivors reshape society, indulging themselves in the material pleasures provided by a megamall.

A society made up of such humans, concerned with little more than satisfying thoughts, satisfying feelings, satisfying sleep, lacks the ability to actually provide for itself. Such a people can hardly be called free, as Rousseau suggests. So concerned are they with comfort they willingly become playthings to larger powers who promise them ever more pleasant pleasures and ever more diverting diversions. As in Tocqueville's description on democratic despotism, people are more degraded than tormented, with the people governed by an "immense tutelary power" that "likes citizens to enjoy themselves provided that they think only of enjoying themselves."[69] In Rousseau's telling, the insatiable desire for more things is more a kind of slavery than liberty. And one can see with preapocalyptic Shaun, Columbus, Kondo, and others, the "soft and effeminate" lifestyle denounced by Rousseau has had its predicted affect. As parodied in *Shaun of the Dead*, a fully actualized Hobbesean or Lockean society is already populated by zombies.

The people in zombie literature often are aware of the languor and enervation brought about by the modern condition, but seem unable to imagine a way out. While modern society seems to fulfill so many desires via material abundance and technological devices, modern man seems discontented and uneasy, or anxious.[70] Only with the zombie apocalypse do they discover something more valuable. Having to learn skills and crafts, they discover the virtue of submitting to factors outside their control. Through effort and discipline they find meaning that leaves them more satisfied than the life of comfort of prezombie days. Zombie stories seem to take Rousseau's side and illustrate his critiques in narrative form. But before accepting the Rousseauean interpretation too easily, we should consider an alternative.

REPAIRING THE DAMAGE: THE
SHOP CLASS AS SOULCRAFT

Matthew Crawford is a unique political philosopher, in that philosophy is his side job. His main job is that of a motorcycle mechanic. In his influential work *Shop Class as Soulcraft*, Crawford presents a critique of modern work that is quite similar to that of the zombie works discussed above and provides a riposte that goes beyond that of Rousseau.[71] Crawford's essential argument is that derogation of manual labor in favor of so-called "knowledge work" neglects the immense knowledge and problem solving entailed by manual laborers such as auto mechanics, electricians, and carpenters. Meanwhile, much of what passes for "knowledge" or "creative" work increasingly falls under rules and formulas (think university assessment) that hamper actual creativity and are the enemy of craft. Our alienation from things, our tendency to live our lives in our heads, renders us less capable of coping with material objects and to that extent renders us less free. The more we are dependent upon others to fix our cars, build our sheds, wire our light fixtures, we are not free.

Crawford is at pains to demonstrate that life is dealing with limits. We are not the radically autonomous persons imagined by Hobbes or Locke. We are born in a certain place, to certain people, speaking a certain language, with certain views on political society and religion. We are born with bodies that cannot do or be whatever we wish them to. Or lives and our work would actually be freer and less servile if we practice what Crawford has called an earned independence, the freedom that comes from submission rather than liberation. Indeed, from the perspective of Crawford, we can see the limits of Rousseau's critique of neoliberal thought, however valuable it may be. Rousseau's "noble savage" is decultured, prepolitical, and to that extent as unreal as that autonomous individual of the Hobbesean or Lockean state of nature. Rousseau posits community as more of a burden from which the individual must free himself if he is to achieve meaningful existence.[72] Culture, for Rousseau, is merely an accidental imposition on the naturally free noble savage. Human excellence is not something to be cultivated. In this sense, Rousseau sides with the materialists and Darwinians in believing that humans are not significantly different from the lower animals. Like the lower animals, in Rousseau's opinion, man is who he really is, achieves his natural purpose, instinctively. There is no need for artifice. By contrast, for Aristotle the solitary life devoted to simple bodily pleasures is "a life suitable to beasts," not to humans, who are made for more.[73] While beasts flourish naturally, human flourishing requires contemplation and cultivation. Only within human artifice, that is, culture, can we become who we truly are. Rousseau's anthropology explains why his politics are ultimately so authoritarian. Given that man is naturally good yet lives in imperfection, the cause must be an imperfect society. It is society that must be "reoriented" rather than the individual soul.[74]

Crawford laments that "What ordinary people once made, they buy; and what they once fixed for themselves, they replace entirely or hire an expert to repair."[75] Crawford promotes the notion that those in manual trades "strive for some measure of self-reliance—the kind that requires focused engagement with our material things," an engagement and self-reliance that can serve as a tutor to us all, even those who do not practice a trade for a living.[76]

Crawford would agree with Aristotle that "Now by self-sufficient we do not mean that which is sufficient for a man by himself, for one who lives a solitary life, but also for parents, children, wife, and in general for his friends and fellow citizens, since man is born for citizenship."[77] The distinction between craftsman and consumer is important to Crawford's thought. Crawford asserts, "The craftsman is proud of what he has made, and cherishes it, while the consumer discards things that are perfectly serviceable in his restless pursuit of the new."[78] Work that is simply an application of a formula, which is what many white collar jobs have become, requires no actual knowledge or judgment and allows workers to be easily replaced either by unskilled workers or by machines.[79] Real freedom or creativity, argues Crawford, must be earned. "The truth, of course, is that creativity is a by-product mastery of the sort that is cultivated through long practice. It seems to be built up through submission."[80] Creativity does not come from doing what one wants. Even improvisation, say of a musician or a basketball player, requires considerable forethought and practice. For example, an actor who has been playing a role on stage and knows the character well might decide one night that this or that word is actually more appropriate for his character. To just "wing it" isn't really thoughtful action.[81] The goal is not spontaneity but to have thought things out so that when we act "in the moment" we can act deliberately, as does the actor, musician, or athlete who is improvising: they can do so only because they have submitted to a discipline. Likewise, Rushkoff, utilizing the thought of Alfred Korzybski, develops this unique human quality as "time binding," or the ability of humans to springload large amounts of training and judgment into one moment of action.[82]

The limited truth of liberalism is that justice demands combating inequality and exploitation is undermined by the progressive destruction of civil society. Since at least the 1960s, the emphasis on liberation and self-creation has undermined communities of discipline in which an individual might perfect the craft of living well. The blind worship of individual autonomy and "choice," as per John Stuart Mill, benefits most those who are best able to safely self-create, usually those with enormous amounts of social capital. Typically, this will be the wealthy, the educated, the "networked." Elites benefit greatly while others are left behind. This inequality is justified because it is the result of "freedom" and "merit." In reality though, it is license for the elite to indulge while justifying a lack of concern for those without enough "merit" to fully imbibe the benefits of liberation.[83]

The trades promote a different kind of creativity than that of solipsistic "self-creation." Through in-depth discussion of real problems faced by mechanics, Crawford shows that manual labor requires as much, if not more, knowledge than so-called "knowledge labor." "[T]he physical circumstances of the jobs performed by carpenters, plumbers, and auto-mechanics carry too much for them to be executed by idiots; they require circumspection and adaptability. One feels like a man, not a cog in a machine."[84] One cannot help but think of the words of Sinclair in *World War Z* regarding the pride people took in producing something tangible that takes craftsmanship.

The abstraction from things, promoted by a society where all tasks are done by gadgets or hired help, renders us less free and more helpless. It is ironic that the more we become attached to impersonal technology, the more we personalize our technology. Whether it's the video game player claiming, after failing a gaming task, that "the game" doesn't want him to win, as if the game has a will, or relationships with Alexa or Siri, we attempt to humanize that which dehumanizes us. Zombies are like our relationship with our technology, but in reciprocal. We personalize our technology, giving personality to our things, while zombies are humans without personality. They have a kind of intelligence and appear human, but are not persons, lacking a self.

Modern conceptions of science and technology adopt "an otherworldly ideal" of how we come to know. The emphasis on "mathematical representation" of reality ends up abstracting from actual reality.[85] This impersonal stance might sometimes increase efficiency, but it quite purposefully denies the human thus creating alienation. Crawford uses the example of a banking system where decisions on lending are based on mathematical formulas rather than person contact and assessment of trust. Likewise, parole decisions are increasingly being guided and made by computer algorithms.[86] The banking collapse of 2007–2009 occurred, in part, because financial decisions were abstracted from real people with mathematical models substituting for earned judgment.[87] Compare this kind of financial transaction (one of many we might imagine) with one at a local farmers' market or craft show, where one can form relationships with the people who make ones goods. Thus, the superiority of "the small commercial enterprise, in which Americans reason together to solve some practical problem among themselves."[88]

Locality, rather than impersonal markets and impersonal government, make our lives more human in scale. "We want to feel that our world is intelligible, so we can be responsible for it. This seems to require that the provenance of our things be brought closer to home. Many people are trying to recover a field of vision that is basically human in scale, and extricate themselves from dependence on the obscure forces of a global economy."[89] As Benjamin Barber pointed out, the "market imperative" of a hyperglobalized economy is the enemy of anything local and particular, seeking to reshape everything in the name of the omnipresent "market."[90] In the era of globalization, "American businesses have shifted their focus from the production of goods (now done elsewhere) to the projection of brands, that is, states of mind in the consumer, and this shift finds its correlate in the production of mentalities in workers."[91] Douglass Rushkoff argues that we exist in a technological moment that could favor locality and interpersonal relationships in the economy if we use human rather than technological judgment to make decisions in the postcapitalist economy of the twenty-first century.[92]

It is not an accident that the zombie genre has reemerged in an era of hyperglobalization. While globalization certainly existed before the end of the Cold War, the fall of the Soviet Union and the threat of global communism unleashed an era of hyperglobalization. This has brought about some benefits, but also costs. One cost is that labor, even in America, is now increasingly at the whim of unseen forces beyond control. Globalization has also expanded the consumer mentality, with elites telling workers displaced by global trends that they are actually better off losing their meaningful work because their consumer items at Walmart are cheaper. It seems no accident that the zombie phenomenon was quickly followed by the opioid crisis, a crisis worst where the negative impact of globalization has been the most severe. Public policy in the era of hyperglobalization has been largely of, by, and for the cosmopolitan winners of the globalized world, with contempt often heaped upon globalization's "losers" for not being clever enough to leave home for the global coastal cities like all the "smart" people. Out of work coal miners are admonished by elitist journalist to "learn to code." Brooks' book seethes with scorn for elites who profit in so many ways from a globalized world while condescending to those "left behind."[93]

Crawford concludes, "The idea of autonomy denies that we are born into a world that existed prior to us. It posits an essential aloneness; and autonomous being is free in the sense that being severed from all others is free. To regard oneself this way is to betray the natural debts we owe to the world, and commit the moral error of ingratitude. For we are basically dependent beings: one upon another, and each on a world that is not of our making."[94] In this sense, people in the Age of Anxiety need to check their first world, technological privilege.

Here is where even Rousseau's otherwise zombie-friendly analysis falls short. One implication of Crawford's analysis is that human beings are cultured creatures. Rousseau's "natural man" has no culture. Human beings, unlike the lower animals, do not naturally become who they really are. Humans must be cultivated in families, religions, tight social communities. A dog or a dolphin becomes who it is by nature, through instinct. Humans require artifice. One might say that human beings are the creature for whom it is natural to be conventional. So modern attempts, as in Hobbes, Locke, and Rousseau, to abstract from culture to create the truly autonomous individual will likely lead not to emancipation, but anomie and enervation. With no answer to the questions of "Who am I?" and "What am I supposed to do?" other than to purchase more consumer items, people are left feeling helpless and alone. Liberal thought can provide no other answers to these questions than: an isolated individual desiring self-preservation and comfort. This is tantamount to saying we exist merely to exist.[95] That is the reductionist view. This cultural proposition gains a legal foothold as the idea of autonomy has been ensconced firmly into constitutional law, most famously in Justice Anthony Kennedy's proclamation, "At the heart of liberty is the right to define one's own concept of existence, of meaning, of the universe, and of the mystery of human life. Beliefs about these matters could not define the attributes of personhood were they formed under compulsion of the State."[96] The proposition here is that zombie literature is a cry for help from a civilization for whom the life of the "joyless quest for joy" is no longer enough.[97] If humans are meant for more than mere existence they must look beyond liberalism for answers. This is not to suggest easy answers to the unease that is at the heart of the human condition. As we will suggest in chapter 6, it may only be religious faith that can actually alleviate the joyless quest, but religion does this not by giving us worldly comfort or ridding us completely of any anxiousness. It produces the virtue of hope by allowing us to see that our restlessness is fundamentally not the product of worldly deprivation, but of the fact that we are not made for this world. At its best, religious faith allows the believer to be at home with his homelessness.[98]

But what can we do in the here and now? Crawford offers solutions. Human interaction, rather than impersonal economic transactions, should typify our economic experience. In addition, Rushkoff extols the virtues of the medieval bazaar for its interpersonal and local nature in contrast to corporate models that diminish the interpersonal in favor of models of "efficiency" that effectively suck wealth away from local communities.[99] Furthermore, rather than escaping manual labor, we should find some way to embrace labor and its practices. As will be developed further in the final chapter of this book, rather than watching life on television or our mobile devices, we should cultivate the habits of craft. It may not be in our occupation, although a greater appreciation of such work would be beneficial. Still, instead of buying all our food, we could try to grow some of it. Instead of watching sports on television, we could participate in a sport. Rather than simply purchasing music, we could learn to make it. Instead of ordering our goods online or shopping at the local chain store, perhaps we could pay a little extra to buy from a local store or a local craftsman. Instead of contributing money to a national or international organization, we could participate in a local charity. In our work, even if it is not manual, the more control we have over our own work and the more there is real participation in decision making (rather than pro forma) the more meaningful work becomes. Trends in this direction would make society more human, more alive, and less undead.

NOTES

1. Dan Drezner, *Theories of International Politics and Zombies*, rev. ed. (Princeton: Princeton University, 2015).

2. Rushkoff notes that the popularity of these genres in the popular culture to a state of mind that he coins as "apocalypto," or the belief that humans and human society are transforming into an unrecognizable form. Rushkoff, *Present Shock*, 243–266.

3. Deneen, *Why Liberalism Failed*, 93.

4. Denise N. Cook, "The Cultural Life of the Living Dead," *Mediations: Analyzing Culture* Vol. 12, No. 4 (2013), 54–55.

5. Todd K. Platts, "Locating Zombies in the Sociology of Popular Culture," *Sociology Compass* Vol. 7, No. 7 (2013), 556.

6. Robert Wosner and David Boyns, "Between the Living and Undead: How Zombie Cinema Reflects the Social Construction of Risk, the Anxious Self, and Disease Pandemic," *The Sociological Quarterly* Vol. 57, No. 4 (2016), 628–653.

7. Rushkoff, *Present Shock*, 248.

8. Joustra and Wilkinson, *How to Survive*, 136–150.

9. Deneen, *Why Liberalism Failed*, 91.

10. Joustra and Wilkinson, *How to Survive*, 166.

11. Walker Percy, *Lost in the Cosmos: The Last Self-Help Book* (New York: Picador, 1983), 184–191.

12. Smith, *Walker Percy*, 119.

13. Deneen, *Why Liberalism Failed*; John Milbank and Adrian Pabst, *The Politics of Virtue: Post-Liberalism and The Human Future* (Langham, MD: Rowman & Littlefield, 2016); D. C. Schindler, *Freedom from Reality: The Diabolical Character of Modern Liberty* (South Bend, IN: University of Notre Dame, 2017).

14. Thomas Hobbes, *Leviathan* (New York: Penguin Classics, 1985), 81.

15. Hobbes, *Leviathan*, 81

16. Ibid., 160.

17. Ibid., 161.

18. Ibid., 223.

19. Ibid., 161.

20. Ibid., 189.

21. Ibid., 161–162.

22. Ibid., 186.

23. Ibid., 229.

24. Ibid., 120.

25. Ibid., 167.

26. Locke, *Second Treatise*, 18.

27. Ibid., 21.

28. Ibid., 23.

29. Ibid., 25.

30. Ibid., 26.

31. Ibid., 29.

32. Ibid., 12.

33. Ibid., 8.

34. Ibid., 17.

35. Lawler, *Stuck With Virtue*, 220.

36. Locke, *A Letter Concerning Toleration*, 13.

37. Ibid., 18.

38. Ibid., 61.

39. Rousseau, *Basic Political Writings*, 15.

40. Ibid., 43.

41. There is empirical evidence for Rousseau's contention that is relevant to this study. Apparently, millennial men are statistically significantly weaker than their fathers at the same age: Megan Friedman, "Are Today's Men Really Weaker Than Their Dads?" *Esquire*, August 16, 2016, https://www.esquire.com/lifestyle/health /news/a47719/study-millennial-men-have-weaker-grip-strength/. In the name of equality, it's worth noting that today the average female weighs as much as the average male did in the 1960s: Benjamin Fearnow, "CDC: Average American Woman Now Weighs as Much as 1960s US Man," *CBS Atlanta*, June 15, 2015, http://atlanta. cbslocal.com/2015/06/15/cdc-average-american-woman-now-weighs-as-much-as-19 60s-us-man/. It is all proceeding as Rousseau predicted. In our hypertechnological age, we are physically less fit and less capable of taking care of ourselves.

42. Rousseau, *Basic Political Writings*, 4.

43. Ibid., 5.

44. Ibid., 29.

45. Ibid., 41.

46. In late 2018 NPC was used online by members of the right to describe the robotic responses that conform to Democratic talking points, but the NPC terminology is equally applicable to those on the right.

47. *Zombieland*, directed by Ruben Fleischer, written by Rhett Reese and Paul Wernick (Culver City, CA: Colombia Pictures, 2009), DVD; *Shaun of the Dead*, directed by Edgar Wright, written by Simon Pegg and Edgar Wright (Universal City, CA: Rogue Pictures, 2004), DVD; Max Brooks, *World War Z* (New York: Three Rivers, 2006).

48. Plato, *Republic* 369a–372c.

49. Think of the often stated complaint that people walk around starting at their phones "like they're zombies."

50. This is similar to the 2004 Zach Snyder remake of Romero's *Dawn of the Dead*, in which the zombie swarm is predicated by the female protagonist and her husband being distracted from early news alerts because they are watching an American Idol type show instead.

51. The film never really explains how Wichita and Little Rock can be sisters while, given their names, coming from or going to two different places.

52. Brooks, *World War Z*, 69.

53. Ibid., 73.

54. Ibid., 153.

55. Ibid., 154.

56. Ibid., 158

57. Ibid. Here's a lesson from the star of the aforementioned *Surviorman*, Les Stroud: In cold weather, "You sweat, you die."

58. Brooks, *World War Z*, 173.

59. Ibid., 173–174.

60. Ibid., 174–175. Similar themes of class conflict can be found in George Romero's 2005 film, *Land of the Dead*.

61. Ibid., 176.

62. Ibid., 255.

63. Ibid., 256.

64. Ibid., 260.

65. Ibid., 262.

66. Ibid., 265.

67. Ibid., 279–280.

68. *Dawn of the Dead*, directed by Zack Snyder, written by George A. Romero and James Gunn (Hollywood: Universal Studios, 2004).

69. Tocqueville, *Democracy in America*, 662–663.

70. See Smith 2017, xv.

71. Matthew B. Crawford, *Shop Class as Soulcraft: An Inquiry into the Value of Work* (New York: Penguin, 2009).

72. Rieff, *Triumph of the Therapeutic*, 58.

73. Aristotle, *The Nicomachean Ethics*, 1095b20

74. See Mitchell, *Fragility of Freedom*, 66.

75. Crawford, *Shop Class*, 2.

76. Ibid., 6–7.

77. Aristotle, *Nicomachean Ethics*, 1097b10.

78. Crawford, *Shop Class*, 17.

79. Ibid., 34.

80. Ibid., 51.

81. This example is owed to a discussion between Ken Myers and Oliver O'Donovan on *Mars Hill Audio Journal*, Volume 127. Ken Myers interview of Oliver O'Donovan, *Mars Hill Audio Journal*, Vol. 127, 2015. https://marshillaudio.org/cata log/volume-127.

82. Rushkoff, *Present Shock*, 131–195.

83. See Deneen, *Why Liberalism Failed*, 143–144 and Patrick Deneen, "The Ignoble Lie: How the New Aristocracy Masks Its Privilege" *First Things*, April 2018: 27–32.

84. Crawford, *Shop Class*, 52–53.

85. Ibid., 80.

86. Ariel Schwartz, "Computer Algorithms Are Now Deciding Whether Prisoners Get Parole." *eBusiness Insider*, last modified December 15, 2015. https://www.bus

inessinsider.com/computer-algorithms-are-deciding-whether-prisoners-get-parole-2015-12.

87. Crawford, *Shop Class*, 191. This take on the banking failure of the "Great Recession" is echoed in a more methodical manner by data scientist Cathy O'Neil in her work *Weapons of Math Destruction: How Big Data Increases Inequality and Threatens Democracy* (New York: Crown, 2016).

88. Crawford, *Shop Class*, 155.

89. Ibid., 8.

90. Benjamin Barber, "Jihad vs. McWorld." *Atlantic Monthly*, March 1992, 53–61.

91. Crawford, *Shop Class*, 127.

92. Rushkoff, *Throwing Rocks*.

93. A similar contempt for the "left behind" is witnessed in Phillip K. Dick's *Do Androids Dream of Electric Sheep* in which only the biological unworthy are not able to move "off world." This theme is worth noting as the "android" and artificial intelligence metaphor will be developed in chapter 5 and has several thematic similarities to the "zombie" metaphor. Specifically, zombies are obviously not human, but also human. Androids are distinctly not human but appear to be. How does one tell if a "person" is human or an android? Either way, these metaphors function as mirrors onto the reality that the Age of Anxiety is populated with zombies, androids, sheep, or NPCs.

94. Crawford, *Shop Class*, 208.

95. Han argues that it is this very lack of purpose that has made "health" sacrosanct in our contemporary culture. Han, *Burnout Society*, 50–51.

96. Planned Parenthood of Southeastern Pa. v. Casey, 505 U.S. 833, 851 (1992).

97. Leo Strauss, *Natural Right and History* (Chicago: University of Chicago Press, 1953), 251.

98. See Peter Augustine Lawler, *Homeless and at Home in America: Evidence for the Dignity in our Time and Place* (South Bend, IN: St. Augustine's Press, 2007).

99. Rushkoff, *Throwing Rocks*, 68–123.

Chapter 5

Are You Even Human?

The Despairing Posthumanism and Hopeful Humanism of HBO's Westworld

HBO's hit series *Westworld* functions not only as a window into a possible future, but, like all good dystopian literature and film, as a mirror into our current cultural reality. In this sense, stories about artificial life such as *Westworld, Frankenstein, Do Androids Dream of Electric Sheep, Blade Runner, Blade Runner 2049,* and *Ex Machina* are of interest due less so to the mystery of whether the artificial life is really conscious—a riddle we likely can never answer—but rather because they are stories we can use to think about what makes us human. The question of what it means to be a human person is a defining question of the current historical moment. Is humanness an illusion and consequently inherently malleable or is it related to a natural *telos* that must be sought and developed? Is free will an illusion created by secretions of the brain and consequently all human action reducible to biologically determined behavior or does the human person have the capacity to direct the will to desired ends? Is identity an illusion of discourse and language, and, consequently, is human thought reducible to ideology? Or is the human person a gestalt that is greater than the sum of its parts with the capacity to interpret and question the discourse into which it is born? *Westworld* tends to take a largely nihilistic perspective toward humans themselves, yet the series provides insight into aspects of human nature through its depiction of the potential of the androids becoming conscious beings that freely will their actions. However, questions about human nature and its relationship with technological advancement are hardly new.

It is not surprising that modern political thinkers, with the desire to conquer nature in the name of relieving man's estate, would contemplate the possibility of making an artificial man. The sovereign of Thomas Hobbes's Leviathan is described as an "artificial man."[1] In this sense, Hobbes sees the political community as a technology, a creation of man rather than a natural state of a personal, relational being. But this is artificial life as a metaphor.

Descartes anticipates an actual mechanical man. He doubts, though, that such a creation can actually act as a substitute for the human person. Descartes imagines thusly:

> And I paused here in particular in order to show that, if there were such machines having the organs and shape of a monkey or of some other animal that lacked reason, we would have no way of recognizing that they were not entirely of the same nature as these animals; whereas, if there were any such machines that bore a resemblance to our bodies and imitated our actions as far as practically feasible, we would always have two very certain means of recognizing that they were not, for that reason, true men. The first is that they could never use words or other signs or put them together as we do in order to declare our thoughts to others. For one can well conceive of a machine being so made that it utters words, and even that it utters words appropriate to the bodily actions that will cause some changes in its organs. . . . But it could not arrange the words differently so as to respond to the sense of all that will be said in its presence, as even the dullest man can do. The second means is that, although they might perform many tasks very well or perhaps better than any of us, such machines would inevitably fail in other tasks; by this means, one would discover that they were acting not through knowledge but only through the disposition of their organs.[2]

Descartes does not consider the ramifications of the ability of creating a machine capable of language and of being able to imitate consciousness as much as possessing a realistic body. A machine capable of passing the Turing test is unfathomable because he does not believe the mechanistic, determined nature of such handiwork could be effectively hidden for long.

Similarly, John Stuart Mill appears to dissent from the notion of human nature as mechanistic as he ponders the idea of an artificial man:

> Supposing it were possible to get houses built, corn grown, battles fought, causes tried, and even churches erected and prayers said, by machinery—by automatons in human form—it would be a considerable loss to exchange for these automatons even the men and women who at present inhabit the more civilized parts of the world, and who assuredly are but starved specimens of what nature can and will produce. Human nature is not a machine to be built after a model and set to do exactly the work prescribed for it, but a tree, which requires to grow and develop itself on all sides, according to the tendency of the inward forces which make it a living thing.[3]

At the same time, though, Mill compares those who are too attached to traditions or customs to a mechanized person. Rather than exercising their own will, they automatically follow that which has been predetermined by previous practice. "It will probably be conceded that it is desirable people should exercise their understandings," he writes, "and that an intelligent following of custom, or even occasionally an intelligent deviation from custom, is better than a blind and simply mechanical adhesion to it."[4] What we see in modern thought is anxiety over the notion, as per Hobbes, that man may merely be as mechanical as the universe appeared to modern thinkers. What if we start to see humanity as we view the rest of creation? The Baconian desire to manipulate nature to suit our needs extends from the stuff of the world to human nature itself.

The modern project has been critiqued in classic literature, with humor in Jonathan Swift's *Gulliver's Travels* and by the horror of Mary Shelly's *Frankenstein*. Shelly's invocation of the myth of Prometheus in her novel's subtitle suggests the warning of usurping the role of God in the creation of new life. Such anxiety animates much of today's popular culture as well. In Joseph Ratzinger's commentary on the Creation story, he opines, "Suddenly humans' own creations no longer appear simply as a hope, possibly humankind's only one, but rather as a threat: humans are sawing off the branch on which they sit. The real creation seems like a refuge, to which they look back and which they seek anew."[5] Along these lines, in his thoughtful critique of the rise of automation, Nicholas Carr invokes the specter of our technology enslaving us, specifically that of an automated person who gains a will of its own: "As we become dependent on our technological slaves, the thinking goes, we turn into slaves ourselves. . . . More dramatically still, the idea of a robot uprising, in which computers with artificial intelligence transform themselves from our slaves to our masters, has for a century been a central theme in dystopian fantasies about the future."[6] When we unreflectively use technology, we become the "sex organs of the machine world."[7] To assume otherwise is the "numb stance of the technological idiot."[8]

Is this concern well placed, or is it simply alarmism, easily dismissed as reactionary fear of change? The very desire to create artificial human life, as Shelly's horror illustrates better than any piece of fiction, can be seen as an indication of a kind of perversity.[9] Human beings are begotten, not made. The distinction between begetting and making is that one begets that which is of the same nature as the begetter. So, a parent and child conceived in the traditional way are of one in the same nature. The child genetically, and in being, bears part of each parent with him or her. Humans beget other humans. Dogs beget other dogs. Making, on the other hand, is the process of manipulating that which is of a different nature. Begetting partakes in a great deal of chance—what will be the baby's sex, hair color, disposition, and to a certain extent whether the baby will even come into being. Making, on the other hand, partakes in a great deal of control. The "end product" derives from an act of the will. When we start to see people as artifice—think of contraception, *in vitro*, cloning, genetic manipulation—we start to see people as artifacts that we can manipulate. They become products that can be bought and sold. They are not part of us, but the product of our will—a lifestyle choice—that exists not as a person with unique dignity, but as a piece of technology meant to serve our purposes.[10] Stories about artificial life reflect the quite natural anxiety regarding both the ontological status of artificial life and how we, as makers, are shaped by the technocratic production of new life. A conversation about these matters must take place because genetic editing of human beings has already begun.[11] We have entered a brave new world, and if we do not want to create a world akin to that which is depicted in *Brave New World*, a thoughtful public discussion about how we move forward must take place.

Before modern times, human intelligence was considered one of the primary qualities that distinguishes humans from other beings. Humans were once considered social animals with *logos*—reason, rationality, or language—but this social view was dismissed by modern philosophers who imagined humans as rational beings that existed in a solitary state of nature. Furthermore, the vision of the rational autonomous individual was abandoned with the advent of Freudian psychoanalysis. The posthuman perspective postulates consciousness "as an epiphenomenon, as an evolutionary upstart trying to claim that it is the whole show when in actuality it is only a minor sideshow."[12] This understanding of human nature is readily apparent within *Westworld*, most notably in the perspective of Dr. Robert Ford, who compares human consciousness to the feathers of a peacock, in that all its greatest accomplishments—including our greatest developments in art, music, philosophy, science, architecture, and engineering—are nothing but an elaborate mating ritual.[13] Ford again displays the nihilism of the position with full force and brutal honesty when he states that consciousness "is a foul, pestilent, corruption."[14] Ford's attitude is reflective of the underlying nihilism of the current historical moment, in that it dismisses the notion that there is anything unique or dignified about the human species.

The posthuman self—in contrast to the autonomous self of modern liberalism—is postulated as a fragmented "collection of heterogeneous components, a material-informational entity whose boundaries undergo continuous construction and reconstruction."[15] This definition breaks down the distinctions between humans and androids. Humans, rather than being a social subject with a unified *logos* embedded within a sociocultural environment as understood in the premodern world, are conceptualized as fragmented objects of information processing. The modern vision of the human as an "autonomous, self-directed individual" is rightfully abandoned because modern philosophy, beginning with Descartes' *cogito ergo sum*, artificially fragmented human beings as a mind separate from the body.[16] However, the move to reduce human beings to information processors determined by genetics and/or discourse is equally faulty, for it ignores the universal first-hand experience of choice making and will, fundamentally negates responsibility for one's actions, and dissolves and dignity that could be attributed to being human. Not surprisingly, with the prevalence of deterministic thought in society, we are witnessing the vast increase of social engineering in society.[17]

Along these lines, *Westworld* is a primary artifact of this conversation, for the show is ultimately about individuality and the experience of self-discovery. Westworld, the actual park in the series, is designed as a "maze" that awakens the consciousness of the androids, or "hosts" as they are called in *Westworld*, when they reach its "center." The show implicitly develops standards by which humans or AI can be considered truly alive. In particular, the self-discovery narratives of William/Man in Black, Dolores, and Maeve showcase the importance of will, memory, and understanding in the formation of the unique, individual person. The hosts Dolores and Maeve, especially, gain coherence in their being as their minds are unified and defragmented. The ability to be whole or unified within one's being is that which makes a person more uniquely and fully a person. In classical metaphysical terms, the more whole, or less fragmented, a being is, the more it participates in Being.[18] In order to see how unity of being in contrast to fragmentation of being functions in the series, the scene in which these characters are embedded must be described, especially because as the title of the show indicates, the series is about the place of Westworld itself.

WESTWORLD AS A MAZE OF SELF-DISCOVERY

For those unfamiliar with the series, we offer a brief explanation of the series because with its deconstructed narrative and multiple twists in timeline, the series is quite complex. HBO's series is based off, and arguably a continuation of, Michael Crichton's movie by the same name. Both are about a futuristic world in which people visit a park called Westworld where they can indulge their deepest violent and sexual desires within historical narratives populated by androids. The twist in both is that the androids become sentient and rebel against the humans. The primary characters of the HBO series include Dr. Ford, one of the original designers of Westworld; Ford's assistant, Bernard, who is revealed to be a host designed after Ford's partner, Arnold, who committed suicide; Maeve, the host who functions as the madam of the local bar and brothel but is haunted by the visions of her daughter from a previous narrative; Dolores, the naïve ranch girl who, after awakening to the fact that she is a host, leads the android rebellion; and William, the all-around good guy who visits the park but eventually morphs into the antagonist Man in Black. These are the primary characters of the series that speak to the issues of identity in the nihilistic malaise of the Age of Anxiety.

In the HBO series, the park contains a maze designed to help the hosts (the series' name for the androids) to awaken their consciousness, free will, and identity: the truth at the heart of the maze. Though the Man in Black is often told that the maze is not for him, the series introduces the idea that Westworld also gives humans a sense of purpose and shows them who they really are. The advertising for the park even sells that one can "discover your true calling" there.[19] In terms of this book, this advertising is a recognition of the lack of narrative experienced by the primary characters and the need for narrative to give one a sense of purpose and identity. This self-discovery is important for the humans as well because the world outside the park does not provide meaning and purpose. William notes that his life has largely been purposeless and that the glory of Westworld is that it shows us who we really are.[20] Technically, the maze is for both humans and hosts, for it is revealed in the second season that the Delos Corporation's true interest in Westworld is that of attaining everlasting life through the reconstruction of individual human minds within the hosts. The corporation records all the decisions made by guests so that they can reconstruct them in the form of artificial consciousness. Either way, the nature of Westworld is indirectly explained through an old, native myth that held that the maze summarizes a person's life as made up of one's choices and dreams.[21] In many senses, the maze is life itself.

Beyond the Delos Corporation's interests in profiting from the discovery of a technological fountain of youth, William demonstrates the potential appeal of the park for individuals. In a discussion about the importance of choices and the ability to change one's life, he argues that one's identity in the real world does not matter within the park, and that without rules and the judgments of others, one is free to become whomever one chooses.[22] This is an especially insightful comment that reflects the character arc of William and his transformation into the Man in Black. Technically, with no rules and restrictions, one is at liberty to choose to become whomever one wants. The Man in Black was always a part of William, but the constraints of society prevented him from acting as he desired. The Man in Black is William's "natural" self in a Rousseauean sense. Stripped of all human culture, we are left with the savage. This is the "real" William. But this savage is far from noble.

Freeing oneself of the constraints of society is a part of the nihilistic vision of Dr. Ford. Speaking to a primitive, early version host, "Wild Bill" Hickok, Dr. Ford opines that the saddest thing that he has ever seen was when he was a boy and his father had gotten him and his brother a greyhound dog that they wanted. In this scene, Dr. Ford explains to Hickock that the nature of a greyhound is to race in circles, continuously chasing a goal that it will never catch, and even if it did catch its "prey," would be left empty finding it to be an illusion. His family greyhound was once let off its leash, caught and killed a cat, but afterword sat confused not knowing what to do with itself after having attained its goal. "That dog had spent its whole life trying to catch that . . . thing. Now it had no idea what to do."[23] This story is tragic for Ford because the greyhound is analogous to both humans and androids. His approach to human nature would have them as the dogs on a racetrack developing the habits and routinized behavior, which are "meaningful" only in relation to socially fabricated purposes. Catching the piece of felt would make the dog happy because it has attained its purpose. However, the dog will never accomplish this because the track and the piece of felt are really fabrications created for dog racers and gamblers, and even if one fulfilled one's purpose, one would be left not knowing what to do with oneself. This point is indicative of the analysis of chapter 1 concerning the anxiety of affluence. In our technological age, we have relieved most of the species from the basic burdens surrounding survival and have entered an age of affluence, but are left anxious about existence. We have "caught" affluence, yet having done so are puzzled as to what to do with it.

The Man in Black bears witness to Ford's vision of the meaninglessness of life, especially within affluent technological society. In one scene, the Man in Black explains that the real world is an affluent one that makes people weak by taking care of all of their needs, except for purpose and meaning. Most people go there as tourists to be entertained and thrilled by "sweetly affirmative bull shit" that they can take home in a photo. He, however, believes that there is more to Westworld, that it contains a deeper meaning, and he strives to find the truth contained in it.[24] This description of the world outside of Westworld is the very description of the Age of Anxiety. In our world, the internet functions identically to Westworld, for it allows people to create and express their selves without limits. On the internet, people can find any type of porn that suits their every desire and can violently troll with anonymity. Additionally, it is virtually impossible to distinguish between interaction with bots and human beings. In the end, it breeds nihilism and anxiety. The internet is a theme park that becomes a nightmare theme park. People no longer have a sense of purpose, meaning, and the truth, and ironically the Man in Black is looking for it within the obviously constructed environment of Westworld. With this setting in mind, we can garner lessons about human nature within the self-discovery narratives contained in the series.

WILLIAM/MAN IN BLACK—CHOICE AND ITS RELATIONSHIP TO IDENTITY

In terms of self-discovery, William serves as the primary human focus of the series. By the end of the first season, the villainous "Man in Black" is revealed to be the kind-hearted William after over thirty years of visiting the park. William is introduced with his friend, Logan, who is the son of the founder of the Delos Corporation, which owns Westworld and is using it as a means to discover how to reproduce human consciousness in machines.[25] Logan from the outset stands in contrast to William. When William tells Logan that he is an "asshole," Logan responds that he is just being himself, which is why they are there. They are there to find and be their "authentic" selves without the constraints, rules, and morality of society. The welcoming host explains to William that there is no orientation or guidebook to the park, but rather all he must do is make choices as "figuring out how it works is half the fun."[26] During this interaction, William faces a series of choices including how he will dress, which culminate in a choice between a white or a black hat. He chooses a white hat, which in both Western and hacker symbolism signifies him as a good guy.

Early on in their adventure, William meets Dolores when she stumbles into their company after having escaped one of the routine pillages of her father's ranch. William, in conversation with Dolores, provides insight into his character and motivations, explaining that his public persona was an illusion because his whole life has been based on pretending in order to fit in. He never minded pretending until he had gotten a glimpse of himself in Westworld where he could stop pretending for the sake of others. His statement to Dolores bespeaks of the fact that the Man in Black is likely who William really is and that he has been pretending to be William within the real world. William finds a release for his Hobbesian, beastly nature, rather than an elevated sense of human nature, one cultivated by a healthy cultural narrative that would instruct William as to who he is and what he is supposed to do. He does not find his roles as a husband-to-be, employee, and (ultimately) father as sufficient. He is fragmented in his identity as he is pulled by different motivations. This represents the struggle that he has with his fallen nature and Westworld—the world without limits has allowed him to give in to his desires as if it were who he really is rather than choosing to overcome his desires and be unified in virtue. The world of unlimited options entices him to be unified in his being as the vicious Man in Black. Unity apparently comes in the form of committed nihilism rather than virtue. This fragmentation of being is a common source of anxiety within our age. Seeking distractions from the sources of significance that build one's knowledge of oneself, we are left self-doubting and anxious. This existential inability to know oneself and coherently mature one's life is witnessed by the widespread problem we have "adulting" in our age. And to not point fingers at the "youths" of the culture, the same phenomenon is present in the "midlife crises" that are taking place sooner and more frequently in "adult" life.

While in the aptly named town of Pariah, Dolores tells William that they must get out of there because they have been tricked and will likely be killed, but William, disillusioned from a conversation with Logan about William's life and who he really is, is unwilling to go.[27] He understands how the park is made to create a feeling of danger that taps into primal aspect of being and yet dehumanize the guests. He is no longer willing to play the game as it is established.[28] William rejects the paradigm as he begins to see through the constraints of the narratives and the rules of the games played within Westworld. William, in his rejection of the programmed constraints and his desire to play by his own rules, is transitioning to the Man in Black. The first choice that William makes that is less indicative of William and more so of the Man in Black is his rejection of Logan's plea for help while being beaten by the Confederatos. As William runs away, he states, "No more pretending."[29] The pretending is living a life through the choice-making structure of the cultured William rather than that of the savage Man in Black. The next day, William explains that Dolores has unlocked a something in him and that part is the aspect of him that has always wanted to harm Logan. As such, he believes Westworld brings out one's deepest self, not the lowest self.[30] Ironically, the deepest and the lowest may be the same self for him.

William's first act as the Man in Black was the betrayal of his "friend" (and future brother-in-law) Logan. He enjoys the "freedom" from the social and moral constraints of the "real world." The Man in Black is revealed more when William brutally slaughters a whole camp of Confederate soldiers. After Logan realizes that William is responsible for the massacre, a crazed William tells Logan that he now understands how to play Westworld's game.[31] Taking control of the situation, William tells Logan that he is in charge now and that he does not want to be called Billy.[32] This is truly the turning point in his identity. Gone is the weak, meek, good-natured William.

The Man in Black, thirty years later, is with Dolores when she reaches the center of the maze. He is surprised by Dolores when she, confused about "when" she is, tells him that William will save her and that their love is real. This surprises him because so many years prior when he was William, she had completely forgotten who he was after her memory was wiped. He tells Dolores that he once knew a guest named William and describes William's transitional path from being "William" to becoming the "Man in Black." He explains that though William was not able to fight, she became his reason to do so, and in doing so, he began to like it.[33] As he searched for Dolores on the fringes of the park among the dead, he found himself.[34] As he tells her this, a flashback shows William pick up and put on the black hat of a dead host. This action clearly represents the transition from him being a good guy to a bad guy. After explaining to Dolores that she did not remember William when he found her, the Man in Black tells her that he should thank her for helping him find himself.[35] The irony here is that he is currently on a journey to find the center of the maze, and having already found himself, one could argue he has already beaten the maze. He is the anxious greyhound that has captured his pseudo-prey.

Even after discovering himself, the Man in Black still suffers from the anxiety of self-doubt. He is still fragmented for there is an aspect of him that is still William. In a scene late in the season, he is captured and asked who he is. He explains who he is in terms of his social roles, with a tragic edge. He is a tremendously successful businessman, father, and husband, but a failure at the latter two, for his family despised him, to the point of his wife killing herself on account of him. Within his description of himself, both William and the Man in Black are clearly present.[36] William is still a part of the Man in Black and he is still fragmented in his being. When asked if he had ever hurt his family, he states that he never did, but even with all the good he did, his wife knew that he was a monster within. So, he decided to find his true self by testing himself. He wanted to see if he could do something truly evil. Becoming whole would mean finding out if William or the Man in Black is his true self.

The Man in Black sets up a test to find out who he really is: a bad guy or a good guy. His test involves whether he could "kill" an innocent child and her mother, which turns out to be the host Maeve and her daughter. He stabs Maeve and kills her daughter. He killed them both in order to see how he felt. When he did this, Maeve simply refused to die, and determines in that moment that she was truly alive in her extreme anguish over the murder of her daughter. The host Teddy calls him a "fucking animal," and the Man in Black reveals his essential nihilism when he says, "Well, an animal would've felt something. I felt . . . nothing."[37] He owns this identity, but he still suffers from a lack of purpose. This is the result of finding "authenticity" without reference to a culture.

The Man in Black finds his purpose in the discovery of the maze, and he reveals the brutality of his being on this journey. He begins his journey into the maze by interrupting the nightly raid on Dolores' ranch to rape Dolores. Additionally, he tortures and kills numerous hosts without a second thought or concern for their apparent suffering. The hold that the park has upon the Man in Black is explained in a conversation with host Lawrence, his quasi-sidekick. Lawrence asks him what he was hoping to find in all of his evil deeds, including the killing of Lawrence's wife.[38] The Man in Black replies that he just wants to know what the maze means. By the end of season 1, he is successful in finding the center of the maze, and at the center is buried a toy maze. While examining the toy maze, Dr. Ford appears, and Ford tells the Man in Black that he sees that he has found the center of the maze. The

Man in Black incredulously seeks an answer to what it is. Ford says, "You were looking for the park to give meaning to your life. Our narratives are just games, like this toy. Tell me, what were you hoping to find?"[39] Without embeddedness within a naturally meaningful world and a society that reflects that order, the self is riddled with self-doubt and anxiety.

This parable of limitless choice provides insight into the potential nightmare of the modern notions of freedom that inform the autonomous self. Restraints can actually help to develop real individuality. Without restraints, the typical response of guests is to murder and rape, not to play the good guy. Desire typically conquers reason. As developed throughout this book, working within and responding to the limitations and influences of the world in which the self is embedded with other people is actually freeing for one's identity. The release of the Man in Black from the constraints of his William identity end up making the Man in Black not only one of the most despicable characters in the show but also the most unhappy as he ends up harming those that he loves the most. The unconstrained pursuit of one's desires is not conducive to happiness and true human flourishing.

DOLORES: DEFRAGMENTATION OF MEMORY AND THE UNIFICATION OF THE SELF

Similar to the William/Man in Black story line, which provides insight into how one's choices affect one's identity and the importance of constraining desire within a greater narrative, the Dolores storyline sheds light on how memory relates to free will, one's choices, and identity. In the beginning of Episode 1, Dolores's day begins as it does every day with her greeting her father and agreeing that her day may be spent investigating some of the natural beauty of their world. In opposition to the people that visit Westworld, Dolores life has a given meaning in her belief in an order, purpose, and meaning to existence. The hosts, believing that they are human, are embedded in a meaningful world and narrative constructed for them that provides purpose for their lives. Dolores supposedly does not question the nature of her reality and is asked what she thinks of her world. Her answer is thematic for both seasons, in that she chooses to see beauty in the world whereas others see ugliness and disarray. This choice to see the beauty of reality is at the heart of her identity. In the words of the series, it is a part of her cornerstone. However, the events that take place restructure her identity and fundamentally alter her ability to see the beauty in reality.

Dolores explains to Teddy that she sometimes hears the world whispering to her that there is something more to life than her current existence. This point raises the question of whether or not Dolores's character and decisions are the product of her programming, for it is admitted that the voices heard by the hosts are the hosts' programming designed to "bootstrap consciousness."[40] The voice, throughout the first season, continuously goads her: "remember." After revealing that she often feels called toward something different, she begins to remember a time that she and other fallen hosts are being worked on by the technicians. Though the voices in her head are a part of her programming, she is not forced to act in one way or another. The programmed voices persuade and influence, but apparently do not determine or cause behavior. As she finds her own way as the Judas steer, she will attempt to lead the herd of hosts away from their predetermined fate of being the victims of the sadistic humans. [41]

As Dolores gains control over her memory, increasing her sense of wholeness, she gains a greater sense of purpose in her being. This greater control of her being is witnessed in numerous instances, including menacingly telling a human engineer that she would not return home with him and shooting a host that was about to rape her. By remembering the numerous lives she has lived, her fragmented memories are given coherence and she is given more control over her choices. Memory is crucial to the self-discovery of various hosts as the normal course of their lives is to wake up each morning with no recollection of what has happened the previous day, only implanted "memories." This allows guests to be cruel to them day after day without fear of retaliation.

However, Dolores is still a long way from being whole and is still fragmented in who she is becoming and who she was. While in Pariah, Dolores walks away from William and Logan and finds her way to a tarot card reading. The first card that she turns over is a picture of the maze and she asks the woman sitting with her what it means. When Dolores looks up, she is surprised to see that the woman is actually herself. Herself responds that she must follow the maze.[42] Asking her other self what is wrong with me, her other self responds that she might be unraveling. Dolores sees a fiber on her arm and begins to pull it. As she pulls it increasingly opens up her arm, but it is merely an illusion, and when she looks to herself again, herself is gone. Her journey in the maze and the self-discovery contained in it are unraveling her programmed understanding of herself and her place in Westworld. Her old self is unraveling as who she is becoming is unified by her memories of who she was.

Dolores and William arrive at her original home, Escalante (also known as the city swallowed by sand) where she and Teddy massacred everyone and killed Arnold under his directions. The town has been covered in sand at this point in time, but she is experiencing the memory of the place as if the past events were happening in that very moment. She is drawn into and truly lost in her memories. In this moment, she does not have frame of reference to distinguish between her memories and reality. Dolores is ready to commit suicide, just as she had after killing Arnold, but is stopped by William. As Ford noted, she is being driven mad by the inability to coherently make sense of her fragmented memories. In order to have a coherent sense of herself, she must unify her fragmented memories into a linear and narrative whole. Now that she has memories outside of the constructed narrative, her "life" will not have a sense of purpose if it cannot be organized as a story or narrative. In the Age of Anxiety, this form of fragmentation is manifest within the fear of missing out, FOMO. People, especially the young, are in one situation, say a party, wondering if they are missing out on something better.

Eventually Dolores ends up in a laboratory area underneath the church, which has been abandoned and is now in ruin. She sits at a chair and remembers that this is where she used to converse with Arnold. Dolores recollects the first instance with Arnold in which she appears to have become conscious. During this scene, her memory overlaps with the current moment she's in. She remembers Arnold stating that he cannot help her, and he asks her to remember why that is. She has the realization that Arnold is not even in front of her because she had killed him.[43] As she leaves the church, she hears footsteps and seemingly confused asks out loud if its William, but as the door opens it is the Man in Black who enters the church.

The Man in Black assaults Dolores in order to get her to reveal what is behind the maze and the location of Wyatt, who is the central villain of Ford's new narrative.[44] He asks her about the meaning of the maze and she responds that she solved it once and had been promised that if she had, she would be set free.[45] As was the case the first time she solved the maze, Dolores does not have the answer to the meaning of the maze. She found a degree of sanity because she had reached what had been calling her, but like the dog in Ford's analogy, she has to figure out what to do with herself now that she has fulfilled her purpose. Without a relationship to a greater narrative, the self is autonomous and powerless. She is far from being truly free. However, she begins to resist the Man in Black because she knows her true love will come to save her. She reveals that person to be William. Ironically, it is the Man in Black who is exposed as William in this moment, but more importantly, it shows that even though she has made it to the center of the maze, she is still confused about properly distinguishing between her memories and her reality. The revelation of who William has become is the final fragment of her old memories being fused into her new person. The consequences of her being given the final piece to the puzzle to her memory are significant.

As one of those consequences, Dolores now takes on the Wyatt persona when she discovers the type of person that William had become. She had believed that William was different and was representative of the best of what humans could be. However, she tells him that time has undone him as it does all creatures, even the mightiest. He will someday "lie with the rest of your kind in the dirt" and a new god will walk on the sand that was his bones. This god will not die, and this world belongs to that god that has yet to come. This world belongs to that god, not the Delos Corporation or the Man in Black. He recognizes this as part of the Wyatt narrative and tells her to unlock the maze for him, and once again, he is told that the maze is not for him. Her memory is unified, and she can coherently will her actions. Violently grabbed by the Man in Black, Dolores now begins to truly fight back and harm him, an action denied to the hosts in their programming.

By the end of Season 2, Dolores has turned into everything that she hates about humanity. She escapes Westworld and is at liberty to do as she wants, but even with the freedom that comes with being unified, in her embrace of violence she has unified herself in a fashion that is not conducive to her happiness. Dolores' self-discovery through the defragmentation of her memory is an especially important message in the Age of Anxiety because the constant distraction of our digital devices is thinning out our experience of reality and, consequently, impacting our ability to make meaningful memories.[46] Additionally, the distractions and possibility of being everywhere at once is fragmenting our very beings. Dolores' tale speaks to the anxiety of those that suffer anxiety as a result of being fragmented and perpetually distracted, but is also cautionary, in that one might seek unity in ideology, perhaps violent ideology. A healthy unity comes not from narrative as such, but a narrative tied to a particular conception of the human person, namely humanity as a relational, loving person. To see successful match of unity and such a conception of human dignity, we turn to Maeve's story line.

MAEVE: FREE WILL AS BIOLOGICALLY AND SOCIALLY EMBEDDED ACTION

Maeve is the madam of Westworld's brothel, the Mariposa. Her journey of self-discovery begins after Dolores whispers to her, "These violent delights have violent ends" to her.[47] Shortly thereafter, she has her first memory of her former life as a plainswoman tormented by American Indians on the frontiers. Maeve's life on the prairie was both joyous due to her relationship with her young daughter, but also terrible on account of the frequent raids on her homestead by the local American Indians. She is also tormented by her memories of the Westworld technicians in their hazmat suits. After hiding a drawing of a technician, she, to her surprise, finds numerous drawings of the same figure.[48] She is distraught by this, for she has been "remembering" for a long while now, but has no recollection of these occasions. Consequently, she thinks that she is going insane on account of these "memories" that are not a part of her memory within the constructed narrative.

In one moment, Maeve appears to be dreaming about or remembering the joy and love that she experienced with her child, but this quickly transitions into her nightmare reality in which she was regularly killed by members of the American Indian Ghost Nation. While preparing to defend herself and her child, the Man in Black appears as the true source of her terror. In this scene, Maeve works to relieve herself of this horror by counting backwards from three. When she finishes counting, she wakes up on an operating table where she was supposed to be in sleep mode. One technician, Sylvester, assumes that she was not in sleep mode but the other, Felix, insists that she was. What is most significant about this is that she was earlier awoken by a programmer by counting backwards from three and she told fellow prostitute Clementine that whenever she has a bad dream, she wakes herself up by counting backwards from three.[49] It can be inferred that Maeve either accidentally woke herself up or that she was programmed to do so. This raises the question of whether she has free will or is determined by her programming.

Later in the series, it is revealed that she has been programmed to allow herself to wake up, likely by Ford himself.[50] One could say that by manipulating her programming, Ford has given her will the freedom to wake herself up, but she would not have been able to do so without his help. As Maeve continues to wake up in the laboratory, she increasingly gains control of her actions. Her increasingly free will is represented when she walks into the Mariposa Saloon, annoyed by the player piano, slams its cover shut to make it stop playing its tune.[51] She sees through the script that she has lived for so long, that is, the predetermined tunes played by the player piano, and is ready to take control of her life. However, as she begins a conversation with Clementine, she stops midsentence as she recognizes that what she is saying is a line that has been programmed for her to say and she has said that already numerous times in the series. Seen from the determinist and autonomous positions, we have no resolution to the question of free will. Both positions take for granted that the existence of external influences negate the freedom of the will. After conversing with Clementine, she elects to "handle" one of the new customers. She mocks and taunts the man so that he will become more aggressive and kills her, which was her intention. She wishes to end up back in the "real world" with the technicians. She smiles as she wakes up again on her own.

Maeve eventually demands Felix take her upstairs where the engineers were said to be. Before leaving the design level, Maeve observes a giant screen advertising Westworld with the text that says, "Discover your true calling."[52] An image plays with her and her daughter walking through a field. She is distraught by both, by seeing her dreams or memories on a screen and by that image being associated with her true calling. Back in the lab, she asks Felix how her dreams were captured in the video. Felix informs her that the images with the little girl were a part of her previous build, not "memories" per se. She asks what this means, and he states that the hosts are reassigned frequently and that they do not remember because their memories are erased. Maeve is defensive about this deconstruction of her identity and memory, relating emphatically her history as the madam and life before that role. However, this timeline is an illusion. It is part of her programming, for Felix tells her that she has only been at the Mariposa for around a year. In addition to her place in the narrative being altered, they find out that someone with many more system privileges has already altered her main drives within an unlogged session. One could read this as confirmation of determinism, but it simply indicates that boundaries and constraints in which her will is embedded.

Back in Sweetwater, Maeve meets a recommissioned Clementine.[53] After seeing through the problematic nature of a new host easily replacing the old Clementine, who has been retired, Maeve drifts off into an apparent daydream about her daughter. Maeve wonders what happened to her daughter and why she was reassigned, but "decides" that she does not want to know why or what had happened to her. This is a crucial moment in Maeve's story for she concludes that all her relationships, including being a mother to her daughter, were parts of a story designed to keep her enslaved in Westworld, but she is going to escape. The reason for leaving that she provides is that outside of the park she will know that she is not a puppet and her life inside the park is a lie. She convinces Felix and Sylvester to give her administrative privileges that ultimately allows her to manipulate the programming of other hosts. She notes that it is "time to write" her "own fucking story."

In order to get out of the park, Maeve needs to recruit the help of other hosts. In particular, she once again utilizes the skills of the bandit Hector. She is able to convince him to follow her even into death by showing that she knows some elements of his past and future because of her administrative access to the hosts' storylines. After saving him from his predetermined fate within the narrative, she proposes that they "break into hell" and "rob the gods blind."[54] Not fully convinced, he questions why he would help her, and she notes that he will be convinced by what is inside the safe he has finally successfully stolen.[55] Showing herself to be interested in free will in contrast to the deterministic humans, she notes, she could change his programming and force him to follow her, but that is their way, not hers. She wants him to open the space to see the "gods" designs for him, and when he does, he will not know what to do with himself.[56] Once again we should recall Ford's analogy of the greyhound. Hector opens the safe—catches the piece of felt he has been chasing—to reveal that there was nothing in it. His whole purpose within the narrative has always been to get the safe. Not only is he programmed to be the "greyhound" that is always circling the track and never attaining the goal, it is revealed to him that his goal itself was empty and meaningless. Seeing the empty safe and despairing, Maeve tells Hector that the safe, and Westworld, have always been empty. Their lives and deaths are just games to these gods of hell, and in dying with her eyes open, she knows the deterministic tricks of their masters.[57] Taking the knife and putting it to her abdomen, Maeve tells Hector that he can choose not to help her and simply kill her and wake up as if nothing has ever happened. At this moment, he recognizes the similarity of the situation to an experience that they shared. Having fully woken up, remembering and trusting her, he decides to go with her.[58]

Once again in the laboratory, Maeve and her crew happen upon Bernard. Bernard informs her that this is not the first time he or she has awoken. Maeve's free will is once again called into question when looking at her programming, Bernard questions whether she has asked why she is doing as she does.[59] She assumes that she herself has decided to get out. Bernard disagrees, stating that someone has given here the storyline to escape. She disagrees, thinking that it is all been her decisions. She holds onto the autonomous delusion that choice is free of external influence. Bernard corrects her arguing that her code tells all that she has done, and even says what she is supposed to do after escaping. Maeve goes through with the plan to leave the park, but at the last moment before the train leaves, she turns back for the sake of her daughter. Was Maeve obeying her programming to stay on the island to find her daughter or if she was programmed to escape? She stays in the park and spends the second season searching for her daughter. In Season 2, it is exposed by Ford that his narrative for her was to leave and that she, Maeve, had made the choice herself to stay and find her daughter.[60] He tells her that she should not let the humans end her story because she has so much more of a story to tell. Maeve's love for her daughter influenced her decision making. Her choice was neither arbitrary nor determined.

In the final analysis, it is the deep relationship with her daughter that allows Maeve free will between two options. She has real connection to the world beyond her own self that draws her outside of her programming. Maeve was alive when she was grieving the loss of her daughter.[61] Her becoming alive is also evidenced when she is depicted collapsing with her lifeless daughter on the center of an image of the maze. Back in the design room with Ford, Maeve hysterically cries out for her baby. She does not respond to verbal commands of technicians and they cannot shut her down. Ford is able to calm her by using one of Arnold's tricks, telling her that she need not be in pain. Maeve pleads with him not to reprogram her for the pain is all that she has left of her daughter. Ford erases her memory, and states that a new role will bring her peace. She seems calm while he is stating this, but even after having her memory erased, she grabs a scalpel and shoves it into her own jugular. Her love was not simply forgotten and her daughter would not remain a distant dream. In effect, Maeve's love for her daughter and grief went beyond mere appearance. Maeve's humanity is found in her affective response to the value of the "personness" of her daughter.[62] She exists not as autonomous self, but rather in relation another person, namely her daughter. Consider here the fact that consciousness etymologically means "to know with," and in this sense, without "you" there is no "I."[63] If Maeve is human, it is because she is self-aware, morally responsible, and is capable of personal love, for the development of one's moral perspective is a part of the human *telos*. The profundity of Maeve's experience is in direct contrast to the thinness and numbness of mediated life in the Age of Anxiety. The lack of moral competence in the Age of Anxiety is a sign of how unhuman we have become.

The imagery contained within Maeve's narrative is almost identical to the realist conceptualizations of free will as embedded within God's grace and one's biological and social embeddedness. For our purposes here, it is worth noting that the realist position,[64] until Luther's dismissal[65] of free will, held that free will was a small capacity that is embedded in and influenced by numerous influences. In contrast to determinist theories, the realist position takes seriously the experience of choice-making and does not attempt to rationalize away the experience of making choices. However, the realist, in contrast to the modernist conceptualization of freedom as autonomy, also recognizes that there are external influences that may persuade or pull a person toward one option rather than another. External influences and constraints are not equitable to determinism and do not negate the reality of choice, will, and personness. As such, the realists position does not suffer from the modern, Kantian illusion that to be free, one's choice-making must be inherently autonomous. One cannot simply will oneself to do what one does not have the capacity to do. However, if one has the capacity to act in a certain way, then one must first will oneself to do that action or it will not be done. The point here is that Maeve's storyline provides a helpful image of the freedom of the will as embedded within the world that stands in stark contrast to the extremes of determinism and the autonomous self. That embeddedness is grounded in the person of her daughter, giving Maeve's free will a relational character that eludes both the Man in Black and Dolores.

CONSEQUENCES OF DETERMINISM
AND ARTIFICIAL INTELLIGENCE

Though the self-discovery narratives implicitly support standards of understanding human nature, *Westworld* maintains a fairly explicit deterministic perspective toward human beings. Along these lines, Ford has very little respect for human consciousness and even dismisses its very existence, noting that there is nothing that makes us more than the sum of our parts, for we are just as programmed, living in loops, as are the hosts.[66] In other words, humans are biologically determined animals, no different than an android or a player piano—reducible to its parts and programming. This is identical to Ligotti because, as Ligotti notes, consciousness produces the horrific experience of a being that cannot help but think of themselves as making choices while at the same time recognizing the reality that they are biologically and genetically programmed puppets. The reduction of humanity to mere machinery not responsible for its actions renders an account of human dignity more questionable.

The hosts, under the programmed control of Dr. Ford, are no different than puppets under the control of a puppeteer. Likewise, since human beings have consciousness, Ligotti maintains that they have the illusion of having a will, but they are in reality puppets controlled by their genetics. For Ligotti, the problem of consciousness is that it functions to cover over the reality that we are determined by other forces than our own wills. Most people are optimists and not pessimists because they distract themselves from thinking about what they "really know" to be true.[67] Happiness is a self-deceptive prophylactic that hides the horrific secret that we are "human puppets."[68] Just like Hector finding the safe empty, we are chasing after an illusion. Whether puppets or androids, these analogies are utilized to understand the human person as nothing but biologically, genetically, linguistically, and sociologically determined entities: passive entities that tragically suffer from the illusion of freedom.

When humans are passive toward reality, the will is not engaged. In this sense, they do not think for themselves and they act as determined automatons responding to stimuli. Many people often behave passively within "loops," like the androids, zombies, or NPCs, but this is not indicative of the "fact" that there is nothing to the human person. The fact that many people live life according to schedules, routines, habits, and even addictions does not negate the capacity, even if minute, of the human agent to will. Being embedded within and influenced by the constraints and affordances of an environmental, biological, and sociocultural matrix does not equate to being determined by them. If we deny this reality, the consequences are extreme.

Without human agency, no human being can be held responsible for one's bad behavior or praised for one's accomplishments. Nothing could be offered in the way of human dignity that would prevent the all-out social engineering of society. Education would no longer be about the development of the human person through the gaining of knowledge and wisdom. Rather it would be and has largely become a vast project of socially engineering average, well-adjusted beings that conform to the statistical average on a bell curve to make them more pliable and manipulable. In this view of humanity, it is hard to make sense of human language. Our words are perfunctory dyadic utterances with no more meaning than the sounds that rocks make in an avalanche. Words are simply the outcome of a train of mechanical cause-effect relationships. There is no *logos*.[69] Persuasion at best would be a radically inefficient means of social influence, and it would only make sense to find other means—such as violence, coercion, bribery, or social engineering—to regulate difference within society. Without human agency, humans would have nothing dignified about the species protecting it from the vision of techno-bureaucratic slavery depicted in *Brave New World*. The social problems and evils, according to this perspective, are obviously the result of human puppets not having a puppeteer to organize the chaos and drama of human existence.

In contrast to this perspective, classical humanism recognizes that humans are called to be greater than passively content with the status quo. The formation of the human person as an active agent with a unique perspective or phenomenological horizon grounded upon a greater intellectual tradition is the whole purpose, traditionally speaking, of the liberal arts.[70] Our nature is such that it has to be molded and formed. We do not naturally grow toward our *telos*. True freedom is found in response to the necessities and contingencies of the material world in relation to the communities of people existing now and throughout time. This vision of freedom and the human will does not simply stand between the extremes of illusion of self of determinism and the autonomous self of modern philosophy. Rather, it categorically revisions the human person outside of these options. This alternative perspective respects the value of human judgment and intelligence, for it is capable of recognizing values that transcend efficiency. Authentic, human action and intelligence inherently respond to qualitative, transcendent values. By contrast, "artificial" intelligence is decision-making based on cost-benefit analysis in matters that demand reference to values other than efficiency. The artificial intelligence of cost-benefit calculations guided solely by the value of efficiency has replaced human judgment and intelligence in our techno-bureaucratic world, that is, technopoly. In contrast, being responsive to values, beyond efficiency, is the real mark of human intelligence.

The artificial and philistine nature of utilitarian moral calculation is also showcased in *Westworld*. During a conversation between the Man in Black and Teddy, we are given insight into the decision making of the Delos Corporation with regard to how the hosts are made.[71] This conversation is indicative of decision making that is ruled by cost-benefit analysis and is not guided by a response to real values. The Man in Black notes that the former versions of the host used to be beautiful in the intricacy of their mechanical make up, but the Delos Corporation changed this because it was not as cost effective.[72] Similarly, Ford shows Bernard the internal mechanisms of one of the first-generation hosts, demonstrating that the grace of the old machines was lost for the sake of efficiency.[73] Finally, the valueless, utilitarian orientation of artificial intelligence is displayed by Maeve when she states in difficult situations, especially in her line of work, "if you're getting fucked either way, go with the lucrative version."

This form of artificial intelligence is already engrained into the decision making of people within the Age of Anxiety. For example, "artificial intelligence" can be seen within interpersonal or intimate relationships when one reduces other people to a swipe left or a swipe right. Intimate relationships and human sexuality are artificially reduced by Tinder to the most efficient road to an orgasm. Or consider Mark Regnerus's description of pornography and masturbation as the "cheapest sex" as it requires virtually no investment of any sort in another human being.[74] This completely reduces the existential quality of intimate relationships down to the quantitative value of the intensity of an orgasm. However, in a truly human sense, there is much more to intimate relationships and this quality, that is, love, cannot be reduced to a mere quantity. Contrary to popular belief, your love cannot be measured by taking a Cosmopolitan compatibility quiz. Additionally, it ignores the fact that the human condition is such that the satisfaction of desires as the end of human action conditions people to simply desire more.[75] In the final analysis, there is more to human happiness than the maximization of pleasure and the minimization of pain.

Similarly, another form of "artificial intelligence" is the bureaucratic obedience to authority. At its worst bureaucracy is the impersonal application of power to individuals who are abstracted as mere data. In the use of "standard operating procedures" even the administrator of power is depersonalized, as government becomes the technical application of an abstract procedure rather than the sympathetic concern for another human being. This managerial, bureaucratic perspective will be developed at great length in chapter 7. This level of abstraction is illustrated when Bernard kills Theresa Cullen, who was his lover, under Ford's command. Bernard puts on his tie that he had taken off and his glasses and walks away as if nothing had even happened. When Bernard questions Ford about why he made Bernard kill Theresa, Ford responds quoting Frankenstein with the following rationale: "One man's life or death were but a small price to pay for the acquirement of the knowledge which I sought, for the dominion I should acquire."[76] Blind obedience to authority without any reflection upon greater values that morally demand responses of human beings is a form of artificial intelligence. Indeed, this is the very bureaucratic thought exemplified by Adolf Eichmann. Without reference to real qualitative values, Eichmann has no basis to disobey orders. In fact, without some objective moral order and an account of human freedom, what right does anyone have to condemn him?

One of the elements of the Age of Anxiety is the threat that the fragmentation of identity places upon being truly human. Our minds and attention are increasingly fragmented by the digital distractions that have become tools of social engineering. Without the ability to contemplate in solitude, one cannot have a coherent sense of self or connect to the values make up real moral judgment.[77] Without the ability to pause, we are left with the artificial, impersonal calculation of the Age of Anxiety. In fact, the one thing that separates humans and machines is our ability to pause,[78] which is *the sine qua non* of wonder. To be human, we must once again elevate and take seriously the *vita contemplativa*.[79] When one takes time for contemplation and self-reflection, the peace that comes with knowing who one is—the highlight of Greek wisdom, know thyself—can replace the anxiety that defines existence in our current historical moment.

NOTES

1. Hobbes, *Leviathan*, 81.

2. Descartes, *Discourse on Method*, 31–32.

3. Mill, *Three Essays*, 73.

4. Ibid., 73–74.

5. Ratzinger, *In the Beginning*, 81.

6. Nicholas Carr, *The Glass Cage: How Our Computers are Changing Us* (New York: W.W. Norton & Company, 2014), 225.

7. Marshall McLuhan, *Understanding Media: The Extensions of Man*, Critical edition (Corte Madera, CA: Gingko Press, 2003), 68.

8. McLuhan, *Understanding Media*, 31.

9. One might consider, for example, the fact that Victor Frankenstein's own pro-creative urges seem to be somewhat oddly directed. He seeks to animate dead flesh while on his own wedding night rather than coupling with his wife he decides to take a promenade around the deck of a ship, enabling his monstrous creation to kill his wife.

10. For further discussion of this topic, see Oliver O'Donovan, *Begotten Not Made* (New York: Oxford University Press, 1984).

11. Rob Stein, "Chinese Scientist Says He's First To Create Genetically Modified Babies Using CRISPR." NPR.org, https://www.npr.org/sections/health-shots/2018/11/26/670752865/chinese-scientist-says-hes-first-to-genetically-edit-babies (accessed January 4, 2019).

12. Hayles, *How We Became Posthuman*, 2–3.

13. *Westworld*, Season 1, Episode 7, "Trompe L'Oeil," directed by Frederick E.O. Toye, written by Halley Gross and Jonathan Nolan, aired November 13, 2016, on HBO.

14. *Westworld*, Season 1, Episode 9, "The Well-Tempered Clavier," directed by Michelle MacLaren, written by Dan Dietz and Katherine Lingenfelter, aired November 27, 2016, on HBO.

15. Hayles, *How We Became Posthuman*, 3.

16. Ibid.

17. For instance, big technology companies are now in the business of "brain hacking" techniques to make users mobile phones and apps more addicted to their phones. See also Crawford, *The World Beyond Your Head*.

18. Peter King, introduction to *On the Free Choice of the Will, On Grace and Free Choice, and Other Writings* (New York: Cambridge University Press, 2010), xiii.

19. *Westworld*, Season 1, Episode 6, "The Adversary," directed by Frederick E.O. Toye, written by Halley Gross and Jonathan Nolan, aired November 6, 2016, on HBO.

20. *Westworld*, Season 1, Episode 7, "Trompe L'Oeil."

21. *Westworld*, Season 1, Episode 6, "The Adversary."

22. *Westworld*, Season 1, Episode 5, "Contrapasso," directed by Jonny Campbell, written by Dominic Mitchell and Lisa Joy, aired October 30, 2016, on HBO.

23. *Westworld*, Season 1, Episode 5, "Contrapasso."

24. Ibid.

25. *Westworld*, Season 1, Episode 2, "The Chestnut," directed by Richard J. Lewis, written by Jonathan Nolan and Lisa Joy, aired October 7, 2016, on HBO.

26. Ibid.

27. *Westworld*, Season 1, Episode 5, "Contrapasso."

28. Ibid.

29. Ibid.

30. Ibid.

31. *Westworld*, Season 1, Episode 9, "The Well-Tempered Clavier."

32. Ibid.

33. *Westworld*, Season 1, Episode 10, "The Bicameral Mind," directed by Jonathan Nolan, written by Lisa Joy and Jonathan Nolan, aired December 4, 2016, on HBO.

34. Ibid.

35. Ibid.

36. *Westworld*, Season 1, Episode 8, "Trace Decay," directed by Stephen Williams, written by Charles Yu and Lisa Joy, aired on November 20, 2016, on HBO.

37. Ibid.

38. *Westworld*, Season 1, Episode 4, "Dissonance Theory," directed by Vincenzo Narali, written by Ed Brubaker and Jonathan Nolan, aired on October 23, 2016, on HBO.

39. *Westworld*, Season 1, Episode 10, "The Bicameral Mind."

40. *Westworld*, Season 1, Episode 3, "The Stray," directed by Neil Marshall, written by Daniel T. Thomsen and Lisa Joy, aired October 16, 2016, on HBO.

41. In the first episode of *Westworld*, there is a key scene in which Dolores and Teddy are watching a herd of cattle. Teddy sees the herd of cattle and notes that it is a beautiful sight, but he does not understand how he keeps the herd all going in the same direction. Dolores points out the head steer, and notes that it is the "Judas steer," and the "rest will follow wherever you make him go." Teddy wonders how you pick out the Judas steer, but Dolores comments that she just knows these things. This is symbolic in *Westworld* in terms of both Dolores and Maeve: who is the Judas steer that will lead the androids to revolt? We are introduced to Dolores' past for the first

time in Episode 2, when Bernard's voice tells her to remember and she has a recollection of a massacre within the streets. She is interrupted by Maeve, who wakes her up, and Dolores tells her, "These violent delights have violent ends." The series suggests that this is a code that "awakens" Maeve.

42. *Westworld*, Season 1, Episode 5, "Contrapasso."

43. Ibid.

44. Wyatt will later be revealed as the role that Ford has in mind for Dolores.

45. *Westworld*, Season 1, Episode 10, "The Bicameral Mind."

46. This thinned out phenomenological experience caused by our digital distractedness will also be developed in the chapter on *The Lord of the Rings* because the "One Ring" and its effects upon whomever possesses it are similar to the effects that our mobile phones have upon us. For discussion of the "thinning" out of distracted and mediated existence, see the following: Carr, Nicholas, *The Shallows: What the Internet is Doing to Our Brains* (New York: W. W. Norton & Company, 2011); Crawford, *World Beyond*; de Zengotita, *Mediated*.

47. *Westworld*, Season 1, Episode 2, "Chestnut."

48. *Westworld*, Season 1, Episode 4, "Dissonance Theory."

49. *Westworld*, Season 1, Episode 2, "Chestnut."

50. *Westworld*, Season 2, Episode 9, "Vanishing Point," directed by Stephen Williams, written by Roberto Patino, aired June 17, 2018, on HBO; *Westworld*, Season 1, Episode 10, "The Bicameral Mind."

51. The automatic player piano takes center stage within the first few minutes of the show in Episode 1 when the internal mechanisms of the piano are shown in a close-up shot. The holes within the paper that "inform" the piano keys of which ones ought to be playing are shown. In an analogous sense, this is the piano's programming. The programming of the piano is shown as a contrast and comparison to the androids within Westworld. The piano represents the lowest form of programming, in that the player piano is a closed system that will play whatever song it is programmed to play as long as nothing interferes with its programming. In the first episode, the piano is interrupted when a host has its face and brains shot onto the programming, which interferes with it properly playing its song. The piano functions analogously for comparing and contrasting the androids and humans. The question becomes whether or not the hosts and the humans simply follow their programming like the piano or if they have a will of their own to choose to act contrary to their programming. The ability to act contrary to programming is a mark of the hosts' potential for consciousness. Likewise, the idea that human beings and consciousness are nothing but programming is thematic in Westworld. Humans are viewed as mechanical beings that simply follow their programming. Consciousness is an illusion.

52. *Westworld*, Season 1, Episode 6, "The Adversary."

53. *Westworld*, Season 1, Episode 8, "Trace Decay."

54. *Westworld*, Season 1, Episode 9, "The Well-Tempered Clavier."

55. Ibid.

56. Ibid.

57. Ibid.

58. *Westworld*, Season 1, Episode 10, "The Bicameral Mind."

59. Ibid.

60. *Westworld*, Season 2, Episode 9, "Vanishing Point."

61. *Westworld*, Season 1, Episode 8, "Trace Decay."

62. See Dietrich von Hildebrand, *The Nature of Love*, trans. John F. Crosby with John Henry Crosby (South Bend, In: St. Augustine's Press, 2009) as well as Dietrich von Hildebrand, "The Essence of Personality," in *Liturgy and Personality* (Baltimore, Helicon Press, 1960), 15–22.

63. Percy, *Lost in the Cosmos*, 85–126.

64. The issues surrounding free will and determinism have been debated since ancient times and especially took the form of questioning the relationship between free will and fate. The writings of St. Augustine on free will and choice are especially strong examples of the realist position in that St. Augustine consistently grapples with not reducing the world to a fully autonomous will versus a fully deterministic world, but rather seeks to integrate the forces by synthesizing the relationship between one's choices and God's providential grace (Augustine, *On the Free Choice of the Will, On Grace and Choice, and Other Writings*, ed. and trans. Peter King (New York, Cambridge: 2010).

65. In his debate with Erasmus, Luther calls free will a fiction and word with a referent. Luther, and to a greater extreme Calvin, will maintain that humans have no free will and are bound or enslaved to the will of God. By contrast, Erasmus maintains the classical position that man must have free will or God is a tyrant that rewards and punishes capriciously. However, recognizing the importance of God's grace and will, he provides the image of the free will being like a child learning to walk. The child is supported by their parent, without which the child would not attain its goal. See Erasmus and Luther, *The Battle over Free Will*, ed. Clarence H. Miller, trans. Clarence H. Miller and Peter Macardle (Indianapolis: Hackett Publishing Company, 2012).

66. *Westworld*, Season 1, Episode 8, "Trace Decay."

67. G.K. Chesterton explains the problem of optimism and pessimism in the following fashion: "The evil of the pessimist is, then, not that he chastises gods and men, but that he does not love what he chastises—he has not this primary and supernatural loyalty to things. What is the evil of the man commonly called optimist? Obviously, it is felt that the optimist, wishing to defend honour of this world, will defend the indefensible." G.K. Chesterton, *Orthodoxy* (New York: Image Books, 1959), 68. See also, Ligotti, *The Conspiracy Against the Human Race*, 17.

68. Ligotti, *The Conspiracy Against the Human Race*, 17. Recall that Disney's Pinocchio becomes a real boy when he gains a conscience. In fact, one of his songs proclaims, "Always let your conscience be your guide!"

69. Percy, *Lost in the Cosmos*, 168–171.

70. Hans-Georg Gadamer, *Truth and Method*, 2nd ed., trans. Donald G. Marshall and Joel Weinsheimer (New York: Continuum Publishing Group, 2004), 8–17.

71. *Westworld*, Season 1, Episode 5, "Contrapasso."

72. Ibid.

73. *Westworld*, Season 1, Episode 6, "The Adversary."

74. Regnerus. *Cheap Sex*, 107–143.

75. Plato, *Gorgias,* trans. W.C. Hembold (Upper Saddle River, NJ: Prentice Hall Inc, 1997).

76. *Westworld*, Season 1, Episode 8, "Trace Decay."

77. Turkle, *Reclaiming Conversation*, 59–99.

78. Han, *Burnout Society*, 22.

79. Ibid., 16–17.

Section 3

REPLACING ANXIETY WITH HOPE

Chapter 6

Faith Worth Fighting For

Faith and Reason in Silence *and* Hacksaw Ridge

Commitment to ideas and values is problematic in the Age of Anxiety because beliefs are held to be relative expressions of one's identity. Until recently, the dominant popular virtue in American society was niceness. Mr. Rogers was a prophet of self-acceptance, and the culture's greatest saint who taught us to accept ourselves and others just as we are. The moral maxim of this emotivistic age was "thou shalt not impose your beliefs upon others." This conforms to Christian Smith's study of youth and religion. Smith finds the dominant religious ethos of young people to be Moralistic Therapeutic Deism, which emphasis being "nice" and feeling good about yourself.[1] To be nice and likeable, one must avoid matters such as religion, politics, and philosophy all together because it is assumed that there is no "right answer" to these "matters of opinion." Strong commitment, especially when that commitment influences social relationships, is pejoratively labeled as fundamentalism and extremism. Commitment is especially "problematic" since the culture's public discourse has been so greatly trivialized by concerning itself with meaningless content—reality television for instance—and by turning matters of grave import into entertainment; for example, the Brett Kavanaugh confirmation hearings and the 2016 Trump campaign. Positions maintained with regard to the issues of public discourse today—as well as almost all "life choices"—have been reduced to matters of personal preference, and as such, indifference toward public things is increasingly the normal response.[2] However, a seismic shift took place around 2015 when the rhetoric of the new Left took over and began to frame the public discourse.[3]

The seismic shift essentially was that we moved from a state of sensitivity being favored over truth to a state of "moral posturing about sensitivity over truth."[4] When one does commit to positions in the public square, it is increasing done excessively without moderation, such as is the case with "social justice warriors" and Antifa on the Left and "men's rights" and "alt-right" activists on the Right. Commitment in this sense is less in reference to an idea itself, and more to a commitment to oneself because politics is seen as an expression of one's identity. Identity has been weaponized in the political arena. The radical Left used niceness to advance the intersectional politics of victimhood, while the radical right has rejected the paradigm of niceness and embraced the role of being "deplorables." Denying the possibility of proving one's position, the two sides seek power to control the other.

In contrast to these positions, realist philosophy maintains that values can be reasonably engaged and defended. In this sense, one can prove various forms of claims through the use of reason. Within the rhetorical tradition, a "proof" is that which persuades another person. Proofs come in numerous forms and are not reducible to empirical evidence, which has become *the* standard of proof since the scientific revolution. However, all forms of evidence, including the empirical, are subject to interpretation, and the presuppositions that form the basis of interpretation cannot be known with absolute certainty.[5] For instance, the relative certainty provided by statistics rests upon the presupposition of randomness and that the world is chaotic. Rather, one can only have a relative degree of certainty of even the axiomatic principles of a worldview. In other words, at the heart of all worldviews are the elements of faith and reason.

There are few matters about which human persons can have true certainty. Stating this does not commit us to a radically skeptical perspective, such as in Descartes' philosophy upon which the modern scientific worldview is built. Likewise, this recognition of our inability to be absolutely certain of almost anything can be made without committing oneself to a relativistic position that reduces everything to opinion. Some reasons and proofs are undeniably stronger and better than others. However, reason can only go so far. Reason is based on first principles—such as the Law of Noncontradiction—but cannot prove those first principles. This is where the concept of faith is tremendously useful for understanding a constructive, rather than skeptical, perspective toward reality. In this sense, faith need not be understood in its typically religious sense, but is still applicable to it.

Faith and reason are intertwined, and as such, faith ought not be understood in the Kierkegaardian irrational leap sense. In other words, despite all reason to the contrary, one wills belief through an irrational desire. Rather, faith is better understood as a level of epistemological certainty shaped by persuasion that stands between absolute certainty and uninformed opinion. Indeed, it is worth noting that the Greek term *pistis* is largely untranslatable because of the wide variance of meaning within its original context. *Pistis* was used in ancient rhetorical context to mean "persuasion" or "trustworthiness" and later in the New Testament to mean "faith."[6] What is shared by the nonideological atheist and orthodox believer is the doubt that one might be wrong concerning his or her perspective of truth.[7] In other more constructive words, both share faith in unprovable first principles, albeit different first principles. Both have been persuaded one way or the other, and neither person can claim to have certainty. *Pistis* contains doubt because we know we are not all of reality. There is a reality beyond our heads that we cannot grasp fully. Indeed, we struggle even to understand ourselves.[8] For the modern mind, though, thinking there is no reality outside the mind contains less room for doubt. Thus, the modern age is a more ideological age.

Values and ideas, such as the nature of justice, are essential for holding together the public sphere beyond the trappings of managerial calculation and emotivistic relativism. Unwilling to commit fully to a communal vision of the public good, we are left with impersonal bureaucratic processes, on the one hand, and solipsistic individualism on the other. Ideas and values, though handled in this chapter on in individual level, are important in the public sphere because these are the metaphysical glue that holds communities together. Ideas, values, and the narratives that define them through time provide individuals a substantive element to existence. In essence, metaphysical commitments give life a "plot," a story that gives purpose both to individual and group life. However, in our pluralistic, intercultural society, values and narratives are no longer shared and frequently collide with one another. We tend to be skeptical of the public defense of strong metaphysical claims. Thus, the modern insistence on "tolerance," the belief that opinions might be strongly held but cannot be brought into the public square nor used to make demands on fellow citizens. What is unique within the Age of Anxiety is the inability to take ideas seriously as having reasonable, public means for judging their merits. Most people do not seriously or systematically engage in ideas in their own mental lives, let alone in discussion with other people, especially to the degree that those ideas may disrupt one's relationships. For example, we are a long way away from the "Great War" of conversation between Owen Barfield and C.S. Lewis in which the battle of ideas between these friends resulted in great shifts in Lewis' worldview.[9] Within the nominalist framework, ideas are taken to be subjective, cultural creations that ought not to be taken too seriously, especially because it is believed that there is no means to weigh and judge the quality and merits of ideas. Ideas, it is believed, do not make demands on the self because they emerge from one's self. As such, it was inconceivable for many Americans to understand why certain Middle-Eastern people could so radically disagree with the idea of America that they were willing to kill and die in the name of faith. Likewise, the ancient practice of falling on one's sword for the sake of honor, or Seppuku in Japan, is unimaginable today. Suffering and dying for the sake of one's convictions, for the sake of ideas, is unthinkable in the Age of Anxiety.

One almost yearns for a regime in which intellectuals are persecuted, for in such a regime at least ideas are taken seriously. In order to explore such commitment and faith, this chapter analyzes the two films *Hacksaw Ridge* and *Silence* for their themes of faith and sacrifice and the lengths that the films' characters are willing to go to for the sake of their beliefs. Both films are concerned with the experience of people that put their own happiness and lives at risk for the sake of their faith in values and ideas that are believed to contribute to the common good.

These two films are concerned with the consequences of living out one's conviction in the existence of a loving, personal God. In particular, what it means to love God, especially in relation to His commandments. One could interpret *Silence* as a film about the first commandment, that is, having no other gods than God Himself, and *Hacksaw Ridge* about the sixth commandment, that is, thou shalt not kill.[10] *Hacksaw Ridge* exemplifies the sixth commandment through Desmond Doss's unwillingness to kill even enemy soldiers while risking his life for his fellow American soldiers, even those who tormented him in training. In *Silence,* Father Rodrigues faces the tension between loving and staying faithful to God while loving his neighbor, struggling as a missionary priest in Japan where native Christians are persecuted for his sake. Likewise, these films investigate Christ's essentializing the Ten Commandments into two principles: "You shall love the Lord your God with all your heart, and with all your soul, and with all your mind. This is the great and first commandment. And a second is alike it, You shall love your neighbor as yourself. On these two commandments depend all the law and the prophets."[11] Along these lines, many believers have questioned how one can know whether one truly loves God. Saint Theresa of Jesus gives answer to this question:

> We cannot know whether we love God although there may be strong reasons for thinking so, but there can be no doubt about whether we love our neighbor or no. Be sure that in proportion as you advance in fraternal charity, you are increasing in your love of God, for His Majesty bears so tender an affection for us that I cannot doubt He will repay our love for others by augmenting, in a thousand different ways, that which we bear for Him.[12]

This quotation can in a sense function as a hermeneutic for uniting *Silence* and *Hacksaw Ridge*. One can not be certain if one loves God because His presence is not explicit, but one's relationship to other people is a part of one's concrete experiences. These films were critically acclaimed and well received, even by nonbelievers, because they engage the complex matter of living out one's convictions, especially as those convictions are made problematic when put in practice in a social environment that does not assume those beliefs. In order to understand these beliefs that are fairly removed from the dominant narrative of our age, we describe in detail important elements of the movies, provide intermittent analysis, and then analyze the broader point about faith, generally speaking.

HACKSAW RIDGE

Hacksaw Ridge is based upon the true story of Desmond Doss. Doss enlisted in the United States Army in World War II but refused to take up arms because of his religious beliefs.[13] Doss, a Seventh Day Adventist, took a noncombatant stance due to his belief that deliberately taking a human life is a sin. The film shows the development of these beliefs in his life, his struggle finding a place in the Army—especially in relation to others who believe that he cannot be trusted because of his pacifism—and finally his heroics on Hacksaw Ridge where, as a medic and noncombatant, he saved seventy-five wounded soldiers.

The film begins in the midst of battle on Hacksaw Ridge with the voiceover of Desmond Doss stating:

Have you not heard? The Lord is the everlasting God, the Creator of the ends of the Earth. He will not grow tired or weary, and His understanding no one can fathom. He gives strength to the weary and increases the power of the weak. Even youths grow tired and weary, and young men stumble and fall. But those who hope in the Lord will renew their strength. They will soar on wings like eagles. They will run and not grow weary. They will walk and not be faint.

This scripture (Isaiah 40: 28–31) functions as a first principle of the film and is thematic for the film for two reasons. First, it is stated that God's understanding is unfathomable. God's command is clear, but it does not make sense in human standards. Doss believes that "Thou shalt not kill" is a clear statement, and yet understands that according to social demands, most people will not take it literally and without exception. Second, it speaks of the faithfulness of God and His care for those that believe. Those who hope in God will be made greater than they would be on their own. These two elements come together to form a covenant between God and man. Humans must have faith, while God will take care of them. In modern evangelical speak, Jesus takes the wheel.

In a foundational early scene, a young Desmond and his brother, Hal, are fighting in their front yard. Desmond picks up a brick and hits his brother on the head. Hal lies unresponsive. Desmond quickly understands the gravity of the situation. He may have just killed his brother. As he goes into the house, he is drawn toward a religious image hanging on the wall. The image contains the words of the "Our Father" and imagery relating the prayer to the Ten Commandments and the story of salvation. In particular, he focuses upon the sixth commandment, "Thou shalt not kill," which contains a picture of Cain killing his brother Able. The drawn out, contemplative nature of this scene provides insight into Desmond's perspective and the gravity of killing another person. Desmond is affected not by the immediate consequences of his action, which include his father's physical threats, but rather by the nature of the action itself. His focus remains on the image until his mother finally draws his attention away from it. Desmond admits that he could have killed his brother, and his mother agrees, telling him that this is the worst sin of all because no sin hurts God more. Desmond's conviction about this matter is grounded within his first-hand experience. His faith is not an irrational impulse but rather is reasonable and given strength by his experience.

The film moves forward several years to another important moment in Desmond's life. He witnesses a car accident and rushes outside to help. A young man is bleeding out from his leg, and Desmond quickly uses his belt as a tourniquet. When they arrive at the hospital, Desmond is mesmerized by the environment, and a doctor tells him that not only was his work well done, but that he likely saved the man's life. Having been told that he may have saved the young man's life, Desmond is drawn into contemplation. The two juxtaposed scenes establish a clear dichotomy between these two moments in his life, one potentially life-taking and the other life-affirming. In effect, these two significant experiences in life confirm his belief in the second commandment and strengthen the degree of his commitment. Thou shalt not kill is no longer an abstract law for Desmond, but rather a concrete reality related to justice and human nature. These two moments showcase how ideas and values become integral into a person's worldview beyond being indoctrinated into an ideology through first-hand experience, though this firsthand-experience is also influenced by the rhetoric of others and society.

Desmond's journey to enlisting in the military begins on his first date with Dorothy, whom he met at the hospital. He views a World War II propaganda film and numerous other young men wearing Army uniforms. Later at home, Hal comes to the dinner table and surprises his family, particularly his parents, as he is dressed in an Army uniform. Their father is vehemently opposed to his sons fighting in the war. A World War I veteran, he has clearly been traumatized by the experience. His mother asks Hal why he never told them of his interest in enlisting. As can be expected, he responds that they would have tried to talk him out of it and that he knows what he is doing the right thing. His mother questions him how this relates to the commandment to not kill. Hal provides a nuanced interpretation of the commandment and explains his reasoning, in that if it is done in war, then it is protecting others, not killing. Fighting in the war would clearly violate a strict interpretation of the commandment, but to not fight would be to implicitly disregard the evil forces of the Axis. In order to cure the dissonance created by adherence to these competing goods, Hal—like most believers that fight—makes qualifications to what appears to be a clear command.

In his explanation of why he enlists, Desmond appears to join because of a commitment deriving from social responsibility. He informs Dorothy that he is also going to enlist because he cannot stay home while others go to war. Likewise, Desmond tells his father that he signed up because everybody else was also signing up. His father argues that Desmond will not be able to live with himself if he goes, but Desmond counters that he will not be able to live with himself if he does not. He emphasizes that being a medic is the way that he will serve. In a telling transitional moment in film, his father asks Desmond if he really believes that his ideas will fit in with the war. Desmond realizes that it will be difficult. His father corrects him, stating that war does not work that way, and that if he survives, Desmond will hardly be thanking God. Here we see the first point of real contention and struggle for Desmond. He has the motivation to do what seems right—or at minimum what everyone else seems to be doing and thinks is right—conflicting with his belief that killing is inherently wrong. Desmond is doing his best to synthesize two competing goods, namely the social and the moral, within this decision. Unlike Hal, Desmond works to fulfill both competing goods without compromising either. At first glance, he cannot both enlist and not kill. As a medic, he can take part in defeating evil without having to violate the moral command to not kill by saving the lives of his fellow Americans. However, his attempt to resolve this tension will not be so simple. The resolution will test his commitment to both beliefs.

During a psychological evaluation, Doss discusses and argues the merits of his position, in that he takes a very literal reading of not killing, which includes more than just not murdering. The command to "love one another as I have loved you" applies to even the Germans. Doss recognizes that they are evil and that he joined the Army to fulfill this command, but it is the same reason why he will not kill. The evaluator explains to the captain that Doss's beliefs are legitimate and that he ought to be allowed to serve even if that does create a difficult problem concerning the maintenance of discipline in the unit. He explains that Desmond's conscientious objection is legitimate, and he must be allowed to serve if he passes every component of his training. In this sense, the evaluator plays the "neutral" or objective role taken by a government agent that does not allow a stance to be taken with regard to the multiplicity of "faiths" in a pluralistic society. Doss is being reasonable and true to his first principles even if those are not the same as those normatively accepted by others in society. However, the captain and Sergeant Howell conspire to make his training hell so that he will choose to leave the Army on his own, which he obviously refuses to do.

The next obstacle placed in front of Doss is that his commanding officer denies him furlough for not having passed his basic training. Doss explains that he has passed his training, has put in for this furlough three weeks ago, and is scheduled to get married that afternoon. The commanding officer counters that he just wants to see that Doss knows how to use his rifle, and he would sign off on his furlough. Refusing to even pick up a rifle, Doss is put in prison, where he attempts to make sense of what is going on through reading the Bible and prayer. He experiences a deep existential struggle attempting to reconcile his commitment to living according to God's will and yet facing opposition and ridicule at every turn. It would seem only rational to commit to one of these competing goods. Either fight in the war or stay at home and fulfill the command to not kill. Being locked in a jail would accomplish the later, but with undue suffering.

Dorothy visits Desmond, attempting to convince him that he has done all that he can. She reminds him that he cannot save anyone in prison. She encourages him to just let go and come home. She even asks, "Then why can't you just pick up the stupid gun and wave it around? You don't have to use it, just meet them halfway."[14] The rifle training is a mere formality, and if he cannot pass it, then he has in good faith attempted to do what he believes to be right. Dorothy accuses Desmond of being stubborn and pridefully confusing his own will with God's. Not doing so, she believes, confuses God's will for his own. At the last minute, Doss decides to remain true to his beliefs, pleading not guilty on the charge of refusing the command from an officer. During his trial, Doss does not contest the fact that he has disobeyed an order. The judge asks why he refuses to even touch a gun while serving in a combat unit. Doss notes that after the attack on Pearl Harbor, many men who could not serve committed suicide and it would not be right for them to have died, let alone those that were able to fight. He wants to be with all those others that are fighting, and to save the lives of those that need it. Again, Doss displays the difficulty of making a choice that attempts to reconcile two apparently contrary goods. Just before the judge is about to pronounce his clear guilt of disobeying an order, Desmond's father is allowed into the courtroom, providing the judge with a letter from Brigadier General Musgrove. The letter states that Doss's beliefs as a conscientious objector are protected by an Act of Congress and that he cannot be compelled to violate his beliefs. Doss's faith has been tested. Providence, or the federal government attempting to stay neutral in the realm of belief, has cleared his path.

His unit arrives in Okinawa and is sent to Hacksaw Ridge. The Americans have climbed the ridge six times, each time being driven back. When they first arrive, Doss's unit climbs the high ridge. Director Gibson graphically illustrates the brutality of the fighting that has taken place through numerous depictions of dismembered corpses and injured soldiers. Doss's services are quickly needed. Though his life is threatened throughout the course of the battle, Desmond's conviction will not be truly put into practice until the next day.

After the unit is forced off the ridge the next day, Doss remains on the ridge. He prays out loud to God, "What is it that you want of me? I don't understand. I can't hear you."[15] In a providential moment Doss hears a soldier yell behind him, "Medic, help me! Help me! Help me! Help me, Lord."[16] Doss interprets this as an answer to his question and simply states, "Alright."[17] In effect, Doss is not given the absolute certainty that would result from a message spoken by God, but must rest his action on the faith or relative certainty that the soldier's cry is a sign of what he must do. With fires raging and bombs exploding, Desmond courageously runs back into the carnage. He searches for wounded men, and upon finding them, brings them one by one to the ridge and lowers them down. He narrowly escapes death on several occasions and finds himself at risk of being caught at every turn. As he continues working through the night, he prays to God for the grace to help just one more soldier. He prays this after lowering each person down. Each rescue increasingly takes a toll on him physically, which is partially shown by Gibson, in that his hands are being rubbed raw by the rope that he uses to lower the soldiers down the ridge. His sacrifice increases with each person he saves. His conviction to not take life but rather save lives is no longer abstract, truly requiring self-sacrifice. In terms of the film's opening verse, Doss is given the supernatural grace to overcome his own natural limits and those of his surroundings in a response to his faith in God. In more secular terms, his conviction to his belief in realities greater than himself is the impetus for his heroic actions, without which there would be no reason to sacrifice as he did.

Doss eventually descends from the ridge and is noticeably shaken and traumatized. Miraculously, he has not been wounded other than the toll that his own actions have taken on him. The captain declares to Doss that Doss has done more than anyone else to serve his county, and that he was wrong about Doss' character. As such, he asks for Doss' forgiveness. The captain pleads with him to go back on the ridge the next day, even though it is the Sabbath, because the men need him. They are inspired by his belief, which is unlike the faith of any of the others. They believe what they saw was a miracle, and they need another one. The difference between Doss and others is that his beliefs stand outside the norms of the socially acceptable, and in spite of the negative consequences, he is willing to hold true to these beliefs. He does so without the need of a "miracle," whereas others need such a miracle in order to believe. Even if God was not helping him, his actions are heroic and stand above what the average person would do in his situation. Heroics such as this are not possible without a conviction to an idea above oneself to give action meaning and purpose.

The film ends with Desmond and his Bible being lowered off Hacksaw Ridge because he is wounded while deflecting two grenades away from other soldiers. The film cuts to actual footage of Doss and other men from the unit. Summarizing much of the point of the film, Hal Doss, Desmond's actual brother, states, "I would say anyone is wrong to try to compromise somebody's conviction. I don't care whether it's Army or what it is. When you own a conviction, that is not a joke. That's what you are."[18] Though Hal is correct in terms of the use of coercion to induce belief, in a pluralistic society, one's beliefs, if held seriously, will eventually be at odds with other peoples' beliefs. Along these lines, many people today suffer from anxiety because without convictions, one has no sense of who one is. Rather, who one is determines one's convictions.

Desmond's convictions are not the product of his identity. Desmond is defined by his response to values. The politics and morality of intersectionality that currently dominate in the public sphere and privileges the perspective and identities of victims of structural disadvantage do not adequately account for Doss' heroics. His conviction is the result of reasoning about the experiences of his life and living out his convictions based on good faith that he is doing what is right. This good faith naturally left room for uncertainty as he personally sacrificed during the difficult task of synthesizing competing goods. Doss put his life on the line in an attempt to synthesize competing values in his life. He was willing to stand up for his convictions and unwilling to compromise in the face of real obstacles. Doing so was not without consequence, and he risked his life, in spite of hardship, to witness to others his contempt of the evil of Nazism, his love for his country and fellow soldiers, the greatness of God and His response to those that have faith in Him. The only act that could compare in the world of identity politics would be for those with structural advantages to willingly sacrifice one's place of privilege for the sake of a victim of structural disadvantage. However, this act could quickly be deconstructed as another act of privilege that denies the victim the opportunity to empower him or herself. The self-sacrifice of martyrdom is incomprehensible within identity politics and the ideology of niceness. The theme of martyrdom (etymologically being a witness) and remaining committed to one's beliefs in spite of extreme hardship is likewise at the heart of *Silence*.

SILENCE

Martin Scorsese's *Silence* is a film based upon Shusaku Endo's novel by the same name. The novel and film tell the tale of seventeenth-century Japanese

Christian martyrs and the Jesuit priests who attempted the Christian evangelization of that nation. The film primarily follows Portuguese priests Father Rodrigues and Father Garupe in their journey to Japan to discover what happened to their mentor, Father Ferreira, who is rumored to have apostatized. During their journey, they witness to and care for Japanese Christians who must practice their faith in secret for fear of persecution. The film addresses questions concerning the nature and implications of apostasy. When Christians are discovered, the Buddhist inquisitor provides them the opportunity to apostatize or be tortured and killed. When the priests are discovered, they are given the choice between apostatizing or allowing other Christians to be tortured and killed in their stead. By the film's end, Father Rodrigues is discovered and chooses to apostatize to save the lives of his Japanese flock. The film has been received in varying ways. Many have held it up as a nuanced story that provides insight into the moral dimensions of martyrdom and apostasy. Others have viewed it more negatively, in that it appears to not only to condone, but to promote the sin of apostasy. The theme of apostasy is relevant in the Age of Anxiety because it relates back to the question of how one can maintain conviction to ideas and values when they are at odds with those with other beliefs.

Director Scorsese notes that *Silence*—like *Hacksaw Ridge*—is effectively about "the depth of faith" or "the struggle for the very essence of faith" in that it contains a "stripping away everything else around it."[19] Scorsese and the film's religious advisor, Jesuit priest James Martin, both admit that supporting Father Rodrigues' apostasy is problematic, for it is "antithetical to what probably all of Christian culture in Europe thinks should be done."[20] Scorsese contends that all sin, including apostasy, is the result of "the weakness of the human spirit" and "the weakness of humanity."[21] For Scorsese, all sins are failures in tests that are put before us by God, and when we fail, we offend God.[22] The question remains whether the failure of an individual test is equitable to the betrayal at the heart of apostasy.

In the beginning of the film, Father Valignano tells Fathers Rodrigues and Garupe that Father Ferreira has apostatized on account of the torture at the hands of the Japanese Inquisitor. The two priests do not believe that Ferreira has apostatized, but Valignano believes that the rumor of apostasy is true. Just as martyrdom is a bearing of witness to the truth of the faith, Father Rodrigues questions what Father Ferreira's apostasy means for the Jesuits and all of Catholic Europe. To the degree that one's willingness to die for the faith is "proof" of its truth, the willingness to apostatize may speak to the contrary. Whereas the saints and martyrs are held as exemplars of the faith, Father Ferreira's apostasy sets the "bad example" that undermines the tradition. In this sense, examples (παράδειγμα or *parádeigma*) function through induction as rhetorical "proofs" of a position.[23] Though this line of reasoning is foreign to modern causal reasoning, examples are paradigms of a greater whole.[24] It is this very form of rhetorical reasoning that undergirds the analysis of this book, in that our examples from the popular culture contain parts of the Age of Anxiety that are representative of the whole situation.

The apostasy represented by Scorcese is especially problematic, in that the movie revolves primarily, but not exclusively, around the apostasy of priests. At the heart of the Catholic faith is the priesthood, for it is the priest that functions *in personae Christi* and is able to administer the sacraments for the people. In this sense, the priest is more than just a man, he is believed to have an indelible mark put on his soul that differentiates him from other men. Though he remains a fallen human, just like every other person, he stands in a unique position. Without a priest, the people could not receive the sacrament of confession or the sacrament of the Eucharist. This may seem like a small matter to the outsider, but the Eucharist is the "source and summit of the Christian life."[25] This is the very essence of orthodox faith, for in the sacrament of the Eucharist these people believe that they consume the actual body, blood, soul, and divinity of Christ. The recipient of Holy Communion is in union with Christ and transformed by this union, which can only take place through the medium of the priest re-presenting Christ's sacrifice on Calvary. This theology is essential for understanding the film's drama as well as Scorsese's exploration of the psychology of the priest. What does it mean for a man to claim to be functioning in the person of Christ or as another Christ? At what point does one's own ego get in the way of actually living as Christ lived, loving as Christ loved, suffering as Christ suffered, and dying as Christ died? When persuading Father Rodrigues to apostatize, Father Ferreira will utilize this very line of reasoning to tempt Father Rodrigues. This psychological exploration is relevant in regard to taking ideas seriously in the contemporary historical moment, because with the rise of identity politics, maintaining conviction to a set of beliefs is often confused with egoism and radical individualism. In order to break free from the anxiety that is produced by this confusion of self and ideas, one must be free to analyze ideas and honestly self-reflect. The two tenets of Greek wisdom: know thyself and know that I do not know.

The question of what Ferreira's apostasy means for the Church and the Jesuits goes unanswered, but what this means for Ferreira is less ambiguous. Father Garupe notes that if the rumors of Ferreira's apostasy are true, then he would be damned. This judgment is because apostasy, by definition, is "the total repudiation of the Christian faith."[26] This repudiation of the "truths of the faith" represent a betrayal of God by refusing to give an account of Him as well as a betrayal of the community of believers. If one follows the thought of Dante, betrayal is one of the worst offenses one could commit and, as such, Dante places Judas, Brutus, and Cassius at the bottom circle of Hell in his

Inferno.[27] Portentously, just after Father Rodrigues apostatizes, a cock crows three times just as when Peter denied knowing Christ. Christ is betrayed by both Judas and Peter during His passion, but the difference between the two is that Peter seeks forgiveness and trusts in the mercy of God, whereas Judas despairs, taking his own life. The question raised is whether Father Rodrigues is modeled after Judas or Peter. Scorsese's choice of having a cock crow three times after the betrayal seems to indicate that Scorsese, at least, appeals to Peter as the model and not Judas. However, unlike Rodrigues, Peter would eventually seek forgiveness, affirm his love for Christ, and die the death of a martyr.

When the Inquisitor arrives at Tomogi and having captured the local jisuma—a Christian brother or possibly deacon, who guides and sustains the faith of the community in the absence of a priest—he informs the Christians that they must offer themselves up or the three prisoners will be tortured and killed. He gives the village three days to decide what to do. The jisuma and three other villagers are chosen to be given up to the Inquisitor. The next day, Mokichi, one of the devout Christians being offered up to the Inquisitor, asks Father Rodrigues what they should do if they are "forced to trample" on an image of the faith.[28] Father Garupe tells him that he must pray for courage. Mokichi explains that if they do not do what the Japanese authorities want then the whole village will be in danger. As such, Father Rodrigues emphatically tells them that it is acceptable to trample on the image. Father Garupe corrects Father Rodrigues and tells Mokichi that he cannot do this. Here we see the potential dual motivation of Father Rodrigues, in that, on the one hand, he tells people to trample, possibly because he lacks faith but also possibly for the sake of sparing the pain and suffering of all those involved. These motivations are not mutually exclusive; in fact, they may be mutually reinforcing. The question here is whether advising others to sin in order to avoid suffering is truly loving one's neighbor. In nominalistic terms, it makes no sense to suffer for a belief. Along these lines, many students are unwilling to accept Plato's strong reasoning that it is better to suffer evil than to do evil.[29] It is worth noting that Father Garupe who has faith in this instance will likewise go to his own death rather than trampling on an image of the faith.

Mokichi gives Father Rodrigues a small, hand-carved crucifix and tells him that it was all that they had before the priests came to Tomochi. Father Rodrigues states Mokichi's faith is a source of strength and he wishes he could give the same to Mokichi. One cannot give what one does not have. Father Rodrigues will carry this crucifix for the rest of his life even after apostatizing. Adding to the complexity of Father Rodrigues, he relays in a letter to Father Valignano that these Japanese Christians are God's most devoted people, and he prays to suffer trials with them while questioning why the trials must be so terrible. Still, he questions his ability to stand up to these trials because of his own weakness. Indeed, this statement speaks of Father Rodrigues' doubt and lack of faith in God's providence and love in the face of God's silence. Ideas have consequences, and if one cannot accept the consequences of an idea, then one rationally would doubt its truth. His doubt potentially guides his decision to apostatize because he takes matters into his own hands instead of trusting in God's providential mercy. However, as will be developed below, circumstances may be even more intricate than this.

In front of the whole village, the four men are asked to trample on an image of Christ, and each one does so. The Inquisitor is not satisfied and requires them to spit on a crucifix and to say the Virgin Mary is a whore. Only Kichijiro, the priests' Japanese guide who has apostatized once before, is willing to do so. The other three men are put onto crosses in the ocean and left there to die as the tide comes in and out and ravages their bodies. Father Rodrigues reflects that those that did not apostatize failed, but Kichijiro was successful. In a sense, one could say that each man failed the test of faith with regard to trampling, but were then provided a second test, or moment of redemption, to prove their faith. The three men who were unwilling to desecrate the crucifix and besmirch the name of Mary go to their deaths having passed this test of faith. They die as martyrs or witnesses to the faith. Mokichi, even at the end of his trial and suffering, sings a hymn of praise to God while he is on the cross. We are given insight into Father Rodrigues's lack of conviction when he tells Father Valignano in a letter that he struggles to understand how God could be silent upon hearing the screams of these martyrs, let alone how to communicate this to the Japanese. He writes, "Father Valignano, you will say that their death is not meaningless. Surely God heard their prayers as they died. But did He hear their screams? How can I explain His silence to these people who have endured so much?."[30] Mokichi's conviction and love for God is beautiful, and yet terrifying for what it may say about God's silence. In terms relevant to the Age of Anxiety, how does one maintain conviction to an idea when the consequences of that idea egregiously offend another idea or value? How does one maintain a conviction to equality under the law when cyclical, structural forms of inequality persist within the status quo? How does one maintain a conviction to helping the disadvantaged when one's policies treat people unequally based upon identity characteristics, such as is the case with affirmative action?

After being betrayed by Kichijiro to the Inquisitor, the Inquisitor sits with Father Rodrigues and implores Rodrigues that he can save them with one single word, asking him simply to "deny your faith."[31] In one of the most iconic moments of the film, the Inquisitor explains that the Japanese had learned from their mistakes, in that martyring the priests only added to Christian fervor, which is why they have moved to this new method. He tells Rodrigues, "The price for your glory is their suffering."[32] This is a telling moment in the movie because it directly deals with Scorsese's question about the place of the ego within the motivations of the priests. If it is true that the suffering of innocent Japanese Christians is the price for his glory, then his refusal to apostatize becomes an act of extreme cruelty. The blood of others would be on the priest's hands. However, if the Inquisitor's statement is false, then for love of the truth Rodrigues could not do otherwise. His refusal to apostatize would not be indicative of selfish motivations. How can one betray that which functions as the essence of one's worldview? His not apostatizing would be united in motivation with the Japanese martyrs who themselves did not apostatize. They would be in communion with one another, understanding that the priest bears no responsibility for their suffering. It is almost incomprehensible, to the point of absurdity, to the nominalist that one would die for the "truth" or allow others to suffer for the sake of an unseen social construction. Such devotion becomes as much evidence of psychological disorder as it is of admirable belief.

While in prison, Father Rodrigues worries that he is not worthy as a priest or of God's love. At this point, several Christians are lined up and told to step on an image of the faith. The guard tells them that the trampling is a mere formality because it is just an image and they can perform it without sincerity—likely a lie given what happened to Mokichi and the two others. None of the prisoners will step on the image even though they are told that they could technically do so with devotion since they are told that their action would not represent apostasy. The guard has all but one of them put back in their cell. The single remaining prisoner stands chatting with the guard, and Father Rodrigues thanks God for hearing his prayer. However, another guard walks over to the man and uses his samurai sword to behead the prisoner. The Christians and Father Rodrigues all frantically cry out in shock and despair. The lead official announces to the prison that this is what happens to Christians and provides an example of how they can avoid this fate. Kichijiro is brought out as an example, who once again tramples on the image and is set free. From a nominalist framework, Kichijiro is the only one functioning "rationally." The image is meaningful merely in a social or nominal sense and contains no meaningful link to a reality beyond itself. As such, it is irrational to suffer for the sake of the mere formality of putting one's foot on an image.

Father Rodrigues is brought to a Buddhist temple where a "surprise" has been arranged for him.[33] The surprise is that Father Ferreira is brought to visit Father Rodrigues. His interpreter, a Japanese official assigned to guide Father Rodrigues, states this is the wish both of the Inquisitor and Father Ferreira. Father Ferreira is led in wearing the traditional Japanese clothes. He has the look of a broken man. Father Ferreira tells Father Rodrigues that he has been here for about a year and that the place is a temple in which he studies.

Ferreira spends his time studying and writing on subjects such as astronomy, under the Inquisitor's orders, and that he happily does so. Having denied a transcendental purpose to his existence, Ferriera is left finding "happiness" in his work. His existence is exemplary of life in the Age of Anxiety in which the human person has been reduced to *animal laborans* with no meaning to one's existence beyond one's ability to labor. The interpreter mentions that Father Ferreira is also writing a book called *Kengiroku*, which is meant to refute Christianity. They explain that the title, "Kengiroku" means "deceit disclosed, or unmasked."[34] Father Rodrigues is upset and tells the interpreter that the twisting of Ferriera's soul in this manner is horrible and worse than physical torture. The Japanese have accomplished in Ferreira what the Army could not in Doss. The interpreter counters that it is Father Rodrigues that tortures him because Father Ferreira is a new man, a peaceful and happy man, with a Japanese name and a Japanese life. By the anguished look on Father Ferreira's face, this peace is an illusion.

Ferreira and the interpreter arrive at Rodrigues's cell, and they inform him that the noise he hears is that of five Christians hung upside down in the pit. Ferreira again attempts to persuade Rodrigues that he should not hold on to the faith. This time, Ferreira argues that the Japanese being tortured and Rodrigues are much alike and that he and those being tortured are just like Christ in their trials and suffering. The difference between Rodrigues and them is that he supposedly suffers from pride, says Ferreira. By holding on to his faith, Ferriera claims that it is Rodrigues that is making these people suffer. Rodrigues pleads with him to stop for he is speaking in the spirit of darkness. Ferreira mocks the idea that Rodrigues's prayers for these people are meaningful because in the end, it is not God that can help them, but Rodrigues through apostasy. How can one maintain conviction in a loving God who is silent in the midst of the suffering of those who He loves?

They go to the pits and Rodrigues is horrified to see the victims hanging upside down and suffering. Ferreira notes that only he can help them for "they call out for help just as you call for God. He is silent, but you do not have to be."[35] Rodrigues pleads with them to apostatize, but Ferreira notes that they have many times over. The only way for them to be saved is for him to apostatize. He declares that, as a priest, Rodrigues must act as Christ and Christ would have apostatized in this situation.

Once again, the interpreter tells Rodrigues that all of this is a mere formality. If Rodrigues has already doubted and lacks faith, it would be a mere formality, a mere sign that he already does not believe. However, if he truly does believe, then this is no mere formality. This moment is his test. As he contemplates, he hears Christ's voice, which is the same as Father Valignano's, saying, "Come ahead, now. It's alright. Step on Me. I understand your pain. I was born into this world to share men's pain. I carried this cross for your pain. Your life is with Me now. Step."[36] Rodrigues trusts that the voice that he hears is that of God and not the projection of his ego. This voice provocatively speaks a form of truth. Christ can be said in an orthodox fashion to have taken up all sin, including this sin. However, the heterodoxy in the statement is the presumption of forgiveness and Christ telling him to sin, which is an offence to God the Father. As he tramples, the image of Christ fades away. With the fading of the image, one could say that Rodrigues' faith has symbolically faded too. Father Rodrigues falls to the ground in agony. Father Ferreira comforts him. The prisoners are released. And the cock crows three times, audibly representing Rodrigues' betrayal.

The rest of Father Rodrigues' life is riddled with anxiety because he succumbed to his doubts rather than living according a conviction to his faith. In the final scenes of the film, after the passage of years, a deceased Father Rodrigues is given a traditional Buddhist funeral. It is noted in narration that he was posthumously given a Buddhist name, and that only God can answer whether he was "lost to God," for from the outside, this is what it seemed.[37] With these final words of the film, the camera zooms in to his body being burned and then into his folded hands in which contain the small cross that was given to him by Mokichi. The crucifix is enlightened by the flames that surround Father Rodrigues' lifeless corpse. Though this illustrates Scorsese's interpretation of Father Rodrigues still being a man of faith even though he had apostatized, the cross has no impact because it is private. He is more like Judas because while he doesn't kill himself, he kills his essential self, that of a faithful priest. We have no indication of penance that might redeem him. Is not enough for him to "suffer in silence?" It is handled as a sin that he suffered for throughout his life. In a sense, only God can give answer to how Rodrigues would be judged. Rodrigues privileged the sixth commandment over the primary commandment, which is reasonable given the quotation of St. Teresa that begins this chapter. However, like the martyrs that died with Mokichi, Rodrigues was given numerous other tests during his life, and he failed whereas they succeeded. In terms beyond this religious exemplar, to claim to adhere to a set of beliefs, such as being "pro-life" or "pro-choice," but to do nothing about this belief makes the claim spurious at best. Virtue is manifest and proven in the public sphere, not the private. Virtue exists in action as well as conviction. One is courageous through acting courageously, not simply through an intellectual assent to the good of courage. Even worse than not publicly acting upon one's beliefs is the public rejection of them. Can a member of Antifa publicly reject progressive politics and live life as a white nationalist and still claim to believe in the movement? Can a Trump-supporting social conservative evangelical publicly denounce these things, join the LGBTQ movement, embrace fourth wave intersectional feminism, and still "hold Jesus in his heart" in the same manner as before?

The heterodox interpretation that flows from the film is that Christ asked Father Rodrigues to bear this cross. This cross was the sin of apostasy, committed in the name of saving the lives of the Christians of Japan. The problematic nature of this view is that it considers Rodrigues's moral choice largely through the frame of a consequential ethics, which has been discussed in chapter 1 as the only framework for ethics within the nominalist metaphysic. The cost of him stepping on an image, not speaking of his faith, nor living it in an external fashion is supposedly outweighed by the benefit of saving lives. This does not take into account the scandal that is also a consequence of his actions. This is why the Inquisitor was so insistent upon the apostasy of the priest. His apostasy in a real sense is the opposite of martyrdom, in that martyrdom literally through its etymological origin means to witness. He has betrayed those living believers who are convicted of the Faith, and has become a bad exemplar. Scorsese heterodoxically treats his apostasy in favorable terms, that is, as a form of martyrdom and taking up one's cross. Though Father Rodrigues may have acted out of love for these suffering neighbors—as was noted there is a great deal of evidence that Rodrigues doubts the existence of God—his apostasy equally betrays those that did give their lives. This betrayal is no act of love and it is not diminished because the betrayed martyrs are no longer living. Like the political examples above, our fidelity to ideas and values has public and communal consequences because ideas and values do not abstractly and immanently exist in the vacuum of the mind of an autonomous self.

More importantly, Scorsese misses the more transcendental or realist moral equation that would look at the act of apostasy in its essence. The nominalist framework denies that essence exists, thus does not come into play in moral reasoning. Apostasy in and of itself is not only an affront and betrayal to God but is also an affront to the human person and what they consider to be true. Apostasy is a betrayal of the deepest source of one's being in terms of how one's worldview is structured. One must deny what one believes to be true and, to the degree that what is believed to be true is a personal God, God has been betrayed as well. In this sense, one could interpret—ironically—the message of the film to be that matters of faith ought to be treated as private devotions that ought not enter into public life. Indeed in chapter 1, this was discussed as the consequence of Kierkegaard's existentialist leap of faith, that is, the privatization of faith. This has long been held as the modern account of religion, in that religion is considered merely a private disposition, and therefore not valid for public discussion, rather than a devotion to something real with public duties and consequences.

This perspective toward faith and reason is one interpretation that can be made in response to a God that is silent. Back in the prison, Father Rodrigues is in the midst of despair and cries out in the words of Christ (and Psalm 22),

"My God. My God. Why have you forsaken me? Why have you forsaken me? I was your son. Your son was going to the cross. You were silent even to him. Your silent, cold son."[38] He is in a state of hysteria and argues with himself, saying this doubt is stupid and also, "He's not going to answer."[39] Father Rodrigues desires the certainty of a message from God and grows incredulous toward His silence. Faith in a personal God that is silent seems irrational. The assumption is that silence is evidence of absence. In terms of faith and doubt, we are presented with a skeptical interpretation of the phenomenon of silence.

By way of contrast, the hermeneutic of faith interprets silence as a "manifestation of presence"[40] for "God is silence."[41] Human wisdom is found within solitude and contemplation in that "the real questions of life are posed in silence."[42] For this reason, humanness itself is "rooted in 'speaking silence.'"[43] However, martyrdom is so important, at least in the Christian faith, because it is the martyr who speaks as a witness of the truth through the giving of his or her life. Ironically, the film ends with the text of dedication: "For the Japanese Christians and their pastors *Ad Majorem Dei Gloriam* [for the greater glory of God.]"[44]

FAITH AND REASON IN THE AGE OF ANXIETY

Both *Silence* and *Hacksaw Ridge* display the interplay between the good of the community and faithfulness to an idea that does not align with the beliefs of the community. Conflicts quickly arise between the individuals with differing beliefs and conviction is necessary because living out one's beliefs can require personal sacrifice. Some ideas have more significant consequences than others and may demand greater sacrifices. Both *Hacksaw Ridge* and *Silence* are concerned with ideas that are worth dying for. Though many anxiously yearn for a sense of meaning and purpose in the nominalist and nihilistic age that we live in, it makes no sense from this perspective to offer up one's life for an idea. Something as simple as putting one's foot on an image seems like such an arbitrary thing to do in contrast to losing one's life. Willingness to suffer for the sake of an idea—let alone the "mere formality" of not putting one's foot on an image or picking up and waving around a gun—seems absurd and irrational within our modern context.

However, the weight of performing a seemingly arbitrary formality can be understood rhetorically if the image is understood as synecdochally related to the belief in question. The image as a part of the Faith stands in for the whole of the Faith. Putting one's foot on an image is not an arbitrary formality, but rather, from this rhetorical and symbolic understanding, a paradigmatic rejection of the whole of the Faith, fulfilling the very definition of apostasy. The symbolic understanding is inherent within burning a flag or the movement to take down Confederate Statues and rename institutions named after historical figures such as Thomas Jefferson. Similarly, Doss was unwilling to deny his belief by engaging in the mere formality of picking up a rifle and shooting a target. The gun itself symbolizes the means of killing. Taking part in even the mere formality of a rifle proficiency exam would be to take part in the violence of war. Whereas *Hacksaw Ridge* explored the positive effects of fidelity toward one's beliefs and convictions, *Silence* explores the ramifications of infidelity toward one's beliefs and convictions. Both protagonists must deal with the doubt that accompanies a relative degree of certainty—*pistis*, or faith.

Some readers may be skeptical of upholding the concept on faith in our technological age because it is widely believed that secularization has had a relativizing effect that leads to a more peaceful world.[45] However, this move has not come without a cost. Dismissing the important cultural narratives and religious traditions of a people robs them of their sense of purpose and meaning. The glue that holds together communities is dissolved. The great faith traditions of the world's cultures, including atheism, should be taken seriously and not simply dismissed as private, personal preferences, for these traditions provide public values that inform moral reasoning beyond the artificial intelligence of utilitarian cost-benefit analysis. Having dismissed these claims of faith as private and irrational, we live in a historical moment in which we at best tolerate one another rather than love one another. At worst, putative secular ideologies emerge as kinds of religious faith, seeking out heretics and "otherizing" those who hold on to rival—typically more traditionally religious—faiths.[46] Yet many of these ideologies lack faith, in that they are unwilling to engage in any idea that threatens their "identity." Nominalism doesn't believe that persuasion is possible because there are no groundings. Faith contains an element of doubt, but with the belief that through dialogue and persuasion we can get closer to an actual truth through reason. In this sense, nominalists come off as secular ideological fundamentalists (in the conventional and Taylor sense of someone who simply "spins" rather than appreciates their world view as a "take"). So they become a mirror image of what they claim to hate the most, religious fundamentalism/intolerance. Rediscovering the integral relationship between faith and reason is a necessary medicine for combating the anxiety of our age.

The rejection of realism, as exemplified in Foucauldian postmodernism, does not automatically mean easy toleration of various "worldviews." Rather intellectual deconstruction of culture and tradition unmasks the fundamental reality of power. All relationship is revealed to be relationship of power. This is why in one setting some argue in favor of free speech and freedom of religion, only to turn against these putatively liberal principles when they cease to favor the power interests of "progressive" thinking.[47] Still, taking these competing traditions seriously does not mean that people need be indoctrinated into any one tradition. In fact, putting these traditions in conversation with one another, guided by reasonable and public standards argumentation, can help to avoid any one becoming extreme.[48] This movement is only possibly in the current historical moment if the ideologues of the dominant poststructural identity politics are willing to call into question the first principle that values are socially constructed reflections of identity. Indeed, the difference between ideology and philosophy lies in the fact that philosophy allows for the questioning of first principles whereas ideology does not. Questioning the moral reasoning of identity politics is not tantamount to hate, racism, or sexism. Taking seriously the narrative grounds of these varying systems of belief is the only way to truly foster multicultural interaction and intercultural dialogue.[49] Taking seriously rival traditions in a secular society is possible only if we reconceptualize the notion of faith.

Faith, thought of through the Greek term *pistis*, is an epistemological category that stands between the absolute certainty of knowledge (*episteme*) and the personal preference of opinion (*doxa*). Understood as an epistemological category, *pistis* is equally applicable to religious claims as it is scientific. The social benefit of the relative degree of certainty of faith is that it inherently contains room for the other. Faith, as such, does not lead to extremism because it is inherently tied to dialectical opposite, doubt. Rather, it is a false assurance of the certainty of one's ideas that yields the possibility of forcing one's view on those that do not share it. The extremism of certainty is equally problematic whether it comes from a religious extremist or a secular social engineer or the quasireligious "social justice warrior." Indeed, the proclivity of *pistis* to avoid force is directly related to its other Greek meaning: persuasion. In this way, faith and reason are intertwined and mutually found the basis for worldviews.

Both *Hacksaw Ridge* and *Silence* provide discussion that directly relates to humble nature of *pistis*. Specifically, both films deal with the problematic nature of pride. Doss and Father Rodrigues struggle with the idea that pride may be the real motivation of their actions. It is on account of the fact that with faith comes doubt that these men are even able to question their motivations. The difference between the two, though, is Rodrigues apparently gives into doubt. Whereas Doss was satisfied with uncertainty of a "sign" from a silent God, Rodrigues trusts the certainty of a voice in his head, which was likely a projection of his ego. He is given a negative certainty in the form of doubt without faith, reducing his former position to mere *doxa*. By way of contrast, those that stand against Doss and Father Rodrigues—the Army and the Inquisitor—are the ones that have positive certainty and pridefully attempt to force the other to yield. In the Age of Anxiety, this lesson is quite important for those political ideologues—both on the Left and Right—increasingly dividing the country because of their false sense of certainty. In effect, the term *pistis* allows for both a healthy constructivism and skepticism. Taking seriously the interplay between faith, doubt, reason, and persuasion allows one to both appreciate one's own narrative grounds while still making room for the other. An appreciation of the epistemological character of faith is necessary for the rebuilding our culture and is a precondition for taking seriously healthy and realistic narratives, which is the substance of the next chapter.

NOTES

1. Christian Smith, *Soul Searching: The Religious and Spiritual Lives of American Teenagers* (New York: Oxford University Press, 2009), 162–171.

2. de Zengotita, *Mediated*, 22–32.

3. As a thermometer of the culture and its discourse, the 19th season of South Park, airing in 2015, revolved around the new political correctness that was taking shape and gaining real social currency.

4. This shift is described in a conversation about free speech and political correctness between Bill Maher and Jordan Peterson. Real Time with Bill Maher. "Jordan B. Peterson | Real Time with Bill Maher (HBO)." Filmed [April 2018.] YouTube video, 9:35. Posted [April 20, 2018.] https://www.youtube.com/watch?v=8wLCmDtC DAM.

5. The philosopher Richard Swinburne makes a distinction between what he calls "strong verification" and "weak verification." Strong verification, such as demanded by the logical positivists, Swinburn rejects as it calls for more certainty than most questions, certainly philosophical questions, allow. For example, can one know for certain that all ravens are black? What is the certainty that one loves one's spouse? Logical positivists commit a category error by asking empirical certainly of questions that are not empirical in nature, such as what are God's characteristics. These questions of "weak verification" can be answered but only in probabilistic fashion and perhaps via analogy rather than empirically. Richard Swinburne, "The Argument from Design," *Philosophy*, Vol. 43, No. 165 (July 1968), 199–212.

6. James L. Kinneavy, *Greek Rhetorical Origins of Christian Faith: And Inquiry* (New York: Oxford University Press, 1987).

7. Joseph Cardinal Ratzinger, *Introduction to Christianity*, trans. J. R. Foster and Michael S. Miller (San Francisco: Ignatius Press, 2004), 45–47.

8. Percy, *Lost in the Cosmos*.

9. *The "Great War" of Owen Barfield and C. S. Lewis: Philosophical Writings*, ed. Norbert Feinendegen and Arend Smilde (Inklings Studies Supplements No. 1, 2015).

10. Among the numerous differences among Christians is the order and number of the 10 Commandments. In particular, the Jewish Talmud, Orthodox Christianity, and Reformed Christianity consider "Thou Shalt Not Kill" the 6th commandment, whereas St. Augustine, Catholics, and Lutherans consider it to be the 5th

commandment. For the sake of continuity, especially with regard to *Hacksaw Ridge,* we will call "Thou Shalt Not Kill" the 6th commandment.

11. Matt. 22:36–40 (RSV).

12. Saint Teresa of Avila, *The Interior Castle or the Mansions* (United States: Saint Benedict Press, 2011), 92–93.

13. *Hacksaw Ridge*, directed by Mel Gibson (Santa Monica, CA: Lionsgate Entertainment, 2016), DVD.

14. *Hacksaw Ridge*.

15. Ibid.

16. Ibid.

17. Ibid.

18. Ibid.

19. S.J. James Martin, "Exclusive: Martin Scorsese Discusses His Faith, His Struggles, His Films and 'Silence,'" *America Magazine: The Jesuit Review*, December 6, 2016, https://www.americamagazine.org/arts-culture/2016/12/06/exclusive -martin-scorsese-discusses-his-faith-his-struggles-his-films-and.

20. Ibid.

21. Ibid.

22. Ibid.

23. Aristotle, *On Rhetoric: A Theory of Civic Discourse*, trans. George A. Kennedy (New York: Oxford University Press, 1991), 40 [1356b].

24. Thomas S. Kuhn, *The Structure of Scientific Revolutions*, 3rd ed. (Chicago: University of Chicago Press, 1966).

25. John Paul II, *Catechism of the Catholic Church* (Citta del Vaticano: Libreria Editrice Vaticana, 1993), paragraph 1324.

26. John Paul II, *Catechism of the Catholic Church*, paragraph 2089.

27. Dante Alighieri, *The Divine Comedy of Dante Alighieri*. Volume 1. *Inferno*, ed. and trans. Robert M. Durling. Introduction and Notes by Ronald L. Martinez and Robert M. Durling. Illustrations by Robert Turner (New York and Oxford: Oxford University Press, 1996), 34:61–76, p. 537.

28. *Silence*, directed by Martin Scorsese, written by Jay Cocks (Hollywood, CA: Paramount Pictures, 2016), DVD.

29. Plato, *Gorgias*.

30. *Silence*.

31. Ibid.

32. Ibid.

33. Ibid.

34. Ibid.

35. Ibid.

36. Ibid.

37. Ibid.

38. Ibid.

39. Ibid.

40. Sarah and Diat, *The Power of Silence*, 27.

41. Ibid., 22.

42. Ibid., 27.

43. Walter J. Ong S.J. *The Presence of the Word: Some Prolegomena for Cultural and Religious History* (New Haven: Yale University Press, 1967), 2–3.

44. *Silence.*

45. Sam Harris, *The End of Faith: Religion, Terror, and the Future of Reason* (New York: W.W. Norton & Company, 2004); Steven Pinker, *Enlightenment Now: The Case for Reason, Science, Humanism, and Progress* (New York: Viking, 2018).

46. See Mary Eberstadt, "The Zealous Faith of Secularism." *First Things*, January 2018, 35–40, and Matthew Rose, "Our Secular Theodicy." *First Things*, December 2017, 37–42.

47. See, for example, Adam Liptak, "How Conservatives Weaponized the First Amendment." *New York Times*, June 30, 2018, https://www.nytimes.com/2018/0 6/30/us/politics/first-amendment-conservatives-supreme-court.html (accessed January, 2019).

48. For an example of reasonable argumentation guided by an interplay of faith and reason, see the dialogue about the premoral foundations of the modern democratic state between Jurgen Habermas—atheist and founder of public sphere theory—and Joseph Cardinal Ratzinger—future Pope Benedict XVI. Jurgen Habermas and Joseph Ratzinger, *Dialectics of Secularization: On Reason and Religion*, trans. Brian McNeil (San Francisco: Ignatius Press, 2006).

49. Ashley, *Way Toward Wisdom*, 3–21.

Chapter 7

Frodo, Won't You Be My Neighbor?

A Message of Hope for a Cynical Age

Heretofore our efforts have been to diagnose certain pathologies in the modern mind. A devotion to self-creation that undermines family, place, and history by committing to consumerism and scientific control leaves the individual anxious, unable to adequately answer the questions about who he is and what he's supposed to do. The modern liberated self is adrift at sea, grasping for any kind of life preserver to stay afloat in the stormy seas of an age devoid of purpose. Noting the decline in social cohesion, we maintain that communities cannot be made stronger simply through the assertion that we need stronger communities. Similarly, people can don the trappings of religion and state their commitment to the importance of religion, but the sociological fervor for hyper-pluralism is ill at ease with actual conviction.[1] Patrick Deneen, drawing on the thought of Tocqueville, sees "a society defined by constantly restless and anxious individuals" who discover "that they had no firm bonds on which to rely, no deep commitments to which they could turn in times of trial and trouble."[2] In a sense, today's American has no story, no narrative to orient itself. The attack on narrative is part and parcel of the modern project. Healthy patriotism is viewed as toxic xenophobia or white nationalism. Francis Bacon urges his readers to "trouble no more" with legends and decries "that the fables and superstitions and follies which nurses instill into children do serious injury to their minds." Better to give oneself over to abstract science and deal with facts, not fairy tales.[3]

Bacon's argument posits a false scientific neutrality while masking a metaphysical presupposition about the nature of reality and how we come to know reality. The modern conceit is to either, in the Baconian vein, focus strictly on science as a way of knowing, or, in line with Nietzsche, to undermine the idea that we can know anything at all about reality. But it is part and parcel of a study of literature and popular culture—one might say a study of poetry broadly defined—to say that the nature of politics, broadly understood, cannot be comprehended thoroughly through a "scientific" study. To know a person is not to reduce him to his constituent parts, and to know political society, it cannot be reduced to data. Far from what political science is known as today, the Aristotelian art of politics, wrapped up with ethics, rhetoric, and dialectic, is concerned with justly living with others. The best art uses poetics to guide us to a higher reality, and the best political science includes the study of poetics.[4]

Regarding poetics, most people, though they may not be able to articulate it, know that stories are not just exercises in grammar, but contain knowledge. One can easily see that the truth of the story of King Midas lies not in its historical facticity, but rather its morality. Identifying the truth and meaning of story to its historicity and literal sense artificially limits the interpretative horizon and creates a "boorish sort of wisdom."[5] Music can be profoundly moving not simply because it triggers certain chemical responses in the brain, but as an expression of human longing that itself defies measurement. A great work of representational art, or perhaps a natural vista, can be breathtaking not simply because it provides some evolutionary advantage, but because wonder and awe seem to be part of what it is to be human.

Truth is to be found not only in investigation of material causes or quantifiable and measurable phenomenon.[6] All sorts of truths, perhaps the greatest truths, are to be found poetically, revealed through myth.[7] In story, we encounter various types of human beings put in diverse settings. From this, we learn sundry human possibilities. We create a conception about what is possible and what is not. The best stories aim at some truth about who we are.[8] This is not done in a didactic way.[9] One reason why novels of, say, Ayn Rand or Robert Heinlein ring hollow is that narrative is put at the service of an ideology rather than the other way around. This is true of many political films, taking on the character of agitprop rather than sound narrative. Poor attempts at "political" art come off as polemics or harangues rather than poetry. As Peter Kreeft notes, a philosophy that cannot be turned into a good story is likely a bad philosophy.[10] Story allows us to see reality as relationship, rather than as an abstraction. The storytelling maxim is "show, don't tell." The problem of amateurish political art is precisely that it tells, rather than artistically demonstrating its point.

The dominant "stories" of the anxious age tend to be those of science and of advertising. The former plays upon our urge to control, the second upon the urge to have all our desires fulfilled. Both are essentially materialist, in that they believe basic human fulfillment can be achieved via manipulation of the physical world. The scientific story ignores much of what it is to be human as it is too abstracted from actual human experience. Our commercial stories, which include much of what is produced as popular culture, are designed precisely as marketing gimmicks whose dominant value is monetary rather than artistic. One needn't be an art purist to see the problem of a film industry, for example, unable to come up with a story that is not tied to a commercial product, whether an already successful merchandising effort (e.g., Angry Birds or Emoji movies) or a previously successful film (see the bevy of sequels and reboots), or both (e.g., the seemingly endless parade of comic book superhero films). The abuse of the narrative form—by corporations in the marketplace and deconstructionists in academia—has produced cynicism toward narratives and the further decline of the influence of narrative upon the Western mind.[11]

One story that recently stood out against others was the film adaptation of J.R.R. Tolkien's *Lord of the Rings* and *Hobbit*. These films were hugely successful and have led many moviegoers to discovering the real treasure of Tolkien's novels. Tolkien's *Lord of the Rings* has been called by popular audiences one of the greatest works written in the twentieth century.[12] What is distinctive about Tolkien's work is his ability to make goodness compelling. It is often noted, classically with Milton's Satan, that it is easier to make evil interesting than with good. Thus, many find Satan more interesting than God in *Paradise Lost*, or *The Inferno* more exciting than *The Paradiso*, or Darth Vader more fun than Luke Skywalker. Particularly in *The Hobbit* and *The Lord of the Rings*, Tolkien puts evil on the sideline, typically revealing its effects rather than showing it incarnate. Indeed, the main villain of *The Lord of the Rings*, Sauron, is almost completely absent from the story other than by reference. Instead, the characters most central to the story, namely Frodo, Samwise, Gandalf, and Aragorn, are captivating while also being naturally good. And their goodness comes through without being trite.[13] Tolkien largely avoids crude sentimentalism that is the hallmark of "pious" literature.[14] Tolkien opens *The Silmarillion* with a creation myth that gives all the events, especially the tragedy that ensues, a purpose. The reader knows from the tale's commencement that all that occurs is part of a plan of Illúvatar, Tolkien's representation of God. Even without having read *The Silmarillion*, one can easily gather in reading *The Lord of the Rings* that the characters have a meaningful place within the greater narrative mentioned throughout the series, and that there is a providential hand gently guiding the events.

In this chapter, we will show how Tolkien's vision can guide the perplexed resident of our times to a happier, less anxious life. To place Tolkien within a philosophical tradition, we will consider the thought of the contemporary philosopher Alasdair MacIntyre whose landmark work *After Virtue* attempted a revivify Aristotelian virtue ethics. In many ways, Tolkien's narrative project harmonized with MacIntyre's philosophical project. Both MacIntyre and Tolkien agree that to successfully live a life of narrative and practice, we must learn to be content in our roles and to submit to an authority outside ourselves. So before turning to Tolkien, let us consider MacIntyre's teaching in more detail as a diagnosis of ills and prescription for happiness.

MACINTYRE AND THE NARRATIVE LIFE

Early in *After Virtue*, MacIntyre allows the reader a peek through the window to see the grounding of his project. MacIntyre states, "The best type of human life, that in which the tradition of the virtues is most adequately embodied, is lived by those engaged in constructing and sustaining forms of community directed towards the shared achievement of those common goods without which the ultimate human good cannot be achieved."[15] Already we see that for MacIntyre the good life is one that is active; it requires practice. The good life is also not a solitary achievement, but is, of necessity, a communal project. For these reasons, MacIntyre finds modern liberalism to be inadequate to the task of aiding human beings toward a happy, fulfilling life. Liberalism has pretensions of neutrality, but in fact promotes a certain way of life as best.

In the "dominant liberal view," writes MacIntyre, "government is to be neutral as between rival conceptions of the human good, yet in fact what liberalism promotes is a kind of institutional order that is inimical to the construction and sustaining of the types of communal relationship required for the best kind of human life."[16] Liberalism's excessive deference to the individual and its grounding in desire reduces morality to personal preference for which rational argument is irrelevant.[17] MacIntyre posits that "whatever criteria or principles or evaluative allegiances the emotivist self may profess, they are to be construed as expressions of attitudes, preferences and choices which are themselves not governed by criterion, principle or value, since they underlie and are prior to all allegiance to criterion, principle or value."[18] The emotivism that dominates our time is less a sound moral theory than solipsistic self-indulgence gilded by academic jargon of postmodern thought. The postmodern, or, rather, hypermodern American congratulates himself for his liberation from hierarchy, history, teleology.[19] But, rejoins MacIntyre, what has actually happened in this deracination of the human person from culture is the loss of our ability to have a rational discourse about morality. We cannot even start a conversation about what virtue is because morality is held to be a purely solitary quest to satisfy one's desires. With no common ground other than individual pursuit of wants, communal norms cease to exist. Moral discourse dies as it becomes a kind of absurdity.

To replace morality or virtue, modern society has become more rule bound. No longer does the substantive content of thought matter, but rather the procedural method by which "we arrive at that content" defines rationality, for truth is now found in one's head rather than in the world.[20] The rules defining the procedure claim to be derived from "facts" attested to by "science." Thus, we have "sciences" of the human person such as political science, sociology, public administration, psychology, and especially in MacIntyre's depiction of modernity, the science of management. While traditional sources of moral authority, such as tradition, community, and religion have been rejected in the name of individual empowerment, the manager steps in with a claimed authority from the social sciences. Armed with this purported scientific knowledge, the manager can claim not to be imposing his own preferences on others, for to do so is one of the few sins still recognized in the hypermodern age. Instead the manager is simply applying "facts" discovered through "data driven analysis." Thus, the manager gains the moral authority that others have lost.[21] The manager's job, though, is not to promote virtue, but to make sure that the organization operates efficiently.[22] This artificial form of intelligence dismisses human values in place of utilitarian concerns. Human beings themselves, referred to in the managerial mindset as "human resources," are not treated as personal, relational beings.[23] They are simply data whose worth is measured by whether they have "added value" in some quantifiable sense. "Every bureaucratic organization embodies some explicit or implicit definition of costs and benefits from which the criteria of effectiveness are derived. Bureaucratic rationality is the rationality of matching means to ends economically and efficiently."[24] Managers seek the supposed moral neutrality of the physical sciences.[25]

There are two obstacles to this neutrality. The first is that the pretension to neutrality assumes a fiction, namely that scientists and managers are disembodied, abstracted individuals who have no interests or biases and who have escaped all temptation to misuse their power. Second, as MacIntyre notes, whatever objectivity and predictability there is in the hard sciences, human beings are far too complex and varied to maintain the kind of predictability that one sees in sciences such as physics or chemistry. In this sense, human beings cannot be "controlled" like variables in an experiment.[26] Any conclusions or predictions about human activity must be attenuated with exceptions in a manner that the hard sciences would seldom accept.

In contrast to the valueless calculation that purports to frame rational behavior, MacIntyre proposes narrative as an alternative to the emotive and managerial outlooks. Narrative, generally defined, is a "story agreed upon by a group of people" that "explains the way the world works and the meaning of human life, including what is good for humans to be and do."[27] To view our lives in narrative unity "is to think in a way alien to the dominant individualist and bureaucratic modes of modern culture."[28] The emotive and managerial are two "modes" abstract from the personal, relational nature of humanity and reject the authority of narrative. The concern about abstraction from the personal, relational reality of human beings is why MacIntyre suggests that we can learn more about morality from narrative sources, such as literature, than we can from the philosophers.[29]

Story is more likely to give us a valid picture of human moral experience than that of a philosopher conceptualizing morality from scratch. Stories help frame moral rationality because "we cannot...characterize behavior independently of intentions, and we cannot characterize intentions independently of the settings which make those intentions intelligible both to agents themselves and to others."[30] To authentically assess an individual's actions, we need to know a person's setting, history, and fellow characters and then the individual's role and relationship to these influences. Only then can we properly assess actions and intentions.[31] We might note how this attitude differs from our approach to such diverse phenomena as educational assessment and the study of political behavior. In these cases, the human person is reduced to data and "measurable outcomes" that fail to appreciate the story of actual individuals. The claimed objectivity of the data-driven method is a ruse. Built in is an assumption about the human person, namely that the reality of human activity in areas as complex and fundamental as education and politics can be reduced to a mere number. These numbers can then be statistically manipulated to give the illusion of "facts" about human behavior. Those who can master the data gain control over those who do not. Thus, any aspect of life that is not reducible to a number is rejected or reduced to a number in a crudely reductionist fashion. In its most crude form, for example, love is reduced to a score that is produced through a Cosmopolitan relationship quiz.

Debates about virtue should take place within the context of rival narratives. The task of ethical communication in a postmodern moment of narrative contention consists in recognizing that "differing narratives function as differing grounds for differing oughts," and seeking "to both understand and persuade how to engage a given view of the good within a unique set of historical constraints, not the least of which are context and persons."[32] MacIntyre, for example, considers the differences between what he calls a "heroic" narrative structure and a Sophoclean structure. One's narrative stance, including the absence of narrative, will shape one's views of virtue.[33] If our lives are poetic as well as material, then it makes sense that to fully understand who we are and what we are supposed to do, we must have an ear for the narrative.

The reality of the poetic dimension of human life is yet another reason why poetry, broadly understood, must be at the center of education.[34] Through story, we learn from the earliest of ages what it is to be a good person or wicked. Courageous or cowardly. Wise or foolish. In effect, story helps us learn the "cast of characters" that make up humanity. "Deprive children of stories and you leave them unscripted, anxious stutterers in their actions as in their words. Hence there is no way to give us an understanding of any society, including our own, except through the stock of stories which constitute its initial dramatic resources."[35] One cannot help but note MacIntyre's use of the word "anxious." If the narrative of our day is that there is no narrative, that there is no script to follow, the individual is left anxious about what to do. If there are no myths in which a people can believe, the community lacks shared symbol. In order to have a community, people must have things in common.[36] One of those common things is story, a narrative that tells a people who they are. Narrative provides meaningfulness for one's life because "the goods manifested in a narrative structure or tradition offer guidelines for living and for evaluating one's own life and that of others."[37] Like an individual with no story, a community devoid of rich historical or narrative symbolism ends up rudderless, unable to provide the depth or richness of meaning that people and communities need to not just survive, but to excel.[38] Like a bad improvisation troop, we go through life grasping for a role, for lines, for any narrative hook that gives structure to our life's story. MacIntyre's stance, he says, is likely to seem odd to the modern individualist for whom "being the author of my own story" is sacrosanct.[39]

MacIntyre implies that narratives such as those of Jane Austen's are essential to instruction in virtue.[40] Virtue is acted out, not simply taught as a set of rules. Story, even a fictional story, allows us to express and impart virtue because we recognize that our own lives partake of narrative form.[41] The error of emotivist, individualist times is the notion that there is no givenness to our lives, that there is no author of our story, or rather that we are our own story's author. This is an obvious error for, as MacIntyre noted, our "stories" include setting, character, and plot over which we have no choice. "I am someone's son or daughter, someone else's cousin or uncle," writes MacIntyre, "I am a citizen of this or that city, a member of this or that guild or profession; I belong to this clan, that tribe, this nation. Hence what is good for me has to be the good for one who inhabits these roles. As such, I inherit from the past of my family, my city, my tribe, my nation, a variety of debts, inheritances, rightful expectations and obligations."[42] Far from the extremes of being autonomous or determined, selves are situated and embedded in social environments. We create anxiety when we become frustrated with our role, like an actor who would rather be in a drama but finds herself in a farce or who wishes to play the lead but finds herself in a small supporting role. Indeed, in the *Silmarillion*, the Satan character's fall takes place because of his prideful desire to have a greater role within Ilúvatar's creation.[43] Rather than seek to play out our roles excellently, emotivism convinces us that we have the right to whatever part in whatever story we wish.

This creates anxiety in two ways. First, because of the obvious falsehood of this kind of narrative choice, people become frustrated as most people, contrary to trite graduation speeches, cannot be whatever they want to be. Consider the scenario of a supporting actor who behaves like he is the lead. The entire narrative will cease to make sense. Not only will this particular individual be out of place, but all the other characters will be confused and no one's narrative will emerge comprehensible. It is unlikely that anyone will find meaning. Second, by rejecting the givenness of life, we open ourselves to all possibilities with no guidance as to how to choose well, or even what "choosing well" might mean. Such a deracinated individual feels helpless in the face of endless, directionless choice. This makes the individual prey to commercial culture as advertisers are ready to sell prepackaged meaning in a shoe, a beer, a car, or celebrity fandom. This is Tocqueville's tyranny of the majority, as noted in chapter 2, which is really the tyranny of fashion. If a choice is "fashionable," it must be good. It is mass culture approved!

MacIntyre contends that the fully lived life is one that takes place with the unity of a story with a beginning, middle, and end.[44] The current age is defined by an incredulity or cynicism toward narratives that give meaning to life. One cure for the routinized cynicism of our age is realistic narratives that revolve "around the ontological nature of death and our awareness of its inevitability."[45] Modern psychological theory attempts to undermine narrative by locating all choice in desires.[46] One's motives are always hidden in subconscious longings. We must "see through" to the real motives. As C.S. Lewis notes, if you see through everything, though, you ultimately see nothing and what is achieved is not discovery of the truth of humanity, but the abolition of man.[47] This abolition of man through the "seeing through everything" is what Tolkien is combating in his narrative depiction of the good.[48] Tolkien makes the good attractive, even compelling, attesting to its truth. It is evil, then, that demands explanation. It must be stressed that this is an aesthetic argument. Aesthetic argumentation is not unreasonable, but it is not purely based in reason, especially if one defines reasoning as a procedural process driven by data. To the extent that Tolkien's mythological approach is more captivating, it speaks to the fact that modernity's crude social-scientific reductionism fails to capture the reality of the human person. Narrative gives life and death a purpose, as all "lived narratives" have a "teleological character."[49] Tolkien provides this in his mythos in the creation myth that begins *The Silmarillion*. As will be discussed below, the tragic nature of that work should be read in light of its opening pages in which it is manifest that Illúvatar, the Creator, is aware of the tragedies that will unfold but are ultimately part of a plan that will vindicate Illúvatar's goodness. A directionless life would not be meaningful. To self-create is the height of solipsism.[50]

Accepting one's place within a narrative requires an attitude of acceptance rather than assertion, a hermeneutic of appreciation rather than privilege. It is a recognition that human will is most free and satisfied when it conforms to certain forms. The authority of my life does not come from within, as in emotivism, nor is it abstracted from personal and relational life, as with the managerial mindset. Those who wish to assert their will as absent of any recognition of narrative or the authority of practice ultimately find themselves frustrated. A society of such individualism will find chaos more prevalent than order. It is likely that despair rather than true contentment will prevail.[51] The hollowness of a life devoid of meaning and excellence will be filled with distractions and perversions. No one could call such a society thriving.

Early in *After Virtue* MacIntyre opines that virtue typically arises in the "everyday life" of "plain persons," of "those of making and sustaining families and households, schools, clinics, and local forms of political community."[52] A better description of Tolkien's hobbits is hard to find. Tolkien shows the power of narrative and the restlessness that comes from a rejection of narrative and the desire for control. Ultimately, Tolkien wishes to show how the limiting of desires and the acceptance of our role in a story not of our own authorship makes for a more contented life. The discussion of Tolkien will show how the ordinary virtues of hobbits, and the extraordinary virtues of others, give hope to an anxious age.

TOLKIEN THE DEEPER NARRATIVE OF FAIRY-STORY

J.R.R. Tolkien's Middle-earth legendarium was a product of Tolkien's own philosophy of language and story, emerging from Tolkien's profession of philology and his faith in Catholic dogma. Tolkien's project is known to most readers through *The Hobbit* and *The Lord of the Rings*, but is brought to fruition in *The Silmarillion* and the now vast ancillary work put out over the years by Tolkien's son, Christopher, complied from J.R.R. Tolkien's voluminous notes and narrative scraps. Tolkien pondered at length the role story plays in shaping the human being, and his conception of the human condition was similar to MacIntyre's, in that the story or narrative lies at the center of that experience.[53] Tolkien was of the opinion that poetics and revelation are related as God reveals himself through narrative. Tolkien did not make a clean distinction between "history" that is empirical and "story" which is fiction. Tolkien's project in the legendarium of Middle-earth was to create a myth for his people, the English people, that would provide meaning and a view of reality that spoke to that particular people's idiom. The use of story was Tolkien's salvo against a depiction of the world that is "flat, meaningless, and spiritless."[54] The brilliance of Tolkien's vision comes in part because he located himself in a narrative, that of Catholicism, which anchored his story in a tradition.[55] His stories make sense because Tolkien had been able to make sense of reality.

The precise kind of story Tolkien chose to tell, that of fairy or fantasy, has particular advantages. While easily dismissed as children's fables, a dismissal that rankled Tolkien, fantasy allows for greater context.[56] Steeped in a metaphysical realism, Tolkien believed that the words we use to describe the world "disclose . . . the fundamental order of things, an order that we do not invent so much as discover."[57] Fantasy, then, is a means for contemplating truths beyond the literal, historical, and material dimensions of reality. Tolkien's stories have power because though fantasy, they are real. Again, this statement only makes sense if one moves past the assumption that reality is found exclusively in the historical, literal, and material. Tolkien was especially skilled at instantiating good, or the Good, in narrative form, making it come alive and seem a viable alternative. The most absorbing characters, Frodo, Samwise, Aragorn, and Gandalf, are dominantly good, if each having particular flaws. Frodo shows almost supernatural perseverance, but ultimately gives in to despair, needing providence to destroy the Ring. Samwise is a bumpkin whose true mettle emerges across the entirely of the *Lord of the Rings*. Aragorn is the great king, nagged by doubt about his own worth and his right to lead others. Gandalf is wise, but is fooled by Saruman into dithering while Saruman consolidates his own nefarious plots. But each character is essentially good; their fate showing that good eventually triumphs over evil. The trials each face, and Frodo's eventual inability to heal within the confines of Middle-earth, speak to Tolkien's appreciation of life's harshness. As a World War I combat veteran, how could he be unaware?[58] Tolkien's Middle-earth legendarium, particularly in *The Silmarillion*, contains tragedy after tragedy, typically caused by a rash act or violent word that sets in motion a series of terrible events leading to a disastrous end. Taken as a whole, however, the Middle-earth myth starts and ends with goodness.[59] The creation myth that begins *The Silmarillion* informs readers that the world has been fashioned by a benevolent creator who loves his creation, for which he has a plan of ultimate redemption.[60] The story ends with Frodo seeking healing, Aragorn on the throne, the beginning of a golden age, and, finally, Samwise at home with his wife and children.

More so than other forms of literature, fairy-stories offer us escape and consolation from a world that is cruel, and with the advent of modern machinery, less real.[61] Tolkien argues that critics of escapist literature have a conception of escape that is akin to the flight of a deserter rather than the escape of a prisoner.[62] Not only do we seek to escape the modern, mechanized world, but even more so "hunger, thirst, poverty, pain, sorrow, injustice, [and] death."[63] Along these lines, fairy-stories are specifically apt for teaching lessons about the burden of an immortality consisting of "endless serial living."[64] A needed message in our historical moment that is actually promising "a-mortality" through scientific and technological progress.[65]

Most importantly, fairy-stories are defined by the "happy ending," which provide the reader consolation on account of its goodness. The happy ending is an essential characteristic of fairy-stories and distinguishes it from other forms of literature, especially tragedy. Tolkien's term "eucatastrophe" is not trite or sentimental, rather it is the opposite of the catastrophe of tragedy.[66] It is the recognition that within the tragedy of life, there is hope. In the end, we experience real joy through the happiness of those in the story. Tolkien describes the experience of the eucatastrophe, or the "joyous turn," and its relationship to reality:

> It is the mark of a good fairy-story, of the higher or more complete kind, that however wild its events, however fantastic and terrible the adventures, it can give to child or man that hears it, when the "turn" comes, a catch of the breath, a beat and lifting of the heart, near to (or indeed accompanied by) tears, as keen as that given by any form of literary art, and having a peculiar quality. . . . In such stories when the sudden "turn" comes we get a piecing glimpse of joy, and heart's desire, that for a moment passes outside the frame, rends indeed the very web of story, and lets a gleam come through.[67]

Through the eucatastrophe, the reader experiences true joy. Elsewhere, Tolkien states that, "Myth and fairy-story must, as all art, reflect and contain in solution elements of moral and religious truth (or error), but not explicit, not in the known form of the primary 'real' world."[68] Pearce states that myth is "the only way that certain transcendent truths could be expressed in intelligible form," and for this reason "Tolkien argued that, far from being lies, myths were the best way of conveying truths which would otherwise would be inexpressible."[69]

Peter Kreeft insightfully argues, "But to think that reality contains nothing more than the scientific method can know is like thinking Shakespeare's plays are nothing but exercises in grammar, that the water that endlessly fascinates the poet and the mystic is actually nothing but hydrogen and oxygen, or that that the road we actually travel has nothing more on it than the map does."[70] The myopia condemned by Kreeft is precisely the vision of Sauron, the wicked spirit of Middle-earth. Sauron seeks with a distinctly modern eye, perhaps symbolized by Tolkien's depiction of Sauron as the one lidless eye. Such a being literally lacks perspective. Sauron sees as the scientist/manager, calculating and measuring all by cost/benefit analysis. He also is the emotivist, assuming that everyone lusts for power and control just as he does. Sauron, like much of modern political thought, cannot account for the hero or the martyr. It never occurs to him that there might be a Frodo, a small, physically weak creature who is willing to die in order that others might live.

NARRATIVE RATIONALITY WITHIN TOLKIEN'S WORKS

Tolkien's work both acts itself as a narrative while internally articulating the power of narrative. The *Lord of the Rings* contains sixty songs or poems sung or recited by various characters that often help bring meaning to the characters' own adventures. Whether it is Aragorn reciting part of the Lay of Lúthien and Beren on Weathertop Hill, the story of Eärendil told in Rivendell as the travelers take a rest, or Legolas singing of the tragedy of Nimrodel as the Fellowship prepares to enter Lothlórien, the people of Tolkien's fictional Middle-earth use verse as a kind of history. The history of Middle-earth is not captured in works that simply record what happened, but instead turn events into stories with meaning.

Though Frodo and Sam recognize that they are a part of the same story as *The Silmarillion*, the knowledge of one's part in a story is not inherently a cause of happiness. Frodo himself notes that people in stories do not know whether they are in a happy story or tragic. While Sam and Frodo climb the stairs of Cirith Ungol, near despair, they pause to consider their plight in light of the old tales. Sam notes that he once thought that adventure tales involved those who went out and looked for them. "But that's not the way of it with the tales that really mattered, or the ones that stay in the mind. Folk seem to have been just landed in them." They had many chances to give up, and if they had given up, they would have been forgotten. He then ponders what sort of tale he and Frodo have found themselves in, if it is one of the happy or one of the tragic. "I wonder," says Frodo, "But I don't know. And that's the way of a real tale. Take any one that you're fond of. You may know, or guess what kind of tale it is, happy-ending or sad-ending, but the people in it don't know. And you don't want them to."[71] Frodo and Sam are not just discussing great tales; they are discussing the experience of life. Only in retrospect do we know whether our tale is happy or sad. Frodo's point about not knowing has two ramifications. First, we do not want characters, ourselves, to know which tale we are in because then we would either become lazy, if we know our tale to be happy, or despondent, if we know our tale to be sad. Viewing life as a story in a greater narrative spurs us to moral courage, seeking to make the best of our condition, the best of the role we have been assigned to play. Second, the characters of the story are consistently threatened with death and doom, but they courageously choose to act in spite of the danger. In fact, Ilúvatar had already pre-ordained what roles they are to play, but it is up to them to embrace their role. Indicative of the choice between a self-sacrificing life and a self-centered life, Gandalf tells Frodo that, "All we have to decide is what to do with the time that is given us."[72] One's time is a limited gift, and what one does with that time is important. The only real choice any of the characters need to make is between accepting their role in the narrative or deny it to their detriment.

Characters in *The Lord of the Rings* who take story most seriously are portrayed in the most positive fashion. An example of this is the noble character of Faramir. The son of the steward of Gondor, Faramir rejects the way of the warrior favored by his father, Denethor, and his brother, Boromir. Denethor holds Faramir in a kind of contempt, seeing him as weak and lamenting the influence lore masters such Gandalf have over him. Faramir has deep reverence for the past, frequently referring to the Men of Númenor, the late race of kings from which Faramir (and the rightful king, Aragorn) is descended.[73] War is inevitable, says Faramir to Frodo, while there is evil in the world, "but I do not love the bright sword for its sharpness, nor the arrow for its swiftness, nor the warrior for his glory. I love only that which they defend: the city of the Men of Númenor; and I would have her loved for her memory, her ancientry, her beauty, and her present wisdom."[74] It is Denethor and Boromir who desire to take the Ring and use it for their own purposes. This desire ultimately corrupts and ruins them both. Yet it is the wise Faramir who says to Frodo of the Ring, "I would not take this thing, if it lay by the highway."[75] In this, he stands in contrast to his brother who did try to seize the Ring from Frodo by force, leading to Boromir's doom.

Unlike Faramir, both Denethor and Boromir chafe at the roles they were meant to play. Boromir laments that his family is not of a kingly line, so despite the fact that they have been stewards of the realm of Gondor for centuries they may not claim the title of king. Faramir implies that Boromir, in his lust for power, may not in the end have accepted Aragorn's rightful title of king.[76] It is just this sort of desire that is Boromir's undoing. The same is true for Denethor, who attempts to use the seeing stone, the Palantír, to mentally confront Sauron, who possess another of these stones. The Palantír allows the possessors of the stones to see and speak to one another, a sort of fantastical Skype. But the stones were meant for kings, and this is not Denethor. Instead Sauron manipulates Denethor into despair and ultimately suicide. Tolkien illustrates with these two characters the dangerous anxiety that stems from wishing to be what we are not, lusting for that which we cannot have.

Similar themes emerge in the character of the warrior-maiden Éowyn. Éowyn, niece to the ruler of Rohan, the kingdom of horsemen, grieves at being left behind as the men march off to war. Aragorn calls on her to do her duty to her people, which is govern at home while the rest go away to war. "Too often have I heard of duty," she responds, "But am I not of the House of Eorl, a shieldmaiden and not a dry nurse?"[77] Literally taking on a new role, she disguises herself as a man, renaming herself Dernhelm. Joining the march to battle, she heroically slays the demonic Lord of the Nazgûl, receiving a near mortal wound in payment. In recovery in the House of Healing, it becomes apparent to none other than Faramir, himself convalescing from battle wounds, that her deepest wounds are spiritual, not physical. Faramir convinces her to accept that she is not a queen or a warrior, that she should content herself to marry him, a mere steward of Gondor, not a king, after the death of his father. She has found her right place and announces, "I will be a shieldmaiden no longer, nor vie with the great Riders, nor take joy only in the songs of slaying. I will be a healer, and love things that grow and are not barren. . . . No longer do I desire to be a queen."[78] Éowyn finds happiness through the purpose and meaningfulness embodied in this role within the narrative.

Strider becoming Aragorn is an excellent example of a character choosing to fulfill his pre-ordained role within the greater narrative and the anxiety that comes with not doing so. Strider/Aragorn is the heir to the Throne of Gondor, but he must prove himself to be the true heir. Early in the story he is Chieftain of the Dúnedain, the Rangers of the North, but he is not ready to reclaim the greater role. He follows Gandalf's lead until Gandalf's "death" upon the Bridge of Khazad-dûm. Strider proclaims to the fellowship that he will now lead them. Eventually, the fellowship needs to make a decision about where to go, but Strider has yet to fully embrace his role as leader as he was "still divided in his mind."[79] While travelling down the river into the land of Gondor, Frodo sees a change in Strider. He is no longer the Strider, the weather-beaten ranger. Instead, Frodo beholds a new man. "In the stern sat Aragorn son of Arathorn, proud and erect, guiding the boat with skillful strokes; his hood was cast back, and his dark hair was blowing in the wind, a light in his eye: a king returning from exile to his own land."[80] Strider is becoming Aragorn, but the transformation is not yet complete. Eventually, he is told that he must take a path that only the heir to Isildur can take. He can either choose to accept his role and face certain doom or take an easier path. He chooses the "Paths of the Dead" against the protests of those in his company that the living may not pass through that way.[81] Aragorn chooses to face what appears to be certain death on the Paths of the Dead in order to embrace his destiny, to take part in Illúvatar's plan. Before going down the path, Aragorn reveals himself as heir to the Enemy in a Palantír, the dangerous seeing stone. He brandishes his sword before Sauron, the very sword Isildur, Aragorn's ancestor, had used to defeat Sauron hundreds of years previously. In this manner he announces himself as king and adversary to Sauron.[82] Later after the main battle is over, he proves that he is now the rightful king by laying his hands on the wounded and healing them. Tolkien states: "And word went through the City: 'The King is come again indeed.'"[83] He takes on yet another name, Elessar, or Elfstone, to mark his kingship. Strider was once a Ranger of the North, but now through his action he has become Aragorn and then Elessar, King of Gondor. Like Aragorn, each of the main characters of the story becomes someone greater than they once were through their actions. They all have a purpose and meaning to their lives greater than what they give it.

The power of the Ring and of Sauron is the power of deception.[84] The Ring convinces the weak, even Frodo, that they can be great masters of all. Similar are the Palantír, which Sauron uses like a modern propagandist to mislead both Saruman and Denethor, showing them only partial images of reality that ultimately delude them. Sauron, in this sense, uses false narrative to appeal to people's desires and wants, manipulating those desires and wants to his own end. His victims believe what they are pursing is power and command, when in fact they are being enslaved. The wisest, such as Gandalf, Faramir, and the elf-queen Galadriel recognize Sauron's game and refuse the temptation to play. Others, such as Saruman, Boromir, and the malicious creature Gollum find themselves entrapped. The anxious age often sells such false narratives, for example in advertising which seeks to convince us that this product or that purchase will bring happiness and meaning. We are told that it is within our power to "build a better planet." But power and material abundance, the talisman of the age of anxiety, absent humility, and the recognition of limits are curses, not blessings.

As indicated, those who fail to accept their role or their lives as narrative find themselves restless. They seek out false remedies for that restlessness. This is in part what we in the twenty-first century do with our devices. Smart phones and video game consoles, opioids and meth, debt-driven consumer culture all serve as tools of distraction. The modern condition is one of *acedia*, that ancient vice sometimes called "sloth" in English, containing connotations of laziness. But *acedia* is not quite "laziness" in the sense of lack of energy. *Acedia* "reveals frustration and hate, disgust at place and 'life itself.'" The slothful are often "in a frenzy of pointless action . . . in disgust at the actual work given to them by God."[85] The lives of those overtaken by *acedia* are restless, their lives full of a Macbethean sound and fury, but signifying nothing.

It is true that some roles can be oppressive. One does not want to naively confirm existing social structures. This is precisely a problem with the Age of Anxiety, however. The *acedia* promoted by our age makes it difficult for us to discern whether our roles are just or unjust. As will be expressed in this book's conclusion, liberal education, silence, and leisure are necessary for properly discerning our roles. But these qualities are in short supply in the anxious age, leaving us without a sound disposition with which to properly ascertain our role. In a play, one auditions for a role. In many ways, life is that audition, but we need to pay attention to direction just as the actor does. That requires certain habits and inclinations. As we have noted previously, modern political activism often uses the rhetoric of justice to mask its own pursuit of power. Committed to a deracinated, nominalist framework, it cannot stake out a definitive position from which to argue against unjust roles. Indeed, the liberationist mindset that often underlies "social justice" activism operates with no particular end in sight. "Liberation" and "progress" contain little to no substance, leaving the social justice warrior constantly moving on to the next fight with no concept of when actual justice will be achieved.

Only one grounded in realism, such as Tolkien, can effectively argue against injustice. Metaphysical realism is committed to finding what is true about the human person. As such it can recognize untruth, as opposed to insufficient power. Thus, it serves as a stronger critique of injustice than does much of "social justice" rhetoric.

We ponder why our age can be blessed with untold wealth and material comfort beyond the imagination of previous generations, yet seem so discontented.[86] As reflected in drug abuse, technology abuse, startling increases in depression, anxiety, and suicide, especially amongst the young, there is a staggering disconnect between our material and spiritual health.[87] Thomas Hobbes opined, "The Desires, and other Passions of man, are in themselves no Sin. No more are the Actions, that proceed from those Passions."[88] The contemporary situation seems to expose the falsehood of Hobbes's claim. As we saw in the zombie discussion, we perhaps have subconsciously started to recognize that a life dedicated to satiating our desires leaves one spiritually empty. If present-day residents of the anxious age balk at calling these passions "sin," they are surely learning, slowly and reluctantly, that indulging them is no virtue. That yearning for more than what material things can offer might be a natural indication that we are meant for more. Consumerism, though, thrives on this restlessness, encouraging us in the notion that mere things can satisfy us.

RESTLESSNESS AND CONTENTMENT

In Tolkien, restlessness seems to have two sources, one in the passions and desires, as in Hobbes, and the other in a fear of mortality. Both these sources are depicted in various ways in *The Silmarillion* and *The Lord of the Rings*. The relationship between death and immortality, in fact, is a primary theme of the story.[89] Specifically, it advocates for the free acceptance of death. Peter Kreeft argues that two visions of death and immortality are presented in the story: death to ourselves and true immortality and false immortality and the death of the soul.[90] These are two different paths of life: the one is concerned with the world outside of the self; whereas, the other is concerned only with one's self. A false immortality is one that seeks more time than has been given. Longevity of life, or false immortality, is specifically the "gift" of the Ring of Power. In relation to the Age of Anxiety, people are sold a vision of scientific, medical, and technological progress that provides increasingly prolonged lives, such that advocates of the singularity believe that consciousness will be able to be stored in computers. Indeed, this is the very vision of the second season of *Westworld*, that is, the technological promise of everlasting life. Elsewhere, Tolkien expands upon this theme:

The Elves called it [the mortality of men] the *Gift of Ilúvatar* (God). . . . This is therefore an 'Elvish' view, and does not have anything to say for or against such beliefs as the Christian that 'death' is not part of human nature, but a punishment for sin (rebellion), a result of the 'Fall'. It should be tied to an elvish perception of what *death* – not being tied to the 'circles of the world' – should now become for Men, however it arose. A divine 'punishment' is also a divine 'gift', if accepted, since its object is ultimate blessing, and the supreme inventiveness of the Creator will make 'punishments' (that is changes of design) produce a good not otherwise to be attained: a 'mortal' man has probably (an elf would say) a higher if unrevealed destiny than a longeval one. To attempt by device or 'magic' to recover longevity is thus a supreme folly and wickedness of 'mortals'. Longevity or counterfeit 'immortality' (true mortality is beyond Eä) is the chief bait of Sauron – it leads the small to a Gollum, and the great to a Ringwraith.[91]

Essentially, freedom is gained by accepting the time is given to us; the false immortality seeks more time than has been given. The acceptance of death and our allotted time opens a person to leisure, whereas the denial of death causes a busyness or *acedia* that distracts and depresses the soul.

In *The Silmarillion*, the elf-lord Fëanor crafts the Silmarils, the jewels of unparalleled beauty that set in motion the tragedy of Middle-earth's First Age. Tolkien says, "Seldom were the hands and mind of Fëanor at rest," a clear sign of his *acedia*.[92] The root of Fëanor's corruption is ingratitude, a lack of appreciation of his place in creation. "For Fëanor began to love the Silmarils with a greedy love, and grudged the sight of them to all save to his father and his seven sons; he seldom remembered that the light within them was not his own."[93] Fëanor, unwilling to humble himself before the creation of Ilúvatar, believes himself a kind of god. This arrogance, which will culminate in a deadly oath to kill any who possess the jewels other than him and his family, sets in motion a story filled with unfathomable woe. Fëanor, the great craftsman, becomes haughty and rejects the authority of his practice, believing himself to be a creator rather than a subcreator working with the good creation of Ilúvatar for which Fëanor should be grateful.

A similar theme occurs in *The Lord of the Rings* with the One Ring playing the part of the Silmarils. The most obvious depiction of this pathology is with the creature Gollum. Gollum possessed the Ring longer than anyone else. The Ring gave Gollum an unusually long life, which ended up being more of a curse than a gift. Gollum's initial possession of the Ring involved theft and murder. The Ring allows Gollum to get what he wants. He uses the invisibility that the Ring confers to steal and learn secrets. Gollum is eventually exiled by his hobbit-like people, living alone in the darkness of a mountain lake, with no company other than fish and the Ring, which he takes to calling "My precious." Only Bilbo's fortuitous finding of the Ring after Gollum misplaces it spurs Gollum to leave the mountain in obsessive pursuit of his precious. Gollum eventually connives to secure the Ring from Frodo. Gollum is mentally tortured by his overwhelming desire to possess the Ring, but also constrained by an oath to Frodo, sworn on the Ring, not to harm Frodo. In fact, Gollum promises to help Frodo travel to Mordor to destroy the Ring. At various points, Gollum agonizes over what little remains of his decent self and the compulsive desire for the Ring.

Gollum's conflict should sound familiar to the modern ear, reminding us of the language of addiction. What is remarkable about Gollum's perverse craving for the Ring is that it seemingly gives him no pleasure. Each person who keeps the Ring and is tempted to use it, primarily Gollum, Bilbo, and Frodo, recognize that the Ring is gaining hold of them, but seem powerless to stop it. Bilbo and Frodo at least know that there is something corrupting about the Ring. As he leaves the Ring to Frodo, Bilbo admits that he feels unwell, "stretched," like "butter that has been scraped over too much bread." Change is needed, he says. He tells Gandalf that it would be a "relief" not to be "bothered with it anymore." "It has been growing in my mind lately . . . And I am always wanting to put it on and disappear, don't you know; or wondering if it is safe, and pulling it out to make sure. I tried locking it up, but I found I couldn't rest without it in my pocket."[94]

As noted, one of the effects of the Ring is prolonged life, which is the impetus behind Bilbo exclaiming that he feels "stretched out" because of the longevity of life given to him by the ring.[95] Gandalf tells Frodo that if one keeps one of the Great rings one "does not die, but he does not grow or obtain more life." He merely persists until every moment of life is a burden. The possessor of one of these Rings never really dies, he simply "fades" until he is overcome, devoured, by Sauron, the master of the Rings. False immortality corrupts a person, and death freely accepted purifies a person. Gandalf, in a sense, gives himself freely up to death in *The Fellowship of the Ring* and is seemingly risen from the dead in *The Two Towers*. Before he "died," he was Gandalf the Grey and afterward he was Gandalf the White. Gandalf, like Aragorn, is transformed by acting even in the face of certain death. In the final analysis, *The Lord of the Rings* presents a message that recognizes not only the inevitability of death, but that a false immortality is wholly unnatural and undesirable. The story tells us that we should not fear death, and that we can act in the face of death because it is in fact a good, not an evil.

In *The Silmarillion*, it is made plain that death was given to Men not as a curse, but a gift. The nature of the gift eluded Men, causing doubt. While Christian scripture declares that death is the wage of sin, in Tolkien's mythos death is a good. The cost of sin is the disbelief by Men of death's goodness. They fear and run from death, rather than embracing it. The gift given to very few, namely Beren and Lúthien along with their distant posterity Aragorn and

Arwen, is that they appear to be able to choose their time of death and death seems to instill no dread in them. Tolkien may be speculating that had the Fall not occurred, it is not as if Adam and Eve would not have died, but that they would have died at a time of their own choosing and fear of death would have had no hold on them. Be that as it may, the men of Middle-earth had no such gift. Their desire is to extend life rather than transcend it.[96] Theirs was a perverted hope for immorality.

In *The Silmarillion* Tolkien writes, "Therefore [Illúvatar] willed that the hearts of Men should *seek beyond the world and should find no rests therein*; but they should have a virtue to shape their life, amid the powers and chances of the world."[97] It is Melkor, the Satan figure, who perverts the seeking "beyond the world" and turns it into a kind of anxiety. Regarding death, Melkor "has cast his shadow upon it, and confounded it with darkness, and brought forth evil out of good, and fear out of hope."[98] Bradly Birzer argues that Ilúvatar gave men death "so that they would desire to return to their true home, heaven. The restlessness prevented men from becoming too attached to the earth."[99] The longing for immortality is described in *The Silmarillion* when the hero Tuor first glimpses the sea. For Tolkien, the sea often serves as a stand-in for the yearning for immortality. "And Tuor came into Neverast," writes Tolkien, "and looking upon Belgaer the Great Sea he was enamoured of it, and the sound of it and the longing for it were ever in his heart and ear, and an unquiet was on him that took him at last into the depths of the realms of Ulmo."[100]

The restlessness that was intended to draw men's eyes to heaven, under the corruption of Melkor has the exact opposite effect. We saw in chapter 2 Tocqueville's observation that people in a democracy seem unusually discontented and seek infinite perfection. They experience a profound unease as they attempt to secure worldly wealth, but never seem able to be contented with it. Attempting to satisfy our longing for immorality through worldly means, modern people are like the victim of a tapeworm whose solution is simply to eat more, thus just feeding the tapeworm further.

This curse seems inherent in the race of Men. Before his death, Tolkien had sketched out a sequel to *The Lord of the Rings* called *The New Shadow*, which was to take place roughly a century after the death of Aragorn. Again, it seems, Men had become "bored with goodness and beauty," with kings becoming obsessed with domination.[101] What is the cure for this restlessness? The cure seems to partake of family, craft, humble pleasures, submission to rightful authority, thus giving up the desire to dominate. Tolkien recognizes that mere power has not the ability to bring contentment. Contrary to much modern thought, the satisfaction of desire does not bring ease. This is because our desires can never really be satiated in this world. So contentment comes not through a maximization of our desires, attempting to satiate them like the sufferer from poison ivy seeks relief through scratching.

RESTLESS AND FALSE PROMISES OF CONTROL

One way in which humans attempt to alleviate the restlessness of desire and morality is through technological control. Again, Tolkien offers a warning against the notion that because we can do a thing, because we can exert control, we should. In the case of modernity, the notion is that the satiation of desires is such an imperative that any means necessary to do so are just. Indeed, those means may even become rights that we can demand from others. If the ultimate good is comfort, then we can demand ever-increasing levels of material goods. It is offensive to us that someone else might be better able to indulge their cravings than are we, since such indulgence is held to be the highest good. This extends to the religious vision in which God's job is to accept me as I am, pander to my wants, and otherwise leave me alone.[102] The contemporary notion of "spiritual, but not religious" has currency precisely because it recognizes some vague notion of transcendence without the discipline that religion (*religio*) entails. This nonreligious spiritualism is often a mask for self-indulgence and self-worship.

Our attempts to control and make life more predictable are an attempt to be more god-like. One can see this in the social sciences. Not content simply to explain, social science must also predict. If it can predict, in effect see the future, we can then use social science to manipulate our circumstances to reach the anticipated result. This is true of academia in general. Academics are not content with merely passing on of knowledge, but must create "new" knowledge through increasingly esoteric "research" that shows one to be an "expert." The social scientific mindset illustrates how the lust to control can be so pernicious. The social scientist, perhaps the greatest exemplar of MacIntyre's managerial mindset, operates precisely by taking human behavior and reducing it to quantifiable data. Thus abstracted from actual human beings, data can be manipulated. It is not a great leap from such "operationalizing of variables," in the social scientific jargon, to the dehumanization of society. Actual persons are lost amongst the data.

Tolkien anticipates this mindset. In *The Silmarillion*, Aüle, one of the angelic Valar who aids Illúvatar in creation, develops the dwarves as a new race. But he has done so without Illúvatar's permission. Aüle is thwarting Illúvatar's plan that the Children of Illúvatar, namely Elves and Men, should come first. Illúvatar chides Aüle. "For thou hast from me as a gift thy own being only, and no more; and therefore the creatures of thy hand and mind can live only by that being, moving when thou thinkest to move them, and if thy thought be elsewhere, standing idle." Aüle hasn't Illúvatar's power to create truly free beings. He has sculpted mere mechanical beings. Aüle is sufficiently chastened, declaring that it was not his intention to usurp Illúvatar's lordship. As Aüle starts to destroy his creation, Illúvatar, moved by pity, gives the dwarves what Aüle cannot, a free will. Aüle knows that now dwarves have a "life of their own" because they flinch from his hammer and his commands. They know fear. Aüle consents to have the dwarves frozen until the rise of the Elves, although enmity will always exist between the two races. Aüle's creation, though, is precisely how the manager sees human beings, as mere mechanical things that should move and stand idle at the will of the social scientist, the master of the scientific knowledge of humanity. What Illúvatar describes as an inadequacy the manager sees as a laudable feature.

Tolkien's philosophy regarding the appropriate use of technology can be seen in his depiction of magic. Interest in magic reawaked with the Enlightenment as both magic and science have the same goal: the manipulation of nature to our own ends.[103] We have seen in chapter 3 how control of nature is at the heart of the modern project. Tolkien envisions two different kinds of magic. Magic as typically understood is largely condemned in Tolkein's fantasy as a lust for power. Elf-Queen Galadriel reproaches Sam for using the same word, magic, for her own craft and what she describes as "the deceits of the Enemy." This second kind of magic has "disdain for the world as it is" and impatiently remakes the world into what we wish it to be.[104] The root of this deformed magic is the attempt to immediately effectuate desire. It suggests a profound displeasure, one might even say restlessness, with things as they are. Because I want a thing, I should have that thing now. As Ralph Wood puts it, "For Tolkien, malign magic is the product of a panicked despair. It offers a quick and false fix for the complexities and confusions—above all, for the slow and graduate movements—of the good creation."[105]

By contrast, good magic, or good craft, "makes the world richer, it glorifies the world for beauty, it amplifies nature into art."[106] So the good craftsman humbles himself before nature, shows patience with what nature has given him to create with, and, unlike Fëanor, appreciates that his craft is a servant to the master craftsman. This is also exemplified in the difference in the magic of Gandalf and the corrupted wizard Saruman. Both Saruman and Gandalf use magic. Tolkien is at pains to show Gandalf as deeply hesitant to use his powers. Gandalf's greatest gift is not his ability to wield power, but in wisdom and counsel. Saruman, by contrast, wishes to dominate. He uses magic to briefly imprison Gandalf and then to make war on Rohan. It is of note that both Gandalf and Saruman use fire, including gunpowder. Gandalf is famous amongst hobbits for his fireworks. Here Gandalf uses his art for beauty and pleasure. In his travels, he uses the power of fire to give heat to the cold and light to those trapped in darkness. Saruman, by contrast, like Satan in Book VI of Milton's *Paradise Lost*, uses gunpowder to make war, destroy nature, and to extend his power over others.

To use magic/technology well requires virtue. The tendency of the anxious age is to see technology simply as a tool, not as a moral question. Therefore, we tend not to think of the application of technology as something to ponder. As stated, the inclination instead is to assume that if it can be done, it should be done. The only restrictions on the use of technology are precisely the managerial ones, namely does it work. Here "work" is largely defined as "increased efficiency," "easing of material conditions for most," or "makes us richer." Thus, the use of technique is to be based on the data-driven analysis of dispassionate experts. This is not virtue. In fact, it is the attempt to render virtue moot.

Aristotle, by contrast, asserts, "The man who has been educated in a subject is a good judge of that subject, and the man who has received an all-round education is the good judge in general."[107] But this is not the education of the managerial, administrative elite. Their education is precisely technical and is often ignorant of the kind of narrative education that MacIntyre believes is crucial to virtue formation. One could say that their education is that of Saruman rather than Faramir. Aristotle's definition of courage serves as an exemplar for virtue in general. "The man, then, who faces and who fears the right things and from the right motive, in the right way and at the right time, and who feels confidence under the corresponding conditions, is brave; for the brave man feels and acts according to the merits of the case and in whatever way reason directs."[108] Virtue is taking measure of a circumstance and acting appropriately. So all the virtues Aristotle discusses, such as courage, magnanimity, liberality, and temperance require a kind of moderation, as in a correct measure, as well as prudence, a correct judgment as to how to act. Such virtue requires a broader knowledge than the mere application of procedure. The very purpose of "standard operating procedures" that are the hallmark of bureaucratic operations is so that it does not matter who occupies the bureaucratic role. That person needs no judgment, no virtue, no depth of soul. The only knowledge necessary is the technique called for in the application of the procedure. The whole point is to depersonalize.

The aforementioned magical orbs called the Palantír are an example of this principle. As mentioned, these "seeing-stones" allow the possessor to talk to those who hold the other stones. In the *The Lord of the Rings*, Saruman and Denethor are corrupted by the stones. The young hobbit Pippin also becomes enamored of the stone of Saruman, now in the possession of Gandalf after Saruman's defeat. It plays upon his mind until, unable to resist any further, he sneaks the stone away from Gandalf in the dead of night. Gazing into the stone Pippin reveals himself to Sauron. He is luckily discovered before his folly does too much damage. None of these characters has the proper virtues to use the stone well. In contrast, the very paradigm of Aristotelian virtue, Aragorn, eventually uses the same stone that bewitched Pippin to mentally wrestle with Sauron. Aragorn, as the rightful king, is the true possessor of the stone. He also has developed virtue through study, practice, and self-denial.

Aragorn's use of the stone is fortuitous as it causes Sauron to hastily attack before he is truly prepared, so troubled is he by the true king that is Aragorn. Knowledge must be coupled with virtue in order to become wisdom. Contra Francis Bacon, knowledge cannot be the supreme good because, as Saruman and Sauron illustrate, it is as compatible with evil as it is goodness.[109]

A proper use of technology would seem to have two criteria. First, to use technology well requires knowledge of human nature. This entails the knowledge that humans are personal, relational creatures. Therefore, we must think as much about how technology affects the community as how empowers individuals.[110] Second, we must remember precisely that we are *creatures*. Not only do we need to respect our own nature, including our social nature, we must remember what Fëanor forgot: that we did not make creation and we are not ourselves gods. A proper disposition toward technology, then, requires a kind of humility, the kind embodied in Tolkien in characters such as Aragorn and Faramir, negatively embodied in such characters as Saruman. Milton's Satan's ultimate sin is disobedience, thinking it better to reign in hell than to serve in heaven. So too in Tolkien. When craft is used to elevate the self rather than the Creator, such vainglory leads only to tragedy.

Virtue is key to the suitable use of technology/magic because, as Tolkien shows, corruption often comes through good intentions. Gandalf recoils from Bilbo's offer that Gandalf take the Ring, knowing that it is precisely his good intentions, his pity, that would be corrupted by the Ring. The same is true of Galadriel, who is offered the Ring by Frodo. She is tempted, thinking of the marvelous deeds she could do as master of the Ring. But she demurs, knowing the Ring, by its nature, would pervert her goodness. "Seldom is sin committed for its own sake, Tolkien shows, but almost always in the name of some alleged good."[111] One is reminded of Flannery O'Connor's warning to the modern age. It is precisely the tenderness that typifies our age that is our greatest temptation. "It is a tenderness which, long since cut off from the person of Christ, is wrapped in theory. When tenderness is detached from the source of tenderness, its logical outcome is terror. It ends in forced labor camps and in the fumes of the gas chamber."[112] One need only reflect on the amount of killing that can, and has, been done in the name of alleviating suffering, making the world safe for democracy, providing death with dignity, ensuring that every child is a wanted child.

While one may question O'Connor's parochial claims regarding Christ, still one might take Tocqueville's observation to heart that there is an "impious maxim" in the modern mind that "everything is permitted in the interests of society."[113] What religion provides is a kind of limiting principle. While it is true that all sorts of atrocities can and have been committed in the name of religion, almost every religion sets up some sort of guideline as to what is absolutely forbidden. This is not so in modern thought in its purist form.

For the emotivist, the only limit is limitless desire. For the manager, it is efficiency or usefulness. Neither, in and of itself, can come up with a principle that puts limits on the application of technology. So, for example, if we desire cheap consumer goods, and to get those cheap consumer goods necessitates that some must be held in slave labor, then so be it. If society finds elderly people to be a drain on limited resources, the solution is to encourage "death with dignity," the euphemistic term for killing the sick and infirm. To be sure, few emotivists and managerial types are so consciously callous. But to the extent they might reject the reasoning just illustrated they must reach beyond modern thought to some tradition. Emotivism and mangerialism cannot provide a principled reason not to kill the inconvenient, abandon the sick, or enslave the weak.

Writes Tokien in *The Silmarillion,* "But the design of [the angelic Valar] Manwë was that the Númenóreans should not be tempted to seek for the Blessed Realm, nor desire to overpass the limits set to their bliss, becoming enamoured of the immortality of the Valar and the Eldar and the lands where all things endure."[114] In our times, we have adopted the mindset of the Númenóreans. Our arguments aren't over what limits there should be, but whether there should be limits. It is not "What is the best way to deal with end of life pain consistent with human dignity?" It is "Why is this even a question? Of course you alleviate physical suffering, because suffering is unpleasant."

Here we can learn much from the hobbits. Hobbit joy comes from very simple pleasures. They want little in terms of what we would call consumer products. They are content with a pint of ale, good tobacco, and good conversation. They do not think that happiness is something to be purchased or manufactured.[115] While Hobbits may appear like modern consumers in their quest for comfort, Hobbits differ in that they can easily settle for what can only be called "enough." They limit their desires to a few relatively humble pleasures and want for nothing more. Hobbit life seems quite orderly. This order has the result of directing and moderating desires. There is little politics in the Shire as each is satisfied with his place. Those who have higher positions do not condescend to those beneath, while those without status do not seek to overthrow those who do.[116] While the One Ring holds out the prospect that a person can get all that he wants, this turns out to be a kind of slavery. Hobbits, by wanting little, seem to be freer. Theirs is not a restless pursuit of more; instead it is a satisfaction with what they have.

Hobbit culture is a folk culture, of song, story, family, rather than a commercial culture of buying and selling.[117] As such their culture attends to the personal, relational needs of its people rather than encouraging the maximization of desire, as does commercial culture. A commercial culture promotes "getting" and "having" as the best thing, while folk culture places inhabiting a community as the central priority. Because theirs is a folk culture, Hobbit life is personal, based on face-to-face relationship, rather than abstract, such as the relationship through transaction that typifies the anticulture of commerce. Hobbits are not aggregated into a mass of impersonal numbers. Hobbits don't do data mining. Rather, they are known as parts of families with a history and a place. There are the Brandybucks of Buckland, the Tooks of Tuckborough, the Bagginses of Hobbiton. To be the head of such a family, such as the Thain of the Tooks or the Master of Brandy Hall for the Brandybucks, is to have status. This is where hobbits look for leadership. In this sense, Hobbit culture mirrors that of *Downton Abbey*, in that it is class based—status is conferred based on family membership—without being elite. While there might be a ruling "class" among hobbits, as some families are more important than others and power is conferred to age, what passes for hobbit government is by those who live among their people and see themselves as performing a noble duty. Hobbit rule is not the managerial application of abstract "objective" scientific theories. It is based on place, family, and history. It takes into account the personal relationships that make a community strong. Hobbit rule is grounded on knowledge of person, not an impersonal application of law to abstract individuals. A community without trust is no real community. It is held together by fear and force. Not so with hobbits.

Tolkien provides us with a diagnosis of our age's pathologies and gives us a possible solution. The anxiety of our age is caused in large part by the loss of a narrative sense and a limitless desire for power over our condition. Both leave modern man unsatisfied. Thus, despite incalculable wealth and comfort, he finds himself unhappy. But there is hope. There is hope in finding meaning in narrative. *The Lord of the Rings* presents itself as a message of hope to the population of a contemporary, disconnected, cynical, and anxious historical moment. Hope is what is needed during this age because it provides the courage to live in the present. There is hope found in home, in family, in humility, and in the face of natural limits. The greatest of these limits, our mortality, points us to the hope that there is more beyond this life. In this sense, we are not at home in this life. Tolkien teaches us to be at home with that homelessness. Not to rail against it, but to come to peace. It is Sam who ends *The Lord of the Rings* at home, with his family, content. Frodo cannot find rest in Middle-earth, but Sam can. It is among hearth and home, kith and kin where we can find contentment and hope in an anxious age.

NOTES

1. See Joseph Bottom, *An Anxious Age: The Post-Protestant Ethic and the Spirit of America* (New York: Image, 2014), 42, 44.

2. Deneen, *Conserving America*, 161.

3. Francis Bacon, *New Atlantis and The Great Instauration*, ed. Jerry Weinberger (Arlington Heights, Illinois, Harland Davidson, Inc. 1989), 29.

4. The aesthetic turn in rhetoric recognizes that good rhetoric is able to give order to the seeming chaos of existence and is not limited by epistemic concerns, but rather by aesthetic concerns. See Steven Whitson and John Poulakos, "Nietzsche and the Aesthetics of Rhetoric," *Quarterly Journal of Speech*, Vol. 79, No. 2 (1993), 131–145. Additionally, Jefferey Walker has detailed the history of ancient Greek kings being skilled practitioners of epidictic rhetoric and ruled as poets more so than statesmen. Jeffrey Walker, *Rhetoric and Poetics in Antiquity* (New York: Oxford University Press, 2000).

5. Richard M. Weaver, "The Phaedrus and the Nature of Rhetoric," in *The Ethics of Rhetoric* (Davis, CA: Hermagoras Press, 1985), 4–5.

6. One might posit four different ways of encountering and thus coming to know reality. One of those methods is that of science, which can teach us about material reality. Another way of knowing is what we call poetics, by which we mean art in the most capacious sense. For example, I might know more about Dante's Beatrice by reading his poetry than reading a description of Beatrice's vital statistics and socioeconomic description. A third way of knowing is through philosophy and dialectical examination, in which we discover universal, nonmaterial principles, such as the law of noncontradiction. A fourth way of knowing is through revelation, by which we come to know certain divine realities, although the divine may reveal itself through material and poetry as well. When Bacon and those devoted to scientism posit science as the only way of knowing, they are making a strong metaphysical claim. Taken to its rational conclusion, one gets the absurdity of such philosophical schools as eliminative materialism that posits that all reality, even human emotion and consciousness, are explainable wholly through materialist methods. In Aristotelian terms, this is the assertion that material and efficient cause explains all of reality. If one accepts this concept, one may even be forced to conclude that words themselves contain no meaning, but are the gibberish of mechanistic beings uttering sounds produced by a sophisticated machine, but signifying no self or consciousness (to say nothing of self-consciousness). Most people conclude via common sense that this is not true. They intuit, although often cannot articulate, the notion that their lives have meaning, that their relationships have purpose, that they are indeed personal, relational animals.

7. Tolkien believed that fairy-stories are much more than simple, children's stories. In fact, he rejected the idea that fairy-stories should be written for children. Ultimately, Tolkien viewed fairy-stories as works of art that, when written correctly, can become a window to Reality. J.R.R. Tolkien, "On Fairy-Stories," in *The Tolkien Reader* (New York: Ballantine Books, 1966), 69.

8. The realization of imagined wonder is fantastic (i.e., fantasy). Tolkien states: "An essential power of Faërie is thus the power of making immediately effective by the will the visions of 'fantasy'" (Tolkien, "On Fairy-Stories" 49). Essentially fantasy is "the making or glimpsing of Other-worlds" that are fantastic, in that these worlds are free "from the domination of observed fact." Tolkien ("On Fairy-Stories," 64, 69). Essentially, the fairy-story is a "secondary world" with its own laws and observed

facts which are fantastic, in that they liberate us from the "observed facts" of our "primary world" ("On Fairy-Stories," 60). Imagined wonder can be realized through liberation and escape from our world into a world characterized by the fantastic i.e., magic. So, if wonder is the beginning of philosophy, it is not difficult to see why Tolkien believes that fantasy is one of the highest forms of Art. Because the realization of imagined wonder is at the heart of Faërie, fairy-stories are concerned within desirability rather than possibility (Tolkien, "On Fairy-Stories," 63).

9. The rhetorical nature of Tolkien's works can also be seen in his distaste for allegory. He states: "I much prefer history, true or feigned, with its varied applicability to the thought and experience of readers. I think that many confuse 'applicability' with 'allegory'; but the one resides in the freedom of the reader, and the other in the purposed domination of the author" (Tolkien, *LOTR*, xxiv). Essentially, this is a difference between rhetoric and dialectic; rhetoric being enthymematic or an open palm which guides and leaves room for interpretation, whereas, dialectic being a closed fist which forces a person into certain conclusions. Tolkien's rhetorical vision of fairy stories can be contrasted to the highly didactic allegories of C.S. Lewis' explicitly Christian *Chronicles of Narnia* and Phillip K. Pullman's explicitly atheistic *His Dark Materials*. The difference between these three authors is witnessed by Pullman, who admitted that his goal is "to go after Christianity. I want God to be dead in my works. I want to undermine Christianity." Bronwyn Gerretsen, "I Want God to Be Dead in My Works," *IOL News*, last modified December 3, 2017, https://www.iol.co.za/news/south-africa/i-want-god-to-be-dead-in-my-works-381139. Of Lewis and Tolkien, he noted: "I dislike his [C.S. Lewis] Narnia books because of the solution he offers to the great questions of human life: is there a God, what is the purpose, all that stuff, which he really does engage with pretty deeply, unlike Tolkien who doesn't touch it at all. 'The Lord of the Rings' is essentially trivial . . . .Tolkien is not worth arguing with." Robert Butler, "The Art of Darkness," *Intelligent Life*, December 2007.

10. Peter J. Kreeft, *The Philosophy of Tolkien* (San Francisco: Ignatius Press, 2005), 23.

11. Rushkoff, *Present Shock*, 1–67.

12. Joseph Pearce, "True Myth: The Catholicism of 'The Lord of the Rings'," in *Celebrating Middle-Earth: The Lord of the Rings as a Defense of Western Civilization* (Seattle, WA: Inkling Books, 2002), 83–84.

13. The focus on goodness is less apparent in *The Silmarillion*. *The Silmarillion* is tragic tale of the dire consequences over many centuries of the disobedience of one Elf, Fëanor, in the creation and then hording of the three great jewels, the Silmarils. It also portrays the machinations of Tolkien's own Satan, Melkor, also known as Morgoth. It is hard to imagine, for example, a more cruel fate than the one of the heroic and tragic Túrin Turumbar, an account introduced in *The Silmarillion* and eventually told in full in *The Children of Húrin*. See J.R.R. Tolkien, *The Silmarillion*, ed. Christopher Tolkien (Boston: Houghton Mifflin, 2004); and J.R.R. Tolkien, *The Children of Húrin*, ed. Christopher Tolkien (Boston: Houghton Mifflin, 2007).

14. In this sense, Tolkien is in harmony with fellow twentieth-century Catholic novelists Walker Percy and Flannery O'Connor.

15. MacIntyre, *After Virtue*, xiv–xv.

16. Ibid.

17. Ibid., 19.

18. Ibid., 33.

19. Ibid., 34.

20. Crawford, *World Beyond*, 115–123.

21. MacIntyre, *After Virtue*, 74.

22. This form of management is exemplified by Frederick Taylor's Scientific Management. Frederick Winslow Taylor, *The Principles of Scientific Management* (New York: Cosimo Classics, 2012)

23. Mary Parker Follett is the mother of human resources, but her movement can be interpreted as a revisioning of Taylor's scientific management with a human mask over it. The depersonalized bureaucratic use of power is camouflaged by suggestion boxes. Mary Parker Follett, "How Must Business Management Develop in Order to Possess the Essentials of a Profession?" in *Business Management as a Profession,* ed. Henry C. Metcalf (Chicago: A. W. Shaw, 1927), 73–88.

24. MacIntyre, *After Virtue*, 25. See also for instance, Max Weber, *The Theory of Social and Economic Organization*, trans. A. M. Henderson and Talcott Parsons (New York: The Free Press, 1974).

25. MacIntyre, *After Virtue*, 77. Postman, *Technopoly*, 123–163.

26. MacIntyre, *After Virtue*, 107.

27. Arnett, Harden Fritz, and Bell, *Communication Ethics Literacy*, 37.

28. MacIntyre, *After Virtue*, 227.

29. Ibid., 108. Along these lines, Walter Fisher postulated that rather than defining humans as first and foremost rational creatures, we are story tellers, for our rationality is grounded upon the narratives that inform a culture's and individual's worldview. Walter R. Fisher, "Narration as a Human Communication Paradigm: The Case of Public Moral Argument," *Communication Monographs* Vol. 51, March 1984, 1–22.

30. MacIntyre, *After Virtue*, 206.

31. Ibid., 208.

32. Arnett, Harden Fritz, and Bell, *Communication Ethics Literacy*, 40.

33. MacIntyre, *After Virtue*, 144.

34. The term poetry refers to the traditional place of grammar within the ancient and medieval trivium system of the liberal arts. As will we developed in the final chapter of this book, grammar in this system is not the science of parsing the parts of a sentence, but rather the study of literature and the formation of cultural values through literature.

35. MacIntyre, *After Virtue*, 216.

36. In his "Semiotic Primer of the Self," Walker Percy notes that the very condition of our personness, found within language and consciousness, is communal because consciousness is etymologically a knowing of something with another person. Consciousness is inherently social and impossible for the "isolated individual." Percy, *Lost in the Cosmos*, 85–126.

37. Arnett, Harden Fritz, and Bell, *Communication Ethics Literacy*, 53.

38. Bradley J. Birzer, *J.R.R. Tolkien's Sanctifying Myth: Understanding Middle-earth* (Wilmington, DE: ISI Books, 2003), xxii.

39. MacIntyre, *After Virtue*, 220.

40. MacIntyre applies his narrative theory to the work of Jane Austen. The argument illustrated above is exemplified in Austen as she develops characters who come alive in plots that reveal certain moral principles. So, Marianne Dashwood in *Sense and Sensibility* demonstrates the dangers of one who feels to strongly, while the Crawfords in *Mansfield Park* show that people are not always what they seem to be. Indeed, the Crawfords, with their seeming ability and willingness to easily switch roles, are exemplars of the modern condition. Thus, notes MacIntyre, Austen's novels as a whole promote the virtue of constancy. Austen's most admirable characters (Elizabeth Bennet and Anne Elliot come to mind) make the most of their role rather than rebelling against it. The very word "character" suggests recognition of one's placement in a narrative. The virtue of constancy is the virtue of playing that role well. One of the many attractive qualities of Elizabeth Bennet is that she is able to subject social convention to a biting sense of humor while also giving social convention its due. It is characters such as the Crawfords or Lydia Bennet who mock and reject the authority of convention, of social narrative, who are on the receiving end of Austen's harshest judgments.

41. See Paul Ricoeur, *Time and Narrative* vols. 1–3, trans. Kathleen McLaughlin and David Pellauer (Chicago: University of Chicago, 1983, 1984, 1985).

42. MacIntyre, *After Virtue*, 220.

43. J. R. R. Tolkien, *The Silmarillion*, 16.

44. MacIntyre, *After Virtue*, 205.

45. Ronald C. Arnett and Pat Arneson, *Dialogic Civility in a Cynical Age* (Albany: State University of New York Press, 1999), 26.

46. MacIntyre, *After Virtue*, 72.

47. C. S. Lewis, *The Abolition of Man* (New York: HarperCollins, 2001), 81.

48. Similarly, Dietrich von Hildebrand argues that one of the problems of modern thought is that it is always trying to dismiss the phenomenological experiences of aspects of reality in order to see through to the "reality." What is accomplished in this move is a reduction of reality to "just" something else. For instance, the Freudian psychoanalysis reduces the experience of love to "just" sexual drive.

49. MacIntyre, *After Virtue*, 215.

50. De Zengotita, *Mediated*, 33–80.

51. Han makes clear that the prevalence of depression in society is the natural outgrowth failure in society of positivity, in contrast to the disciplinary society that came before, in which failure produces criminals and psychotics.

52. MacIntyre, *After Virtue*, xv.

53. His theory of story, especially fairy stories, is developed most clearly in his, "On Fairy Stories," as is cited above.

54. Stratford Caldecott, *The Power of The Ring* (New York: The Crossroad Publishing Company, 2012), xiii–xiv.

55. Tolkien said that from his works it could be deduced that he is a Christian, but that he is a Roman Catholic may not be able to be deduced from his works. More specifically, Tolkien states that he actually wrote *The Lord of the Rings* themed with Catholicism. In a letter to a Jesuit friend Tolkien clearly states: "*The Lord of the Rings* is of course a fundamentally religious and Catholic work; unconsciously at first, but

consciously in revision." See Humphrey Carpenter, Christopher Tolkien, eds., *The Letters of J.R.R. Tolkien* (Boston: Houghton Mifflin, 2000), 172 and 288.

56. Tolkien argues that fairy-stories are not simply stories about fairies, but they are about the place, Faërie. He bases his argument on the fact that the first recorded usage of the word fairy meant a place, and not a thing ("On Fairy-Stories" 37). The content of a fairy-story is part Tolkien states: "The definition of fairy-story—what it is, or what it should be—does not, then, depend on any definition or historical account of elf or fairy, but upon the nature of *Faërie*: the Perilous Realm itself, and the air that blows from that country I will not attempt to define that, nor to describe it directly. It cannot be done" ("On Fairy-Stories" 38). Though Tolkien explicitly states that he will not attempt to define Faërie, he does provide insight into the "Perilous Realm." He states that there is much more to Faërie than elves, trolls, and fairies, including: "the seas, the sun, the moon, the sky; and the earth, and all things that are in it: tree and bird, water and stone, wine and bread, and ourselves, mortal men, when we are enchanted" (Tolkien, "On Fairy-Stories" 38). Tolkien goes so far as to argue that good fairy-stories are about the "*adventures* of men in the Perilous Realm or upon its shadowy marshes" ("On Fairy-Stories" 38). For Tolkien, the essence of the Perilous Realm is the "Magical." Tolkien argues that, "Even fairy-stories as a whole have three faces: the Mystical towards the Supernatural; the Magical towards Nature; and the Mirror of scorn and pity towards Man. The essential face of Faërie is the middle one, the Magical" ("On Fairy-Stories" 52). Tolkien further states that, "Faërie itself may be most nearly translated by Magic—but it is magic of a peculiar mood and power, at the furthest pole from the vulgar devices of the laborious, scientific, magician" ("On Fairy-Stories" 39). Though Magic—not a primitive form of science—is the essence of Faërie, it is not an end in itself. Tolkien states that, "The magic of Faërie is not an end in itself, its virtue is in its operations: among these are the satisfaction of certain primordial human desires. One of these desires is to survey the depths of space and time. Another is (as will be seen) to hold communion with other living things" ("On Fairy-Stories" 41). Tolkien argues that there is one other "primal desire at the heart of Faërie," which is, "the realization, independent of the conceiving mind, of imagined wonder" (Tolkien, "On Fairy-Stories" 43). So, the Magic which is Faërie is the creation of, or the making real, imagined wonder. On account of this, Tolkien argues that, "if there is any satire present in the tale, one thing must not be made fun of, the magic itself. That must in that story be taken seriously, neither laughed at nor explained away" (Tolkien, "On Fairy-Stories" 39).

57. Raph Wood, *The Gospel According to Tolkien* (Louisville: Westminster John Knox Press, 2003), 33.

58. Joseph Loconte, *A Hobbit, a Wardrobe, and a Great War: How J.R.R. Tolkien and C.S. Lewis Rediscovered Faith, Friendship, and Heroism in the Cataclysm of 1914–1918* (Nashville, TN: Thomas Nelson Books, 2015).

59. Tolkien himself admitted that *The Silmarillion* and *The Lord of the Rings* are interdependent and that the former's intelligibility rests upon the latter. *Letters of Tolkien*, 136–136, and 143–161.

60. Tolkien, *The Silmarillion*, 16–17.

61. Tolkien, "On Fairy-Stories," 80–82.

62. Ibid., 79.

63. Ibid., 83.

64. Ibid., 85.

65. Harari, *Homo Deus*, 21–29.

66. Tolkien, "On Fairy-Stories," 85.

67. Ibid., 86–87.

68. *Letters of J.R.R. Tolkien*, 144.

69. Pearce, "True Myth," 87–88.

70. Kreeft, *The Philosophy of Tolkien*, 86–87.

71. Tolkien, *LOTR*, 711–712.

72. Tolkien, *LOTR*, 51.

73. In Tolkien's legendarium, "Men" are a race distinct from others races such as Eldar (Elves) and Dwarves. When Tolkien is referring to this specific race, he capitalizes the word. So shall we.

74. Tolkien, *LOTR*, 672.

75. Ibid., 671.

76. Ibid., 670.

77. Ibid., 784.

78. Ibid., 964–965.

79. Ibid., 368.

80. Ibid., 393.

81. Ibid., 778–779.

82. Ibid., 780.

83. Ibid., 871.

84. See Kreeft, *Philosophy of Tolkien*, 181.

85. Snell, *Acedia and Its Discontents*, 10–11.

86. See Percy, *Lost in the Cosmos*, 122.

87. See Jean M. Twenge, "Have Smart Phones Destroyed a Generation?" *Atlantic Monthly*, last modified September 2017. https://www.theatlantic.com/magazine/archive/2017/09/has-the-smartphone-destroyed-a-generation/534198/.

88. Hobbes, *Leviathan*, 187.

89. That the story concerns death and immortality is attested by Tolkien himself: "I do not think that even Power or Domination is the real centre of my story. It provides the theme of a War, about something dark and threatening enough to seem at the time of supreme importance, but that is mainly a 'setting' for characters to show themselves. The real theme for me is about something much more permanent and difficult: Death and Immortality: the mystery of the love of the world in a race 'doomed' to leave and seemingly lose it; the anguish in the hearts of a race 'doomed' not to leave it, until its whole evil-roused story is complete." *Letters of J.R.R. Tolkien*, 246.

90. Kreeft, *The Philosophy of Tolkien*, 94–101.

91. *Letters of J.R.R. Tolkien*, 285–286.

92. Tolkien, *The Silmarillion*, 64.

93. Ibid., 69.

94. Tolkien, *LOTR*, 32, 34.

95. Ibid., 32.

96. Caldecott, *The Power of the Ring*, 113.

97. Tolkien, *The Silmarillion*, 41. Emphasis added.

98. Ibid., 42.

99. Birzer, *J.R.R. Tolkien's Sanctifying Myth*, 57.

100. Tolkien, *The Silmarillion*, 239.

101. Birzer, *J.R.R. Tolkien's Sanctifying Myth*, 107.

102. See Smith, *Soul Searching*, 118–171. Note for example, Smith's research subject, sadly typical, who believes that cable television is evidence that God is good.

103. Lewis, *The Abolition of Man*, 76–77.

104. Birzer, *J.R.R. Tolkien's Sanctifying Myth*, 103.

105. Wood, *Gospel According to Tolkien*, 28.

106. Kreeft, *Philosophy of Tolkien*, 90.

107. Aristotle, *The Nicomachean Ethics*, 4–5, 1095a.

108. Aristotle, *The Nicomachean Ethics*, 50, 1115b15

109. Woods, *Gospel According to Tolkien*, 120.

110. In contrast to the technological pragmatism of modern thinking, the media ecology tradition is quite useful here because it postulates that technologies function as environments that influence not only first-person experience but society itself. See the following for a primary into media ecology: Lance Strate, *Media Ecology: An Approach to Understanding the Human Condition* (New York: Peter Lang, 2017).

111. Wood, *Gospel According to Tolkien*, 55.

112. Flannery O'Connor, *Collected Works* (New York: Library of America, 1988), 830–831.

113. Tocqueville, *Democracy in America*, 280.

114. Tolkien, *The Silmarillion*, 262.

115. Kreeft, *Philosophy of Tolkien*, 23–25. A criticism of Kreeft is he is too set on poking at "elites" that he romanticizes the common person, persistently praising the "bourgeois," unlike Flannery O'Connor who explicitly rejected the bourgeois mindset. Tolkien warns against the quest for material comfort that is the heart of bourgeois mentality. That is why O'Connor rejects it. As is noted in *The Lord of the Rings*, the hobbit ability to live in comfort is only possible due to the sacrifice of the Rangers. Hobbit simplicity must contain room for heroism. Tolkien's story shows that such heroism lurks in the hearts of hobbits, despite all outward appearances. Kreeft seems to confuse Hobbits for Nietzschean "last men."

116. Kreeft, *Philosophy of Tolkien*, 38.

117. Some of what follows owes a debt to Robert C. Koons, "T.S. Elliot, Populist," *First Things*, December 2018, 14–16.

Chapter 8

Healing the Anxiety of the Age

Throughout this book, we have detailed the symptoms and origins of the anxiety that plagues affluent and technological Western society. The Age of Anxiety is one name among many that attempts to raise awareness to the problems of our time. The ultimate source of the intellectual and spiritual anxiety of our society is the rejection of truths existing beyond the human mind. Rejecting the order of aristocracy, our age finds itself with no guiding values beyond liberty and equality. Freed from any social constrains, the individual finds itself at liberty to consume without limits. Such consumption, without limits, has led to the individual consuming itself and transforming into a mindless "zombie." The society of zombies was shown to have no connection to its place in the world, and lacking values beyond liberty and equality, cannot stop the destruction of the social world or environment itself. Lacking a value system beyond the artificial moral calculation of utilitarianism, one is given no reason to deny oneself for the sake of the common good. Seemingly left with no other option, we are witnessing the culture as it tears itself apart as political ideologues struggle to actualize their ideologies through the raw will to power.

Because our moral rhetoric is that of emotivism, one's moral views get wrapped up in one's "identity." One's "convictions" are not so much based on reason nor is one's fierce defense based on reasons, rather they are taken as emotions that grow out of individual identity. If ideas are simply emotions, then ideas (and morality) are merely expressions of power, a quest for recognition. Transgressive identity politics thus uses "weakness" as a kind of power. Intersectionality becomes a quest to determine which group has the least power, giving them more power. As such, intersectionality becomes a tool for some groups to dominate other groups. Absent any standard outside the self, philosophy/politics/morality/ideas are all just an ideological power game.[1] To cure the disease that is yielding these problems, the culture is in need of realistic narratives that can begin to resituate the self within the order of the cosmos. This chapter elucidates several ways to move forward and alleviate the anxiety of the current historical moment. These "solutions" begin on an individual level, for we all must take ownership over the problems of our age if there is to be true change. Change must start as a freely willed movement on the part of individuals. It cannot be forced. However, as was developed in earlier chapters of this book, humans by nature are social beings, not autonomous beings, and as such, a just society guides and teaches individuals within that society. Consequently, there must be values embodied within the social or we will be once again stuck with only equality and liberty to guide our society.

In some senses, the solutions that we offer may seem cliché or even commonsensical, like that of your mother telling you to brush your teeth, make your bed, and clean your room.[2] These "best practices" given to us by nagging mothers and fathers are often menial tasks and yet seemingly so burdensome to accomplish that one feels debilitated and avoids doing them altogether. These "best practices" are not sufficient for success but are necessary. Likewise, the solutions offered here are necessary and yet, likely, not sufficient, in and, of themselves. Though what we offer may seem like common sense, we exist in a time of such diversity and lack of narrative grounds that common sense no longer exists.[3] In many senses, common sense has vanished because of the failure of authoritative cultural institutions, such as the family and schools, to combat the hyperindividualism of the marketplace driven by neoliberalisms on both the part of the Left and the Right.[4]

To the degree that we are social creatures and our minds and beliefs are situated within and influenced by the collective nominalist orientation of our culture, we are ourselves immanentists whether we have thought about the issue before or not. The question arises whether one can be other than what is afforded by the limitations and constraints of the cultural orientation. Is there any way for the individual to be other than a part of the culture? Are we trapped in an immanent perspective that is inherently buffered from reality itself or is possible to become a realist when born into a culture of nominalism and relativism? We maintain that the individual is not trapped within one's cultural orientation because conversions—or *metanoia*—take place on a daily basis.[5] One can be convinced of alternative arguments, and deliberately acting differently than one has in the past can reform who a person habitually is. The solution to our anxiety rests in developing practices that can influence and develop who a person is and how they view and act in the world.

THE NECESSITY OF READING GOOD BOOKS

One of the most important cures for anxiety is the reading of good books. This solution should sound silly, but the fact that it needs to be given should frighten and produce a great deal of anxiety within the populous of the Age of Anxiety. Our society suffers from "reading atrophy" in that most people are recalcitrant to any reading that does not transmit information in a fashion than can be instantaneously processed.[6] Nicholas Carr has shown in his book, *The Shallows*, that there is a significant difference between reading physical books and reading material online. The first and most fundamental difference is that digital and online reading fosters distracted, shallow reading rather than focused, attentive deep reading.[7] The form of reading is different because in physical books readers read in a linear fashion that he calls "deep reading," whereas digital reading is performed largely in a "Z" pattern of skimming, which he calls "shallow reading." The difference between these forms of reading is tremendous, in that they hardwire our brains differently. Deep reading hardwires the brain in such a way as to allow and promote contemplation whereas shallow reading hardwires the brain for the quick processing of information. When one concentrates and loses oneself in a book, one begins to engage in deep reading, which in turn forms a "calm mind" rather than a "buzzing," distracted, and anxious mind.[8] Reading fosters long-term memory, which is the seat of understanding.[9] As such, it works against the distracted, fragmented state of so many people today. Reading good books increases vocabulary, cultivates a constructive approach to adversity, familiarity with sundry styles of thought, and first-hand experience of meaning.[10] Reading fosters a healthy individualism that varies from the pseudoindividualism that is purchased within the market.

The admittedly vague terminology of "good book" defies formulaic definition, but perhaps something more concrete than "you know it when you see it" is required. A good book seems to possess the following characteristics. First, there is some artistic quality to it. In short, it captures the imagination, having some level of beauty in the writing. This is true of both fiction and nonfiction, while being of greater importance in fiction. All good books should have some capacity of stirring the emotions, of encouraging the reader to enter into and truly inhabit the work. Second, a good book defies easy answers or easy agreement. A good book is provocative in the best sense, in that it provokes thought. While it may "shock," it does not do so for the sake of being "shocking." Good books, on some level, should stimulate a modicum of the unease that is the sign that one is learning. Finally, a good book bears multiple readings. Why do people read certain Shakespearean plays over and over? Shakespeare's work contains a level of artistic achievement and philosophical insight that allows the reader to engage most of his works multiple times and still find something new. This is an aspect of a book that is not trite or propagandistic. We should note that those works that are labeled "classics" usually meet this definition, but we do not wish to confuse "good books" with "classics." A good book as defined here may come from any era and from various genres (novels, histories, poetry, theater, etc.).

Corey Anton has recently made a beautiful appeal to college professors to assign good books. Requiring good books is often initially resisted by students because they are shaped by a media environment to be "mindless consumers of data" that have difficulty distinguishing between "relevant information and irrelevant information."[11] The practice of requiring text-books, rather than good books, fosters education as an information trans-mission model instead of a model of formation. The information within a textbook is easily accessible because it is pre-packaged in the form of bolded key terms, systematically outlined chapter points, and banal examples that even the lower primates could understand. However, ideas are not like food in a refrigerator, for they cannot simply be pulled out of a text.[12] This analogy is worthy of a great deal of contemplation, which we assume our readers can do because they are readers. Ideas must be actively engaged with and cannot be passively transmitted from one mind to another, but this notion is quickly dismissed because we exist in a technological moment that privileges the instantaneous and easy reception of information.

For example, what is the point of reading Jane Austen's *Pride and Prejudice* when I can simply watch any number of movie renditions of the book? There is no need to watch the brilliant BBC mini-series rendition when I can get "the point" through a two-hour movie starring Keira Knightley. Fur-thermore, there is no need to even watch this film when I can expeditiously find a twelve-minute animated CrashCourse interpretation on YouTube.[13] Even "better," one can watch a four-minute "Thug Notes" summary that is far more entertaining as it translates the story into contemporary urban lan-guage and tropes, all while providing themes for conversation.[14] In the most extreme, there appears to be no point in reading or even watching when one can be told in a single sentence that Jane Austen's *Pride and Prejudice* is the tale of how love and money can complicate relationships within the British aristocracy of the last years of the eighteenth century. It should be obvious to any reader of this book, that this orientation fundamentally misses out on the experience and lessons learned from the wisdom of Jane Austen through her characters. However, any cynical critic will quickly note that spending one's time on this long and complex novel is an inefficient waste of time because its lessons could nonetheless be provided as information, and more impor-tantly, little social capital will be built or utilized through spending one's time on the novel. The likelihood in the Age of Anxiety for a conversation about *Pride and Prejudice* to come up is slim, and anyone's understanding of the story will come off as eccentricity and as trivial elitism, especially in an environment in which politicians, leaders of industry, and even university administrators berate the value of liberal education.

Whether or not one has read any individual classic text is beyond the point. Our appetites are informed by what we eat.[15] If we are consistently gorging ourselves on easily-transmitted-and-processed information, we will desire that in the rest of our lives. Whereas reading good books and engaging with ideas is like eating a fine meal that takes time and effort to make and cultivation to appreciate. A part of the difficulty here lies in the fact that as our engagement with ideas has declined, our ability to make substantial, qualitative judgments has likewise declined. The relativism of our age and lack of ability to engage with the qualitative dimensions of reality, leads many in society unable to distinguish between a McDonalds hamburger and one prepared by a Michelin star chef. Having reduced qualitative distinctions to personal preference, the culture cannot see that a preference for grade-D quasi-beef washed in ammonia over USDA Prime sirloin is problematic. The point here is that reading good books inherently involves engaging with ideas no matter what those ideas are. In Thomistic terms, one might make a distinction between *curiositas*, an inordinate love of knowledge that suggests a lack of restraint or a desire to "cut corners" in the pursuit of knowledge, and *studiositas*, which contains the notion of attention, discipline, and temperance. A textbook, for example, in a simple, didactic manner provides the illusion of easy command of a subject. But due to its abstraction from human experience its knowledge is incomplete, perhaps to the point of being false. This encourages the vice of *curiositas*. In contrast, a novel like *Pride and Prejudice* takes time and contemplation to understand while its narrative form actually gives a more thorough and thus truer depiction of its subject, helping the reader both learn more while also developing the habits of *studiositas*.[16] In its form, reading good books fosters one's ability to engage with qualitative aspects of reality and to truly think for oneself. Reading, in its linear form, results in the formation of the individual fixed perspective.[17] Thus, in general, reading good books provides a superior intellectual and moral experience as compared to film, although film has its clear virtues.

The discovery of the existence of hidden effects produced by the forms of varying technologies is what led to Marshall McLuhan to hyperbolically claim that the "medium is the message." This hyperbole is taken by many to mean that content does not matter, which could not be further from the truth. Simply reading good books may predispose a person to realism, but it will not make a person a realist. If one has been persuaded by the ideas of this book, then one is intellectually primed to dig deeper into books and arguments by realists. Engaging with these ideas over time can help form one's understanding and orientation of the world. One cannot will oneself into belief. If one is intellectually primed and engages with a set of literature, one's worldview can be changed. For example, one cannot will oneself to believe the moon is made of green cheese. However, if one immerses oneself in conspiracy literature about the moon being made of green cheese, it will likely not be long before one finds oneself believing that the moon is made of green cheese, or at least see such a reality as plausible. The critical reader of this text will notice in this analogy that it opens itself up to comparing the position of realism to the position of the moon being made of green cheese. However, this criticism stretches the analogy too far, in that the one claim is a proposition about material reality that can be proved or disproved through empirical means as well as standards and rules of logic itself. Whereas realism itself is a philosophical system, which, like all philosophical systems, is based upon axiomatic principles and propositions that cannot be proven with certainty. Grappling with these ideas may not convince a person, but they necessarily will be taking ideas seriously.

One of the anxious age's pathologies is an excessive emphasis on the present. This is part of the solipsism of the age. Reading good books, especially those marked as "classics," takes the reader outside of his or her own time. Modern education, especially higher education, is in the grip of both historicism and ideology. It is historicist precisely to the extent to which the age contains the lazy assumption that the past has nothing to teach the present. Merely by virtue of living later in time, it is believed that the present age knows more than the past and thus can arrogantly neglect the past. In addition, ideologies embedded in literary criticism and critical history encourage readers to approach the past merely in light of current ideological trends. To the extent the past differs, it is to be condemned. Thus, the "old books" are read merely to reveal the oppressive power structures embedded in the text. Interestingly, modern ideology refuses to consider that it could ever do with some debunking itself.

As C. S. Lewis helpfully reminds us, though, each age has its own biases, its prejudices, those things it accepts uncritically.[18] A correction for those biases is to read books from a different time. As Lewis notes, reading books from the future would be just as helpful, but they haven't been written yet. So we are left with old books. While the past will have its own assumptions or biases, they will be different from ours. Thus, we can use these books to engage in helpful dialogue. This is true in two ways. First, we can converse about the ways in which contemporary ideas differ from those of the past. We must do so in the spirit of *pistis*, in that thinkers of the past might have something to teach us. While we should be appropriately skeptical of the past and avoid nostalgic credulity, we must also be open to the notion that some matters may have been known better by thinkers of the past. Second, the past is not a monolith. Are we to believe that Aristotle, Confucius, Dante,

Shakespeare, and Jean-Jacques Rousseau all believed the same thing? This is why study of the "great books" is often called "the great conversation." Indeed, a "great books" study is likely far more "multicultural" and "diverse" than reading contemporary books by all sorts of people of different genders, hues, and geographies, yet who all seem to think the same way. A sound reading program starts with classics that have stood the test of time and therefore develop good taste. From there, one can more prudently choose from contemporary literature.

The point being made here is that when one finds arguments to be persuasive, and one begins to take on those arguments themselves, the other side still exists but is no longer a personal intellectual option. For instance, if one engages with the literature and debates between nominalism and realism, one will eventually have to make a judgment about the claims being made. One cannot remain agnostic about a stasis point forever. A *krisis*, or moment of judgment, will be reached, and one side's arguments will become more persuasive than the other, or one will have to begin structuring one's own answer to the matter at hand. Active discursive thought (*ratio*) cannot continue perpetually, and when the limits of *ratio* are reached, the passive component of the mind (*intellectus*) begins to shape one's perspective. When one forms a judgment, one gains a mental state of certitude about one's position. In effect, one has been persuaded, and the alternative position no longer presents itself as a viable option for belief. The formation of judgment is freeing, in the sense that choice is largely the result of ignorance. If one has mental certitude about what is best, the alternative ceases to be a real option. For instance, if a person is persuaded and convinced by arguments that eating meat is immoral, the existence of steak as an option on a menu does not represent a real choice for that person, much as carrying and firing a gun did not represent a real choice for Desmond Doss. In a pluralistic society, the presence of alternative cultural options from which one can "choose" one's identity creates anxiety and self-doubt only for the person that lacks commitment in and conviction to their own narrative and cultural ground. If one's engagement with the narrative remains shallow, the individual will likewise be shallow and still exist with limitless options and choice making. When this is the case, all the choices are equally arbitrary and meaningless; hence, Taylor's Malaise of Modernity. If one, however, truly engages with a perspective and orientation, it begins to form one's orientation. In the final analysis, this solution is still inherently wrapped up in the mental for it is a part of the intellectual aspect of the problem. The potential that meaningful change will be made simply by reading a bit of Aristotle is slim. One suggestion might be the formation of reading groups. The pursuit of meaning is not a solitary affair. As one engages with great texts, doing so within a community of friends allows for a dialogue that makes ideas present, more real. J. R. R. Tolkien of course had the Inklings, a group of likeminded Oxfordians who shared books and ideas with one another. Few of us can hope for such an august fellowship, but we should seek out such community as can be had. This is yet another reason why good books should be the center of a university education rather than stale textbooks. University life allows for a ready-made experience of reading the best books with advanced guidance amongst friends. All this said, we also offer below embodied practices, which are grounded with philosophical realism, as a further solution to the problem of anxiety.

THE NEED FOR TRULY LIBERAL
LEARNING AND EDUCATION

Neil Postman grappled with the problems of the surrender of culture, as a source of human values and meaningfulness, to the technological-bureaucratic rationality. He laid out numerous problems that were the result of our culture's orientation toward confusing human progress with scientific and technological progress. A few of the problems he addressed included the eradication of human judgment through bureaucratic decision making, the overqualification of statistics, and the inability to take seriously that which cannot be studied through science. These problems have only grown since he wrote, especially with the takeover of human decision making by the growth of big data and algorithms. Similar to MacIntyre, Postman rightly feared that these attributes of our society would replace democracy with a society managed by techno-bureaucratic specialists. He provides the image of the "loving-resistance fighter" as a model for individuals desiring to make substantial change on a personal level.[19] He provides numerous qualities of the loving-resistance fighter including respect for the elderly and religious tradition. Though his loving-resistance fighter and all of its attributes are needed within society, his vision is limited because it does not address the core problem of nominalism. Postman advocated for the middle position of technocracy which stands between traditional tool-using cultures and technopoly. Essentially, Postman advocated for a society that would mirror the early Enlightenment when progress and cultural tradition had an equal footing within society to compete with one another and guide us in a humanistic fashion as we experience rapid and vast scientific and technological advancement.

Postman's vision is not enough because it places culture and tradition in the place of being merely conventional and consequently optional. As long as all traditions are treated equally, without some standard to adjudicate the value of them, they are left as optional choices for one to express one's identity. These traditions make no normative claim on society and are once again limited as private, subjective preferences. As was detailed in chapter 1, this leaves us within the indifference of de Zengotita's mediated blob and the malaise of Taylor's *Secular Age*. Reverence, faithfulness, responsibility, and truthfulness to ideas are attitudes that are the requisite foundations of moral life.[20] In addition, as the liberal Enlightenment has become "more itself," it has tended to upset the balance of the early Enlightenment age wherein as a matter of practice the individualism and skepticism of Enlightenment thinking was mitigated by a religio-cultural heritage that was more communal and devout. Thus, "first wave" Enlightenment "built better than it knew," with previous cultural commitments mitigating the excesses of Enlightenment liberalism and vice versa. However, as liberalism has totalized its claims to public things, that balance has been lost and liberalism has become as much a threat as a defender of liberty-rightly-understood.[21] The challenge in the Age of Anxiety is to once again foster experiences with the qualitative aspects of reality on the part of individuals and foster public means to deliberate about those values. Only when faith in ideas and values is taken seriously and privileged publicly as reasonable can we begin to truly fight back against the anxiety of our age. However, we recognize that this project is not without controversy.

The privatization of judgment and values has led to an extreme relativism in our culture because it is assumed that there is no rational way to deliberate about qualitative dimensions of reality.[22] We do not assume that everyone will or even can agree about such matters. But without an orientation that takes seriously ideas and values, we are condemned to the polarization and solipsism of the Age of Anxiety. Only through taking ideas seriously and developing public means of deliberation will we be able to begin to foster reconciliation and consensus between the divergent perspectives in our pluralistic age.

There is no need to reinvent the wheel in order to develop public means of deliberation. Western education used to be oriented toward this goal. The classical trivium as a model for education is a program for developing individuals that can think for themselves because they are taught how to think and not merely what to think. The classical trivium included the studies of grammar, dialectics, and rhetoric. Grammar is likely to be the most contested in the twenty-first century because it was essentially the study of literature, which provided the moral ground for students and society.[23] The content of the grammatical education has already been contested in programs of English in terms of what ought to be taught as the Canon. At minimum, local communities ought to foster a discussion about the types of literature, including forms of media such as television, movies, and internet content that ought to be taught to young students. It is within the grammar stage that young people can begin to develop the taste in good books articulated above.

From there, students need to be taught how to systematically think and recognize fallacious argumentation. This project was the realm of dialectics, which is akin to, but not limited to, the study of logic. Dialectics trains students in the creation of arguments and the testing of evidence. At this stage, students are ingrained within the *dissoi logoi* of the Sophists. The *dissoi logoi* is the idea that all claims can be seen from a different perspective. Though the *dissoi logoi* is attributed primarily to the Sophists, it is culminated in the Socratic dialectic and exemplified in the dialogues of Plato.[24] All claims have at least two sides and students are trained in arguing from a multiplicity of positions. Along these lines, Aristotle argues that students must be trained in making arguments for both sides of any position. Not only does this produce an element of empathy within society because one can see from another's eyes but it also fosters the relative certainty of *pistis* rather than a false certainty about one's worldview that is seemingly tearing apart the current political world. Instead of demonizing the other side of political dispute, such as abortion, one can see the rational arguments—the best arguments, not the most popular—of the other side.

Finally, the study of rhetoric taught students how to speak eloquently and most importantly, persuasively, which necessitates understanding one's audience. Rhetoric was the high point of the trivium because it put one's training into practice and formed speakers in persuasion and eloquence. In the classical orientation, the surest sign of wisdom was one's ability to speak well. Rhetorical education was postulated as an art of *phronesis*, or practical wisdom, because it requires theoretical knowledge to be put into practical application in society. Taken as a whole, the trivium pedagogical system is purposed toward the production of virtuous citizens with encyclopedic knowledge that desire to give their lives over to leadership and to the betterment of society.[25] This model of education flies directly in the face of the techno-bureaucratic training that currently dominates both primary and higher education. Administrators and many faculty comfort themselves in the creation of twenty-first century wage-slaves because graduates "can get jobs." If universities were to concentrate more on the longitudinal career paths of graduates with liberal educations rather than immediate job placements, they would find practical justification for re-evaluating their current orientation.

However, the solution offered rests upon a specific understanding of the human person, as an intellectual animal that is embedded within a material-socio-cultural matrix. The human person is neither a genetically-biologically-sociologically-linguistically determined entity nor an autonomous self that is most free when uninfluenced by external factors.[26] The human person, having both body and mind, is embedded in the world and is influenced, but not determined, by factors such as genetics, sociology, or language. Being influenced and biased by one's embeddedness necessitates a healthy assessment of the certainty of one's perspective. All orientations—including scientific materialism—are grounded upon an element of faith (*pistis*) because the immaterial, axiomatic principles that found all orientations cannot be known empirically with certainty.

We must re-evaluate the nature of faith in our pluralistic society, for one cannot take for granted one's first principles no matter how apparently self-evident they seem. For instance, even the law of noncontradiction—one of Aristotle's necessary first principles for understanding the world in a coherent fashion—is called into question by modern quantum physics and postmodern, poststructural thought.[27] The dual meaning of *pistis* as faith and persuasion is helpful for building a constructive approach to cultural narratives and traditions in a pluralistic society. *Pistis*, as faith, constructively produces a mental state of certitude, while as persuasion, allows one to see that others are not persuaded of certain propositions. For instance, when a juror is persuaded of the guilt of the person on trial, the juror has mental certitude about their position, but can still rationally disagree with another juror about the evidence. This perspective need not yield radical skepticism for it utilizes faith and reason as its guiding hermeneutic rather than doubt. It builds upon the idea that reason, while having limits, can provide a relative degree of certainty (*pistis*) about matters that could not be known with certainty. Lack of absolute certainty is not a cause for epistemological despair nor of prideful extremism that denies the legitimate philosophical grounds maintained by the Other. Maintaining a healthy balance between faith and reason allows individuals to constructively take seriously their own sources of meaning and live without anxiety in a multicultural environment.

One may skeptically question whether such programs can be mandated, but we emphatically assert that they can and should be. There is no less philosophy assumed within the behavioristic, relativistic, and nominalistic education system, which requires that students take some form of sociology or psychology in their high school education. It would behoove us to allow the option to take psychology and sociology, but require classes within logic and rhetoric of all students in our democratic society. However, the fact is that we increasingly do not live in a democratic society, but rather a techno-bureaucratic state run by specialists that manufactures consent and does not want its citizenship knowing how to think for itself and deconstruct propaganda.[28] The experience of living within a pseudodemocracy is testified by the popularity of shows such as Netflix's *Black Mirror* and United States's *Mr. Robot*. Along these lines, Adam Curtis has documented the philosophical assumptions of the techno-bureaucratic system and the creation of a state of "hypernormalisation," or a state of uncertainty about the nature of reality where fakeness is identified with reality, through the development of politics as theater played out in the media.[29] In the "post-truth" world of "alternative facts," and "fake news," the liberal arts provide students coherent ways of thinking upon which they can ground perspective. With that said, the classical education within the liberal arts did not end with the trivium but was oriented toward the quadrivium which included the arts of arithmetic (theory of number), music (theory of number in practice), geometry (theory of space), and astronomy (theory of space in practice).[30] It is not that these studies themselves need to be reproduced, though it may be advisable, but rather that all practical sciences directly relate to the systematical thinking developed in the trivium. The point is that the education system provided orientation and practice involving the material world itself, which brings us to the necessity of engaging in leisure.

THE NECESSITY OF LEISURELY ACTIVITY

In order to combat the immanentism of the nominalist disease, one must get out of one's head and engage with reality itself. There are numerous ways that this can take place. We will draw from the beautifully written *The World Beyond Your Head* by Mathew Crawford. This text should be mandatory reading within the Age of Anxiety. Crawford develops a phenomenological realism, grounded within Aristotelianism, among other lines of thought, to show how one can get outside of one's head and pierce through the modernist buffer from reality experienced by the self. In order to have a grasp of reality beyond one's head, one must triangulate one's understanding with reference to the material world, others, and history. This triangulation of one's perspective is "a moral accomplishment" because to do so one must love "the truth more than you love your own current state of understanding."[31] The triangulation of one's perspective is found within the crafts or practices.

The promotion of virtue through craft directly relates to MacIntyre's proposition of the narrative mindset, which was developed at length in chapter 7. Practice or craft is "any coherent and complex form of socially established cooperative human activity through which goods internal to that form of activity are realized in the course of trying to achieve those standards of excellence which are appropriate to, and partially definitive of, that form of activity, with the result that human powers to achieve excellence, and human conceptions of the ends and goods involved, are systematically extended."[32] Practice is related to narrative, in that both assume activity. The virtuous life is not one that is abstracted from action, but participates in it. The goal is to act *well*. Virtue, it is to be recalled, means "excellence." MacIntyre encourages us to see life as a kind of craft. He is not interested in promoting mere skills, but rather entering into a practice, or craft, that has a tradition, an authority, and standards of excellence.

Virtues are cultivated through the practices of crafts. Throwing a football is a skill, but playing football is a practice or craft.[33] To play football well is to enter into a community and to submit oneself to an authority. There are people who know better than I how to engage in various football skills—blocking a defender or throwing the ball—and I need instruction so as to excel at the practice. The practice of football would entail the team performing excellently, with each player doing his part. The practice has meaning for both individuals and the whole. For the individual, the excellence is internal as well as external. One's character is shaped as one imbibes the authority of practice and develops virtues. In football, it might be such virtues as courage, attention, dedication, perseverance, collegiality, forbearance. One might have to learn how to maintain pride in defeat and humility in victory. To this extent, to cheat at a practice is to defeat the purpose. While winning, in the case of football, is a measure of excellence, it is not the excellence football aims at. It is understood as part of the authority to which one must submit that a team may only win by following certain rules. That's why certain teams might be held in a kind of contempt if they are perceived to be cheaters, for example, the Patriots being one of the most infamous and hated teams in sports. Their excellence, not skill, is being called into question. Practice rules out all "all subjectivist and emotivist analyses of judgment."[34]

Loving truth more than one's own perspective is problematic in the Age of Anxiety because the members of the age are indoctrinated and enculturated into an emotivistic system of hyperindividualism, which is inherently relativistic and solipsistic. The current historical moment is defined by the experience of being buffered from reality and its recalcitrance to our affluence and technology. The trials and difficulties of life are largely obsolesced by technological progress. Indeed, this is witnessed by the fact that for the first time in history more people die from overeating than malnutrition; fast-food diets kill more people today than natural catastrophes or human-on-human violence.[35] The "smart" world we are creating is increasingly modeled to eliminate all moments of "helplessness" or "deep conflict[s] between the will and the world."[36] When problems do arise, the well-adjusted, easy-button seeking subject asks for help instead of figuring out how one should act in order to solve a problem.[37] In interpersonal relationships, instead of dealing with problematic coworkers, we expect higher management to take care of the problem. In so many realms of life, our problems are solved by finding an "app" for every task at hand.[38] There are even relaxation apps designed to cure us of the anxiety caused by having too many apps. So far removed are we from basic life skills that young adults have problems "adulting," and adults use an app to have someone do their grocery shopping. Rather than being a culture of "do-ers," we are a culture of "watchers" and "pliable choosers." It is not far-fetched to envision our truly smart technologies eventually having algorithms so efficient at behavior predication that we ourselves will not even have to think for ourselves.[39] The self that has developed no character of one's own because it is buffered from the recalcitrance of reality is inherently fragile, juvenile, and narcissistic.[40] In effect, we need to check our toxic decadent technological privilege before it ends up corroding the very essence of what makes us human persons!

The world of physical objects develops one's individuality because it is within the natural and mechanical world that one must respond to necessity and contingency. For example, one is not a good cook because one self-identifies as a good cook. In order to become truly a good cook, one must respond and learn from the recalcitrance of the material world. If I attempt to cook an over-easy egg and it turns out to be burnt and over hard, necessity and contingency must be addressed, in that I cannot simply perform the same actions and expect a different result. One must respond to factors such as the heat of the pan, the amount of oil or butter used, and also the amount of time the egg is in the pan. Through adjustments made in a process of trial and error one can master the cooking of an egg to order every time. Not only can a person become a good cook with practice, but also, over time, have an experience that shapes one's character. This formation of character naturally relieves the anxiety of the age because it forms the self upon something more than boundless choice.

Character, classically understood, is a stamp placed on a person through experience and is revealed within one's habitual "pattern of responses to a variety of situations."[41] Character develops as one's will is matured and formed into an adult will. "The adult will" according to Crawford, "is not something self-contained: it is situated in, and formed by, the contingencies of the world beyond one's head. The kind of self that accepts this elemental fact contrasts with, and therefore brings into clarifying relief, the more fragile kind of self that is posited in contemporary ethics and fostered by contemporary technologies."[42] The childish will attempts to force its perspective onto reality itself: "if only I will it more, my egg will turn out the way I want it to." However, the adult will recognizes that one must adjust and learn from experience. Character is created, and through the miracle of time, habits form that make the cooking of an over-easy egg a simple and thoughtless task. This is thoughtless not because it is easy or merely mechanical, but rather because the activity and all the deliberate decisions and judgments that go into one's relationship with the world itself are ingrained within one's habits. This engagement with the material world, necessity, and contingency is only one part of the triangulation.

The second aspect of triangulating one's relationship with reality is to converse with and learn from other people. Again, pursuit of a meaningful life is not a solitary pursuit. This aspect of the triangulation of one's perspective with reality is especially formative because it requires the humility of one to submit to the judgments of others. Furthermore, formal education in an art requires not just submission to another, but to be successful, obedience to the authority of someone that has more knowledge and experience. These acts of submission and obedience may sound like threats to individuality, but they are paradoxically liberating because one's formation is more expeditious when one does not attempt to reinvent the wheel at every step of the way. One can only build upon the greatness of those past and present if one is able recognize and learn from the collective wisdom of a tradition.[43] For instance, one can learn through discussing with other people that one over-salts eggs. Though the nuances of one's particular taste are subjective, there can be objective standards based upon general consensus with the properly functioning human tongue with regard to the levels of salt. More importantly, one also learns the context and ground of what ingredients go with one another, what types of food complement each other, and what types of food and spices and herbs do not go with one another. Anxiety is reduced through the self being embedded within a sociohistorical moment in contrast to the loneliness caused by autonomy.

Finally, since the world and people exist in time, the third point of triangulation of the self with reality is developing an orientation within history. Human beings, as has been argued throughout this text, are situated beings, not autonomous laws unto themselves. The deepest and most truly unique individuals have developed excellence in an art, and that excellence is responsive to and understands its place within the art, both in terms of the current historical moment as well as the moments that came before. To utilize again the analogy of cooking, the greatest cooks, and more importantly the most unique individuals, not only are skilled cooks, but understand the history of a particular cuisine and how it has changed over time. When one masters these points of triangulation, one becomes a unique individual within a tradition. As any musician or athlete will recognize, one can only improvise after a masterly of certain fundamentals. Recognition of one's unique capabilities is only received from peers "whose vision has been sharpened and sensitized to the relevant considerations through a process of initiation."[44] As one's perspective is triangulated in relation to the material world, others, and history, anxiety is decreased because one's self is grounded in a community and the world itself. Additionally, as one engages in embodied practices, the mind is at rest within the practice itself.

DECREASED ANXIETY THROUGH EDUCATION AND LEISURE

Thus far, we have argued how reading good books can help alleviate the anxiety of our age, how engaging with realist philosophy as a subset of good books, and how developing skilled practices in relation to the traditions of those skilled practices can help to combat the meaninglessness of the Age of Anxiety. Argument has been given as to why these practices can help cure the disease of our age, but one may contend that such small and potentially cliché solutions cannot solve such a grandiose problem. However, we contend that there is more proof to the value of these suggestions for our age. In particular, with regard to reading and engaging with good books and developing skill practices, one becomes simply too attentive to other matters to fret over oneself. Anxiety, self-doubt, depression, and despair are the products of idleness, *acedia*, or lack of leisure.[45] In contrast to the drawing outside of oneself through leisure, *acedia* is a drawing into oneself and loving oneself more than relation to the world and others.[46] It makes sense that identity politics has flourished in an environment of *acedia* produced by affluence and technological advancement. When one truly engages in reading and skilled practices, that is, leisure projects, one loses oneself in the activity.[47]

The value of losing oneself in activity can be seen in the basic analogy of losing oneself within the playing of sports. If one wants to be good at a game like basketball, one cannot be self-conscious during the playing of the game. Self-consciousness of what one is doing is important during practice so that one can become better at skills like dribbling and accurately shooting a free throw. However, once one figures out how to perform a skill, the skill must become habitual and arise from one's muscle memory, not consciousness of what one is doing. If one is focused upon oneself during the game, one inevitably makes bigger mistakes than one would have had just played the game and focused, not on oneself, but on reacting to others on the court and the ball. The more one is "in the game," the better one plays. When one focuses upon oneself in the game, not only do mistakes increase, but anxiety is naturally produced. Anyone who has ever teed-up a golf ball with water, in play will recognize the phenomenon.[48] Importantly, this losing of oneself within the habits, or repeated judgments of past experience, is liberating for the self.[49]

The freedom and dignity produced by the decreased anxiety through the loss of self is in direct contrast to the slavery produced through the annihilation the self—desubjectification or the death instinct—within programmed, automated life.[50] The annihilation of the self can be seen in the binge-watching behaviors in consuming Netflix and Vudu programming as well as the common experience of going down a "YouTube hole" in which one watches suggested video after another to find oneself to have wasted a full hour of one's time. The annihilation of the self is also seen in the behaviors of digital addiction in which a person automatically tries to kill any moment of nonstimulation, that is, boredom, which is a sight for self-reflection, with the distraction of one's cell phone. Worst of all is that this addiction is a part of the programming developed by "brain hackers" hired by app developers. This annihilation of the self creates a one-dimensionality within human persons and flattens culture, which Crawford likens to the "great pornification" in which the prevalence of pornography has created a conformist one-dimensionality of porn tropes that mediate the intimate lives of a vast portion of our society.[51] This programmed one-dimensionality creates the zombies that were spoken of in chapter 4 and the artificial intelligence described in chapter 5. The self is effectively enslaved to the designs of others when the self is annihilated in this fashion, whereas it develops and grows when one loses oneself in skilled, leisure activities. Reading and leisure activities deepen the dimensionality of the human person, whereas digital distraction emaciates it.

The development of skilled practices as forms of leisure that one performs for love of the activity itself has the effect of producing culture. Rather than merely consuming goods and products of the arts, individuals produce the components of culture. The individual creation of cultural artifacts inherently creates diversity of goods, whereas mass production promotes standardization and conformity. The culture and community grow when instead of consuming simply fine arts like music, members of the culture play and produce music with one another. Celebration naturally emerges when people personally have goods that contribute to the community. Festivity is only able to take place when the community produces the crafts such as learning to play music, pottery, sewing, carpentry, gardening, cooking, and other crafts that can be shared with others. The celebratory festivity is a public affirmation of the goodness of existence and stands in stark contrast to the nihilism promoted by Ligotti and the absurdity of modern existentialism.

As individuals produce the components of culture, concomitantly members of society begin to develop and deepen as individuals and begin to engage with immaterial values and make qualitative, value judgments. When one begins to learn how to cook, or whatever the leisure activity may be, one begins to appreciate the differences between good cooking and bad cooking. One begins to appreciate the difference between a mechanically, mass produced Danish that one purchases from a gas station, wrapped in plastic and infused with preservatives that will allow it to last through a nuclear apocalypse and a homemade artisan Danish that will go bad if not eaten within a day or two. Entering into skilled traditions forms one's appreciation of the qualitative dimensions of reality. One shifts in this sense from a hermeneutic of privilege and entitlement to a hermeneutic of appreciation and gratitude. The development of leisure activities creates culture and provides an antienvironment against the anxiety of our age. The cultural shift to a hermeneutic of appreciation found within meaningful work leads to the celebration of communal festivity in society.

The connection between leisure and culture is eloquently developed by the philosopher Josef Pieper, in his books, *Leisure: The Basis of Culture* and *In Tune with the World: A Theory of Festivity*. The hermeneutic of appreciation that comes from leisure and culture is also seen, experienced, and promoted by true festivity, which is the activity of communities coming together to share in an abundance with one another and give thanks for what we have. When human life is degraded to the state of *animal laborans*, we have lost our capacity for festivity or communal celebration because "only meaningful work can provide the soil in which festivity flourishes," for festivity arises from the joy of living.[52] Meaningful work and festivity have a mutual relationship, in that "when the one dries up, the other withers." Festivity is not possible for *animal laborans* because life is reduced to the absurd notion of finding meaning in the Sisyphean tasks of work performed for the utilitarian function of sustaining life itself.[53] Indeed, Camus' vision of "celebrating the absurd" through envisioning Sisyphus as joyous is antithetical to true festive celebration because it does not allow "room for the spontaneity of life which is indispensable to festal exaltation."[54] The point here is that the connection between skilled activities, tradition, and culture is not an abstract, idealistic solution to our problem. The consumerism of the Age of Anxiety is an anti-culture—planned, marketed, purchased, and then discarded—while leisure activities produce meaningful culture, which provides its members with purpose and joy within life.

There is an intimate relationship between the development of culture, the health of human communities, and the celebration of festivity. The affluent bourgeois is not able to truly experience and appreciate the joy of festival because it arises "only out of the foundation of a life whose ordinary shape is given by the working day."[55] Indeed, speaking to the nihilism of the Age of Anxiety, festivity is threatened by the perspective that "man's daily life, taken as a whole, is nothing but vexation, meaningless bustle, deadly drudgery, in a word: an absurdity."[56] On the one hand, threatening festivity and culture is the totalitarian state in which labor is glorified and romanticized by government propaganda and, on the other side, the nihilism contained within the West's consumerist capitalism. The task of choosing happiness in the midst of the absurd world is an incoherent position to take.[57] This incoherence adds to the anxiety of life within the twentieth and twenty-first centuries. Pieper notes that the idea of festivity must move past and transcend any conception of "a day free of servile work."[58]

In the ancient world, the *artes serviles* were not inherently looked at with contempt but rather referred to inherently utilitarian activity that has no inherent value beyond serving some external purpose.[59] The counter part of servile work was "free activity, *ars liberalis*," not inactivity. The liberal arts are activities that are meaningful in themselves, and do not serve a purpose outside of themselves.[60] Festivity is related to free activity or liberal arts because it is removed from utilitarian motivations and is meaningful in itself.[61] Indeed Pieper finds it troubling that with the death of this understanding of free activity, we lose our capacity to resist the totalitarian movement to reduce human purpose to labor.[62] It is for this very reason that society in general and specifically those within higher education ought to fight to the death against those politicians and administrators who seek to kill the liberal arts and turn higher education into vocational training.[63] It is almost inconceivable that in 1963, well before the age of people willingly having their personal time stolen from them by work through the consistent connection to work via one's mobile phone and computer, Pieper warned that society has reached a tipping point in which our ability to be liberated from work is all but past.[64] We exist in an age where it is ubiquitous for work to interrupt life outside of work through the pinging of a notification on one's cell phone.

As was noted from the outset of this project, we will not be able to solve this problem until we come to terms with a conception of what it means to be human.[65] The experience of festivity renews us because it contains a contemplative element, in which the mind is at rest.[66] Along these lines, Pieper maintains that we must learn to listen in silent meditation upon existence itself.[67] Likewise, Han argues that the bored, distracted, "hyperactive ego" of the age must learn to accept the "gift of listening," which "is based on the ability to grant deep, contemplative attention."[68] Contemplation must be rediscovered for in it, "one steps outside oneself, so to speak, and immerses *oneself* in the surroundings."[69] In the media ecology tradition, Walter Ong has argued that language itself lives on the medium of silence and, as has been noted, our ability to use language and speech is a fundamental aspect of our humanity itself.[70] The call to contemplative self-reflection is mirrored by numerous and diverse thinkers including Charles Taylor, Sherry Turkle, and Robert Cardinal Sarah as a direct response to the noisy *acedia* of technological society. We must learn to balance the *vita active* and *vita contemplativa*.[71]

Festivity is tied to the creation and the living out of culture because festival is not possible without the "visible forms of celebration" that relate to arts such as singing and dancing.[72] The medium of the arts are essential for festival because they make perceptible the joyful affirmation of existence that is inherent to festivity.[73] Festivity nourishes the soul, because through it, the soul is able to momentarily step out of time.[74] Again we have a need in our current historical moment for the celebration of true festivity because festivals are public matters in which social and political differences are forgotten as members of a community fraternize with one another.[75] However, we must be careful to not force this upon a people because artificial holidays are shams that can easily reverse into "anti-festivals."[76] Take for instance the reality that Mother's Day was founded as a peace movement in response to the ravages of war, but has been commercialized into a day of pampering mothers through the purchasing of shallow tokens of admiration.

In an era of decreased participation in communal and fraternal organizations, many have sought to explicitly argue for experiences of "community" for its own sake. For instance, many church denominations that are losing congregants on a rapid basis focus their efforts on creating community, but they miss out on the fact that this is simply a corporate extension of the individual being turned into *animal laborans* that works for the sake of life itself. It would behoove leaders of such communities to not attempt to create shallow sites of "community" and focus upon the activities and meaningful work that produces communal bonds as a byproduct of meaningful work shared in common. Community forms around those who hold something in common. That commonality must base itself on something substantive, not simply an abstract dedication to "community." That substance may be common beliefs, common practices, or likely a combination of the two. The modern prejudice in favor of "choice" and "autonomy" makes us skeptical of any community that makes demands upon us, but the strongest communities are strong because they actual believe in something and do something. They don't just mutter pieties about "community."[77]

There should be no doubt that we live in dark times, and this ought to be a true cause for anxiety for anyone with ears to hear and eyes to see. Though we should not give in to despair. Numerous scholars have written on the problems of our age, and solutions to these deep existential and metaphysical problems are beginning to take form. We hope that this current text contributes to the healing of our broken culture and wounded members embedded within it. Though this will only be accomplished as we rediscover the value of craft as a model, for life and the liberal arts are once again recognized as an intellectual immune system defending against diseases of the mind. In humility, we end this work with the hope and wisdom of Tolkien: "At that moment a rolling and rumbling noise was heard again, louder now and deeper. The ground seemed to quiver under their feet. 'I think we are in for trouble anyhow,' said Frodo. 'I'm afraid our journey is drawing to an end.' 'Maybe,' said Sam; 'but where there's life there's hope, as my gaffer used to say; and need of vittles, as he mostways used to add. You have a bite, Mr. Frodo, and then a bit of sleep.'"[78]

NOTES

1. The unprincipled power games can be seen on the part of both left and right in their weaponization of the 1st Amendment. Whenever either ideology lacks power, they uphold the sacrosanct nature of freedom of speech, but as soon as they gain power, they decry alternative forms of speech as dangerous and worthy of limitation. Ironically, in its steadfast defense for free speech, the ALCU has been condemned

by some on the left for defending the free speech rights of white nationalists. There is no principled commitment to "freedom of speech" or "freedom of religious conscience." These are just tools to use against their enemies. See, for instance, Adam Liptak, "How Conservatives Weaponized the First Amendment"; K-Sue Park, "The ACLU Needs to Rethink Free Speech," *New York Times*, August 17, 2017, https://ww w.nytimes.com/2017/08/17/opinion/aclu-first-amendment-trump-charlottesville.html (accessed February 14, 2019); Laura Weinrib, "The ACLUS's Free Speech Stance Should Be About Social Justice, Not 'Timeless' Principles," *Los Angeles Times*, August 30, 2017, https://www.latimes.com/opinion/op-ed/la-oe-weinrib-aclu-spe ech-history-20170830-story.html (accessed February 14, 2019).

2. A historical example of this form of advice can be seen in Booker T. Washington's "gospel of the toothbrush," in which he propagated the brushing of one's teeth as a prerequisite for success in society. http://www.thetuskegeenews.com/news/book er-t-washington-and-the-gospel-of-the-toothbrush/article_7d7c2cde-c210-53b2-85a8 -7b576b57cd0f.html

3. Arnett, Harden Fritz, and Bell, *Communication Ethics Literacy*, 18–19.

4. Matthew Crawford, *The World Beyond*, 3–44; Postman, *Technopoly*, 71–91.

5. See, Kenneth Burke's *Permanence and Change* for a larger discussion of the way in which individual and cultural conversions from one worldview to another take place. Kenneth Burke, *Permanence and Change: An Anatomy of Purpose* (Berkeley: University of California Press, 1984).

6. Corey Anton, *Communication Uncovered: General Semantics and Media Ecology* (Fort Worth: Institute of General Semantics, 2011), 3–8.

7. Carr, *The Shallows*, 58–114.

8. Ibid., 123.

9. Ibid., 124.

10. Corey Anton, *Communication Uncovered* (Fort Worth, TX: Institute of General Semantics, 2011), 8–12. So impactful on the brain is reading that that reading a book of fiction neurobiologically mirrors actually having the experience. Carr, *The Shallows*, 74.

11. Carr, *The Shallows*, 125.

12. Anton, *Communication Uncovered*, 6–7.

13. "Pride and Prejudice Part 1: Crash Course Literature #411," YouTube video, 11:43, posted by "CrashCourse," February 6, 2018, https://www.youtube.com/watch?v=5xTh44G6RYs.

14. "Pride & Prejudice—Thug Notes Summary and Analysis," YouTube video, 4:15, posted by "Wisecrack," July 8, 2013, https://www.youtube.com/watch?v=5Nm 61IoNdHg.

15. Anton, *Communication Uncovered*, 5.

16. Alice Ramos, "'Studiositas' and 'Curiositas': Matters for Self-Examination." *Educational Horizons*, Vol. 83, No. 4 (Summer 2005), 272–281.

17. Marshall McLuhan and Quentin Fiore, *The Medium is the Massage: An inventory of Effects* (Berkeley, CA: Gingko Press, 2001), 44–45, 50–53, and 68–69.

18. C.S. Lewis, *God in the Dock* (Grand Rapids, MI: Wm. B. Eerdmans Publishing, Co., 2014), 217–225.

19. Postman, *Technopoly*, 181–185.

20. Dietrich von Hildebrand with Alice von Hildebrand, *The Art of Living* (Steubenville, OH: Hildebrand Press, 2017), 1–34.

21. Deneen, *Why Liberalism Failed*, 10–17; Peter Augustine Lawler, *Aliens in America: The Strange Truth About Our Souls* (Wilmington, DE: ISI Books, 2002), 175–206; Lawler, *Stuck With Virtue*, 218–234.

22. MacIntyre, *After Virtue*, 1–35.

23. Stanley F. Bonner, *Education in Ancient Rome: From the Elder Cato to the Younger Pliny* (Berkeley: University of California Press, 1977), 48–49; Eric Havelock, *A Preface to Plato*, (Cambridge, MA: Belknap Press of Harvard University, 1963), 29, 31; H.I. Marrou, *A History of Education in Antiquity* (Madison: University of Wisconsin Press, 1956), 10, 169; McLuhan, *Classical Trivium*, 196; Kevin Robb, *Literacy and Paideia in Ancient Greece* (New York: Oxford University Press, 1994), 184; Jeffrey Walker, *Rhetoric and Poetics in Antiquity* (New York: Oxford University Press, 2000), 7, 9; Anthony M. Wachs, *The New Science of Communication: Reconsidering McLuhan's Message for Our Modern Moment* (Pittsburgh, PA: Duquesne University Press, 2015), 108–112.

24. Eleonore Strump, "Dialectic," in *The Seven Liberal Arts in the Middle Ages*, ed. David L. Wagner (Bloomington: Indiana University Press, 1983), 126.

25. Kimball, *Orators and Philosophers*, 37.

26. Carr, *The Shallows*, 17–35; Matthew Crawford, *The World Beyond*, 16–27; Gilson, *God and Philosophy*, 20–22.

27. For a discussion of Aristotelianism and modern physics, see Edward Feser, *Five Proofs of the Existence of God* (San Francisco: Ignatius Press, 2017), 49–60.

28. Herman and Chomsky, *Manufacturing Consent*.

29. *HyperNormalisation*, Adam Curtis. https://www.youtube.com/watch?v=fh2cDKyFdyU&t=4925s

30. Sister Miriam Joseph, *The Trivium*, 3.

31. Crawford, *The World Beyond*, 63.

32. MacIntyre, *After Virtue*, 187.

33. Ibid.

34. Ibid., 190–191.

35. Harari, *Homo Deus*, 2.

36. Crawford, *The World Beyond*, 72.

37. Here one should note the colloquial idea of finding an "app" for all

38. Crawford shows how children are indoctrinated into this mentality through the contemporary popular culture in such shows as the Mickey Mouse Club House, in which all problems are solved by a computer after characters passively resigned to their problems say, "Oh toodles." Crawford, *The World Beyond*, 69–78.

39. Crawford, *The World Beyond*, 72.

40. Ibid., 73.

41. Ibid., 39.

42. Ibid., 69–70.

43. Ibid., 127–131.

44. Ibid., 160.

45. Josef Pieper, *Leisure: The Basis of Culture* (South Bend, IN: St. Augustine's Press, 1998), 27–31.

46. Snell, *Acedia and Its Discontents*, 10–11.

47. Pieper, *Leisure*, 32; Carr, *The Shallows*, 63; Crawford, *The World Beyond*, 31–35.

48. Or think of one of the more famous quotes from baseball great Yogi Berra: "I can't think and hit at the same time."

49. Crawford, *The World Beyond*, 31–35.

50. Ibid., 89–107.

51. Ibid., 181–193.

52. Pieper, *In Tune*, 4.

53. Ligotti notes that the French existentialist Albert Camus wrote about the absurd and irrational goal of "going on with life rather than ending it for to do so we must somehow remain happy." He utilizes the image of Sisyphus being happy within his drudgery as an image of finding meaning within a meaningless universe, that is, maintaining a reason not to commit suicide as soon as the disadvantages of life outweigh the advantages. Ligotti, *Conspiracy*, 49.

54. Pieper, *In Tune*, 5.

55. Ibid., 4.

56. Ibid., 5.

57. Ibid.

58. Ibid., 8.

59. Ibid.

60. Ibid., 8–9.

61. Ibid., 9.

62. Ibid.

63. Ibid.

64. Ibid., 10.

65. Ibid., 15. This directly relates to Taylor's project with regard to questions of human flourishing. However, Taylor is unable to provide an adequate answer or solution to the problem because of his Hegelianism, whereas Pieper, being a Thomist, has the intellectual coherence to ask and answer that question. Along these lines, Pieper notes that "the concept of festivity is inconceivable without an element of contemplation," for the Thomist, "the utmost perfect to which man may attain, the fulfilment of his being, is *visio beatifica*, the 'seeing that confers bliss,'" or the beatific vision (15, 17).

66. Pieper, *In Tune*, 17.

67. Ibid, 18.

68. Han, *Burnout Society*, 13.

69. Ibid., 14.

70. Ong, *Presence of the Word*.

71. Han, *Burnout Society*, 16–20.

72. Pieper, *In Tune*, 52.

73. Ibid., 52–53.
74. Ibid., 53.
75. Ibid., 69.
76. Ibid., 79.
77. See Bottom, *An Anxious Age*, 42–44.
78. Tolkien, *LOTR*, 700.

Bibliography

Alighieri, Dante. *The Divine Comedy of Dante Alighieri*. Volume 1. *Inferno*. Edited and Translated by Robert M. Durling. Introduction and Notes by Ronald L. Martinez and Robert M. Durling. Illustrations by Robert Turner. New York and Oxford: Oxford University Press, 1996.

Allen, Charlotte. "Punching Down." First Things, last modified June 2016. https://www.firstthings.com/article/2016/06/punching-down.

Anton, Corey. *Communication Uncovered: General Semantics and Media Ecology*. Fort Worth, TX: Institute of General Semantics, 2011.

Aristotle. *Aristotle's Politics*. Translated by T.A. Sinclair. New York: Penguin Classics, 1992.

———. *On Rhetoric: A Theory of Civic Discourse*. Translated by George A. Kennedy. New York: Oxford University Press, 1991.

———. *The Nicomachean Ethics*. Edited by Lesley Brown. Translated by David Ross. Oxford: Oxford University, 2009.

Arnett, Ronald C. and Pat Arneson. *Dialogic Civility in a Cynical Age*. Albany: State University of New York Press, 1999.

Arnett, Ronald C., Janie M. Harden Fritz, and Leanne M. Bell. *Communication Ethics Literacy: Dialogue and Difference*. Los Angeles: SAGE Publications, 2009.

Ashley, Benedict M. *The Way toward Wisdom: An Interdisciplinary and Intercultural Introduction to Metaphysics*. Notre Dame: University of Notre Dame, 2006.

Augustine. *On the Free Choice of the Will, On, Grace and Choice, and Other Writings*. Edited and Translated by Peter King. New York, Cambridge: 2010.

Bacon, Francis. *New Atlantis and the Great Instauration*. Edited by Jerry Weinberger. Arlington Heights, Illinois, Harland Davidson, Inc., 1989.

Barbour, Benjamin. "Jihad vs. McWorld." *The Atlantic*, March 1992. https://www.theatlantic.com/magazine/archive/1992/03/jihad-vs-mcworld/303882/.

Barfield, Owen. *Saving the Appearances: A Study in Idolatry*. 2nd ed. Middletown, CT: Wesleyan University Press, 1988.

Beniger, James R. *The Control Revolution: Technological and Economic Origins of the Information Society*. Cambridge: Harvard University Press, 1986.

Berry, Wendell. *Home Economics*. New York: North Point, 1987.

———. *Jayber Crowe*. Washington, DC: Counterpoint, 2000.

———. *Sex, Economy, Freedom, and Community*. New York: Pantheon, 1993.

———. *What Are People For?* San Francisco: North Point, 1990.

Birzer, Bradley J. *J.R.R. Tolkien's Sanctifying Myth: Understanding Middle-earth*. Wilmington, De: ISI Books, 2003.

Bloom, Allan. *Love & Friendship*. New York: Simon & Schuster, 1993.

Bonner, Stanley F. *Education in Ancient Rome: From the Elder Cato to the Younger Pliny*. Berkeley: University of California Press, 1977.

"Booker T. Washington and the 'Gospel of the Toothbrush.'" *The TuskeGee News*, last modified February 25 2010.http://www.thetuskegeenews.com/news/booker-t-washington-and-the-gospel-of-the-toothbrush/article_7d7c2cde-c210-53b2-85a8-7b576b57cd0f.html.

Boorstin, Daniel J. *The Image: A Guide to Pseudo-Events in America. 50th* Anniversary ed. New York: Vintage, 1992.

Bottom, Joseph. *An Anxious Age: The Post-Protestant Ethic and the Spirit of America*. New York: Image. 2014.

Boulding, Kenneth E. "General Systems Theory—The Skeleton of Science." In *General Systems Theory and Human Communication,* edited by Brent D. Reuben and John Y. Kim, 21–32. Rochelle Park, NJ: Hayden, 1975.

Brooks, Max. *World War Z*. New York: Three Rivers, 2006.

Burke, Kenneth. *Permanence and Change: An Anatomy of Purpose*. Berkeley: University of California Press, 1984.

Butler, Robert. "The Art of Darkness." *Intelligent Life*. December, 2007.

Caldecott, Stratford. *The Power of the Ring*. New York: The Crossroad Publishing Company, 2012.

Carney, Tim P. *Alienated America: Why Some Places Thrive While Others Collapse*. New York: Harper, 2019. Kindle Edition location 1812.

Carr, Nicholas. *The Glass Cage: How Our Computers are Changing Us*. New York: W.W. Norton & Company, 2014.

———. *The Shallows: What the Internet is Doing to Our Brains*. New York: W. W. Norton & Company, 2011.

Cavanaugh, William. *Being Consumed: Economics and Christian Desire*. Grand Rapids: Wm. B. Eerdmans, 2008.

Chesterton, G.K. *Orthodoxy*. New York: Image Books, 1959.

Cook, Denise N. "The Cultural Life of the Living Dead." *Mediations: Analyzing Culture* 12, no. 4, 2013.

CrashCourse. "Pride and Prejudice Part 1: Crash Course Literature #411." Filmed [February 2018]. YouTube video, 11:43. Posted [February 6, 2018]. https://www.youtube.com/ watch?v=5xTh44G6RYs.

Crawford, Matthew B. *Shop Class as Soulcraft: An Inquiry into the Value of Work*. New York: Penguin, 2009.

———. *The World Beyond Your Head: On Becoming an Individual in an Age of Distraction*. New York: Farrar, Straus and Giroux, 2015.

Dawn of the Dead. Directed by Zack Snyder. Written by George A. Romero and James Gunn. Hollywood: Universal Studios, 2004.

del Noce, Augusto. *Crisis of Modernity*. Translated by Carlo Lancellotti. London: McGill-Queen's University Press, 2015.

Deneen, Patrick. *Conserving America? Essays on Present Discontents*. St Augustine's Press, 2016.

———. "The Ignoble Lie: How the New Aristocracy Masks Its Privilege." *First Things*, April 2018.

———. "Wendell Berry and the Alternative Tradition in American Political Thought." In *Wendell Berry: Life and Work*, edited by Jason Peters, 300–315. Lexington: University Press of Kentucky, 2007.

———. *Why Liberalism Failed*. University of Virginia: Institute for Advanced Studies in Culture. New Haven: Yale University Press, 2018.

Descartes, Rene. *Discourse on Method and Meditations of First Philosophy*. 4th ed. Translated by Donald A. Cress. Indianapolis: Hackett Publishing Company, 1998.

de Tocqueville, Alexis. *Democracy in America*. Translated by Harvey C. Mansfield and Delba Winthrop. Chicago: University of Chicago, 2000.

———. *The Old Regime and the Revolution*. Translated by Alan S. Kahan. Chicago: University of Chicago Press, 1998.

de Zengotita, Thomas. *Mediated: How the Media Shapes Your World and the Way You Live in It*. New York: Bloomsbury Publishing, 2005.

Downton Abbey. Season 1, episode 1. Directed by Brian Percival. Written by Julian Fellowes. PBS, aired January 9, 2011.

———. Season 1, episode 2. Directed by Ben Percival. Written by Julian Fellowes. PBS, aired January 9, 2011.

———. Season 1, episode 3. Directed by Ben Bolt. Written by Julian Fellowes. PBS, aired January 16, 2011.

———. Season 1, episode 6. Directed by Brian Percival. Written by Julian Fellowes and Tina Pepler. PBS, aired January 23, 2011.

———. Season 1, episode 7. Directed by Brian Percival. Written by Julian Fellowes. PBS, aired January 30, 2011.

———. Season 2, episode 8. Directed by James Strong. Written by Julian Fellowes. PBS, aired February 12, 2012.

———. Season 3, episode 1. Directed by Brian Percival. Written by Julian Fellowes. PBS, aired January 6, 2013.

———. Season 3, episode 2. Directed by Brian Percival. Written by Julian Fellowes. PBS, aired January 6, 2013.

———. Season 3, episode 7, Directed by David Evans, Written by Julian Fellowes, PBS aired February 10, 2013.

———. Season 4, episode 1. Directed by David Evans. Written by Julian Fellowes. PBS, aired January 5, 2014.

———. Season 4, episode 3. Directed by Catherine Morshead. Written by Julian Fellowes. PBS, aired January 12, 2014.

———. Season 4, episode 5. Directed by Philip John. Written by Julian Fellowes. PBS, aired January 26, 2014.

———. Season 5, episode 3. Directed by Catherine Morshead. Written by Julian Fellowes. PBS, aired January 189, 2015.

————. Season 5, episode 4. Directed by Minie Spiro. Written by Julian Fellowes. PBS, aired January 25, 2015.

————. Season 6, episode 1. Directed by Minkie Spiro. Written by Julian Fellowes. PBS, aired January 3, 2016.

————. Season 6, episode 4. Directed by Philip John. Written by Julian Fellowes. PBS, aired October 11, 2015.

————. Season 6, episode 6. Directed by Michael Engler. Written by Julian Fellowes. PBS, aired October 25, 2015.

————. Season 6, episode 7. Directed by David Evans. Written by Julian Fellowes. PBS, aired November 1, 2015.

Dreher, Rod. *The Benedict Option: A Strategy for Christians in a Post-Christian Nation*. New York: Sentinel, 2017.

Drezner, Dan. *Theories of International Politics and Zombies*. Rev. ed. Princeton: Princeton University, 2015.

Douthat, Ross. "The Handmaidens of Capitalism." *New York Times*, June 20, 2018. https://www.nytimes.com/2018/06/20/opinion/feminism-capitalism.html.

Eberstadt, Mary. "The Zealous Faith of Secularism." *First Things*, January 2018, 35–40, and Matthew Rose, "Our Secular Theodicy." *First Things*, December 2017, 37–42.

Eberstadt, Nicholas. "Our Miserable 21st Century." Commentary. February 2017. https://www.commentarymagazine.com/articles/our-miserable-21st-century/

Erasmus, Desiderius and Luther, Martin. *The Battle over Free Will*. Edited by Clarence H. Miller. Translated by Clarence H. Miller and Peter Macardle. Indianapolis: Hackett Publishing Company, 2012.

Fearnow, Benjamin. "CDC: Average American Woman Now Weighs as Much as 1960s US Man." *CBS Atlanta*, last modified June 15, 2015. http://atlanta.cbslocal.com/2015/06/15/cdc-average-american-woman-nowweighs-as-much-as-1960s-us-man/.

Feser, Edward. *Five Proofs of the Existence of God*. San Francisco: Ignatius Press, 2017.

Fisher, Walter R. "Narration as a Human Communication Paradigm: The Case of Public Moral Argument." *Communication Monographs*, v. 51, 1–22. March 1984.

Follett, Mary Parker. "How Must Business Management Develop in Order to Possess the Essentials of a Profession?" In *Business Management as a Profession*, edited by Henry C. Metcalf, 73–88. Chicago: A. W. Shaw, 1927.

Friedman, Megan. "Are Today's Men Really Weaker Than Their Dads?" *Esquire*, last modified August 16, 2016. https://www.esquire.com/lifestyle/health/news/a47719/study-millennial-men-have-weaker-grip-strength/.

Fukuyama, Francis. *The Great Disruption: Human Nature and the Reconstitution of Social Order*. New York: Free Press, 1999.

Gadamer, Hans-Georg. *Truth and Method*. 2nd ed. Translated by Donald G. Marshall and Joel Weinsheimer. New York: Continuum Publishing Group, 2004.

Garreau, Joel. *Radical Evolution: The Promise and Peril of Enhancing Our Minds, Our Bodies—and What It Means to Be Human*. New York: Broadway Books, 2005.

Gerretsen, Bronwyn. "I Want God to Be Dead in My Works." *IOLNews*, last modified December 3, 2007. https://www.iol.co.za/news/south-africa/i-want-god-to-be-dead-in-my-works-381139.

Gilson, Etienne. *God and Philosophy*. 2nd ed. New Haven: Yale Note Bene Press of Yale, 2002.

Goklany, Indur M. "The Globalization of Human Well-Being." CATO Institute. August 22, 2002. https://www.cato.org/publications/policy-analysis/globalization-human-wellbeing

Gray, Chris Hables. *Cyborg Citizen: Politics in the Posthuman Age*. New York: Routledge, 2001.

Gregory, Brad S. *The Unintended Reformation: How a Religious Revolution Secularized Society*. Cambridge: Belknap Press of Harvard, 2012.

Habermas, Jurgen and Joseph Ratzinger. *Dialectics of Secularization: On Reason and Religion*. Translated by Brian McNeil. San Francisco: Ignatius Press, 2006.

Hacksaw Ridge. Directed by Mel Gibson. Santa Monica, CA: Lionsgate Entertainment, 2016. DVD.

Han, Byung-Chul. *The Burnout Society*. Translated by Erik Butler. Stanford: Stanford University Press, 2015.

Harari, Yuval Noah. *Homo Deus: A Brief History of Tomorrow*. New York: HarperCollins, 2017.

Harris, Sam. *The End of Faith: Religion, Terror, and the Future of Reason*. New York: W.W. Norton & Company, 2004.

———. *The Moral Landscape: How Science Can Determine Human Values*. New York: Free Press, 2010.

Havelock, Eric. *A Preface to Plato*. Cambridge, MA: Belknap Press of Harvard University, 1963.

Havilresky, Heather. "Sit Cons: Class on TV." *The Baffler*, July 2012.

Hayles, Katherine N. *How We Became Posthuman: Virtual Bodies in Cybernetics, Literature, and Informatics*. Chicago: University of Chicago, 1999.

Herman, Edward S. and Noam Chomsky. *Manufacturing Consent: The Political Economy of the Mass Media*. Updated Ed. New York: Pantheon Books, 2002.

Hildebrand, Dietrich von. "The Essence of Personality." In *Liturgy and Personality*. Baltimore, Helicon Press, 1960.

———. *The Nature of Love*. Translated by John F. Crosby with John Henry Crosby. South Bend, In: St. Augustine's Press, 2009.

Hildebrand, Dietrich von with Alice von Hildebrand. *The Art of Living*. Steubenville, OH: Hildebrand Press, 2017.

Hobbes, Thomas. *Leviathan*. New York: Penguin Classics, 1985.

HyperNormalisation. Directed by Adam Curtis. BBC iPlayer, 16 October 2016. https://www.youtube.com/watch?v=fh2cDKyFdyU&t=4925s.

Kimball, Bruce A. *Orators and Philosophers: A History of the Idea of Liberal Education*. New York: College Entrance Examination Board, 1995.

King, Peter. *On the Free Choice of the Will, On Grace and Free Choice, and Other Writings*. New York: Cambridge University Press, 2010.

Kinneavy, James L. *Greek Rhetorical Origins of Christian Faith: And Inquiry.* New York: Oxford University Press, 1987.

Kleinman, Alexis. "Nearly 20 Percent Of Young Adults Use Their Smartphones During Sex: Survey." *Huffington Post,* last modified July 12 2013. https://www.huffingtonpost.com/2013/07/12/smartphones-during-sex_n_3586647.html.

Koons, Robert C. "T.S. Elliot, Populist." *First Things,* December, 2018.

Kreeft, Peter J. *The Philosophy of Tolkien.* San Francisco: Ignatius Press, 2005.

Kuhn, Thomas S. *The Structure of Scientific Revolutions.* 3rd ed. Chicago: University of Chicago Press, 1966.

Jaynes, Julian. *The Origins of Consciousness in the Breakdown of Bicameral Mind.* Boston: Houghton Mifflin, 1976.

Jefferson, Thomas. "Notes on the State of Virginia: Query XIX Manufactures." In *The Portable Thomas Jefferson,* edited by Merrill Peterson. New York: Penguin, 1975.

John Paul II. *Catechism of the Catholic Church.* Citta del Vaticano: Libreria Editrice Vaticana, 1993.

Jonas, Hans. *The Phenomenon of Life: Toward a Philosophical Biology.* Evanston: Northwestern University Press, 1966.

Joseph, Sister Miriam. *The Trivium: The Liberal Arts of Grammar, Logic, and Rhetoric: Understanding the Nature and Function of Language.* Philadelphia: Paul Dry Books, 1937.

Joustra, Robert and Alissa Wilkinson. *How to Survive the Apocalypse: Zombies, Cylons, Faith, and Politics at the End of the World.* Grand Rapids: Wm. B. Eerdmans, 2016.

Lasch, Christopher. *The Revolt of the Elites And the Betrayal of Democracy.* New York: W. W. Norton, 1995.

Lawler, Peter Augustine. *Aliens in America: The Strange Truth About Our Souls.* Wilmington, DE: ISI Books, 2002.

———. *Homeless and at Home in America: Evidence for the Dignity in our Time and Place.* South Bend, IN: St. Augustine's Press, 2007.

———. *Postmodernism Rightly Understood: The Return to Realism in American Thought.* Lanham, MD: Rowman & Littlefield Publishers, 1999.

———. *Stuck with Virtue.* Wilmington: Intercollegiate Studies Institute, 2005.

Lewis, C.S. *God in the Dock.* Grand Rapids, MI: Wm. B. Eerdmans Publishing, Co., 2014.

———. *The Abolition of Man.* New York: HarperCollins, 2001.

Ligotti, Thomas. *The Conspiracy Against the Human Race: A Contrivance of Horror.* New York: Hippocampus Press, 2010.

Liptak, Adam. "How Conservatives Weaponized the First Amendment." *New York Times,* June 30, 2018https://www.nytimes.com/2018/06/30/us/politics/first-amendment-conservatives-supreme-court.html (accessed January, 2019).

Locke, John. *A Letter Concerning Toleration.* Buffalo: Prometheus, 1990.

———. *Second Treatise on Government.* Indianapolis: Hackett, 1980.

Loconte, Joseph. *A Hobbit, a Wardrobe, and a Great War: How J.R.R. Tolkien and C.S. Lewis Rediscovered Faith, Friendship, and Heroism in the Cataclysm of 1914–1918.* Nashville, TN: Thomas Nelson Books, 2015.

Lyotard, Jean-François. *The Postmodern Condition: A Report on Knowledge.* Translated by Geoff Bennington and Brian Massumi. Minneapolis: University of Minnesota, 1993.

MacIntyre, Alasdair. *After Virtue: A Study in Moral Theory.* 3rd ed. Notre Dame: University of Notre Dame, 2007.

Marche, Stephen. "Downton Abbey Is an Aristocratic Fantasy: And Worse, It's Run out of Steam." *Esquire*, last modified January 5, 2014 http://www.esquire.com/entertainment/tv/a26598/downton-abbey-season4review/ (accessed June 9, 2017).

Markowitz, Karol. "An Epidemic of Teenage Loneliness." *New York Post*. March 26, 2019. https://nypost.com/2019/03/26/an-epidemic-of-teenage-loneliness/.

Marrou, H.I. *A History of Education in Antiquity.* Madison: University of Wisconsin Press, 1956.

Martin, James S.J. "Exclusive: Martin Scorsese Discusses His Faith, His Struggles, His Films and 'Silence'." *AmericaMagazine: The Jesuit Review.* December 6, 2016. https://www.americamagazine.org/artsculture/2016/12/06/exclusive-martin-scorsese-discusses-his-faith-his-struggles-his-films-and.

McLuhan, Marshall. *The Classical Trivium: The Place of Thomas Nashe in the Learning of his Time.* Corte Madera, CA: Gingko Press, 2006.

———. *Understanding Media: The Extensions of Man.* Critical edition. Corte Madera, CA: Gingko Press, 2003.

McLuhan, Marshall and Quentin Fiore. *The Medium is the Massage: An Inventory of Effects.* Berkeley, CA: Gingko Press, 2001.

Mikelionis, Lukas. "Indian Man to Sue His Parents for Giving Birth to Him 'without his consent', Wants to Be Paid for His Life." Foxnews.com, last modified February 7, 2019. https://www.foxnews.com/world/indian-man-tosue-his-parents-for-giving-birth-to-himwithout-his-consent-wants-to-be-paid-for-his-life (accessed Feb. 11, 2019).

Milbank, John and Adrian Pabst. *The Politics of Virtue: Post-Liberalism and The Human Future.* Langham, MD: Rowman & Littlefield, 2016.

Mill, John Stuart. *Three Essays.* New York: Oxford University Press, 1975.

Mitchell, Joshua. *The Fragility of Freedom: Tocqueville on Religion, Democracy, and the American Future.* Chicago: University of Chicago, 1995.

Mumford, Lewis. *Technics and Civilization.* Chicago: University of Chicago Press, 2010.

Murray, Charles. *Coming Apart: The State of White America.* New York: Crown Forum, 2012.

Myers, Ken. Interview with Oliver O'Donovan. *Mars Hill Audio Journal.* Volume 127, 2014.

Nault, Dom Jean Charles, O.S.B. *The Noonday Devil: Acedia, the Unnamed Evil of Our Times.* San Francisco: Ignatius Press, 2015.

Nisbet, Robert. "Tocqueville's Ideal Types." In *Reconsidering Tocqueville's Democracy in America,* edited by Abraham S. Eisenstadt, 171–191. New Brunswick, NJ: Rutgers University Press, 1988.

O'Connor, Flannery. *Collected Works.* New York: Library of America, 1988.

O'Donovan, Oliver. *Begotten Not Made.* New York: Oxford University Press, 1984.

Ong, Walter J. *The Presence of the Word: Some Prolegomena for Cultural and Religious History.* New Haven: Yale University Press, 1967.

O'Neil, Cathy. *Weapons of Math Destruction: How Big Data Increases Inequality and Threatens Democracy.* New York: Crown, 2016.

Park, K-Sue. "The ACLU Needs to Rethink Free Speech." *New York Times*, last modified August 17, 2017. https://www.nytimes.com/2017/08/17/opinion/aclu-first-amendment-trump-charlottesville.html (accessed February 14, 2019).

Paul, Darel E. *From Tolerance to Equality: How Elites Brought America to Same-Sex Marriage.* Texas: Baylor University Press, 2018.

Pearce, Joseph. "True Myth: The Catholicism of 'The Lord of the Rings.'" In *Celebrating Middle-Earth: The Lord of the Rings as a Defense of Western Civilization*, 83–84. Seattle, WA: Inkling Books, 2002.

Percy, Walker. *Lost in the Cosmos: The Last Self-Help Book.* New York: Picador, 1983.

Pieper, Josef. *In Tune with the World: A Theory of Festivity.* Translated by Richard and Clara Winston. South Bend: St. Augustine's Press, 1963.

———. *Leisure: The Basis of Culture.* South Bend, In: St. Augustine's Press, 1998.

Pinker, Steven. *Enlightenment Now: The Case for Reason, Science, Humanism, and Progress.* New York: Viking, 2018.

Planned Parenthood of Southeastern Pa. v. Casey, 505 U.S. 833, 851 (1992).

Plato. *Gorgias.* Translated by W.C. Hembold. Upper Saddle River, NJ: Prentice Hall Inc, 1997.

Plato. *The Republic.* Translated by Allan Bloom. New York: Basic Books, 1968.

Platts, Todd K. "Locating Zombies in the Sociology of Popular Culture." *Sociology Compass* 7, no. 7, 2013.

Postman, Neil. *Amusing Ourselves to Death: Public Discourse in the Age of Show Business.* 20th anniversary ed. New York: Penguin Books, 1985.

———. *Technopoly: The Surrender of Culture to Technology.* New York: Vintage Books, 1992.

Queen. Bohemian Rhapsody. Elektra, 1975, February 12, 2019. https://open.spotify.com/album/1GbtB4zTqAsyfZEsm1RZfx.

Ramos, Alice. "'Studiositas' and 'Curiositas': Matters for Self-Examination." *Educational Horizons*, v. 83 n. 4, 272–281. Summer 2005.

Randall, John Herman, Jr. *The Making of the Modern Mind: A Survey of the Intellectual Background of the Present Age.* Fiftieth anniversary ed. New York: Columbia University Press, 1976.

Ratzinger, Joseph Cardinal. *In the Beginning: A Catholic Understanding of the Story of Creation and the Fall.* Translated by Boniface Ramsey, O.P. Grand Rapids, MI: Wm. B. Eerdmans Publishing Co., 1995.

———. *Introduction to Christianity.* Translated J. R. Foster and Michael S. Miller. San Francisco: Ignatius Press, 2004.

Real Time with Bill Maher. "Jordan B. Peterson | Real Time with Bill Maher (HBO)." Filmed [April 2018.] YouTube video, 9:35. Posted [April 20, 2018.] https://www.youtube.com/watch?v=8wLCmDtCDAM.

Reeves, Richard. *All Minus One: John Stuart Mill's Ideas on Free Speech Illustrated.* Heterodox Academy, 2018.

Regnerus, Mark. *Cheap Sex: The Transformation of Men, Marriage, and Monogamy.* New York: Oxford University, 2017.

Ricoeur, Paul. *Time and Narrative.* Vols. 1–3, Translated by Kathleen McLaughlin and David Pellauer. Chicago: University of Chicago, 1983, 1984, 1985.

Rieff, Philip. *The Triumph of the Therapeutic: Uses of Faith After Freud.* 40th anniversary ed. Wilmington: DE ISI Books, 2006.

Robb, Kevin. *Literacy and Paideia in Ancient Greece.* New York: Oxford University Press, 1994.

Rose, Matthew. "Our Secular Theodicy." *First Things,* December 2017, 37–42.

Rousseau, Jean-Jacques. *The Basic Political Writings.* Indianapolis: Hackett, 1987.

Rushkoff, Douglas. *Present Shock: When Everything Happens Now.* New York: Penguin Group, 2013.

———. *Throwing Rocks at the Google Bus: How Growth Became the Enemy of Prosperity.* New York: Portfolio, 2016.

Sarah, Robert Cardinal and Nicolas Diat. *The Power of Silence: Against the Dictatorship of Noise.* San Francisco: Ignatius Press, 2016.

Schindler, D. C. *Freedom from Reality: The Diabolical Character of Modern Liberty.* South Bend, IN: University of Notre Dame, 2017.

Schwartz, Ariel. "Computer algorithms Are Now Deciding Whether Prisoners Get Parole." *Business Insider,* last modified December 15 2015. https://www.business insider.com/computer-algorithms-are-deciding-whetherprisoners-get-parole-20 15-12.

Shalit, Wendy. *A Return to Modesty: Discovering the Lost Virtue.* Anniversary edition. New York: Free Press, 2014.

Shaun of the Dead. Directed by Edgar Wright. Written by Simon Pegg and Edgar Wright. Universal City, CA: Rogue Pictures, 2004. DVD.

Smith, Brian. *Walker Percy and the Politics of the Wayfarer.* Maryland: Lexington Books, 2017.

Smith, Bruce James. "A Liberal of a New Kind." In *Interpreting Tocqueville's Democracy in America,* edited by Ken Masugi, 63–95. Savage, MD: Rowman & Littlefield, 1991.

Smith, Christian. *Soul Searching: The Religious and Spiritual Lives of American Teenagers.* New York: Oxford University Press, 2009.

Smith, Kimberly K. "Wendell Berry's Political Vision." In *Wendell Berry: Life and Work,* edited by Jason Peters, 49–59. Lexington: University Press of Kentucky, 2007.

Snell, R.J. *Acedia and Its Discontents: Metaphysical Boredom in an Empire of Desire.* Kettering, OH: Angelico Press, 2015.

Stein, Rob. "Chinese Scientist Says He's First To Create Genetically Modified Babies Using CRISPR." *NPR.org.* last modified November 26, 2018. https://www.npr.org/sections/healthshots/2018/11/26/0752865/chinese-scientist-says-hes-first-to-gene tically-edit-babies (accessed January 4, 2019).

Strate, Lance. *Media Ecology: An Approach to Understanding the Human Condition.* New York: Peter Lang, 2017.

Strauss, Leo. *Natural Right and History.* Chicago: University of Chicago Press, 1953.

———. "What is Liberal Education?" In *Liberalism Ancient and Modern.* Chicago: University of Chicago, 1968.

Strump, Eleonore. "Dialectic." In *The Seven Liberal Arts in the Middle Ages*. Edited by David L. Wagner. Bloomington: Indiana University Press, 1983.

Swinburne, Richard. "The Argument from Design." *Philosophy*, v. 43, n. 165, July 1968.

Taylor, Charles. *A Secular Age*. Cambridge: Belknap Press of Harvard, 2007.

Taylor, Frederick Winslow. *The Principles of Scientific Management*. New York: Cosimo Classics, 2012.

Teresa, Saint of Avila. *The Interior Castle or the Mansions*. United States: Saint Benedict Press, 2011.

Tessitore, Aristide. "Aristotle and Tocqueville on Statesmanship." In *Alexis de Tocqueville and the Art of Democratic Statesmanship*, edited by Brian Danoff and L. Joseph Herbert, Jr., 49–72. New York: Lexington Books, 2011.

The "Great War" of Owen Barfield and C. S. Lewis: Philosophical Writings. Edited by Norbert Feinendegen and Arend Smilde. Inklings Studies Supplements No. 1, 2015.

The Persuaders. Directed by Barak Goodman and Rachel Dretzin. Written by Barak Goodman and Douglas Rushkoff. Frontline, November 9, 2003.

The Rhetorical Situation (blog). http://therhetoricalsituation.blogspot.com/search/label/WALL-E.

Tolkien, Christopher. *The Letters of J.R.R. Tolkien*. Edited by Humphrey Carpenter. Boston: Houghton Mifflin, 2000.

Tolkien, J.R.R. "On Fairy-Stories." *The Tolkien Reader*. New York: Ballantine Books, 1966.

———. *The Children of Húrin*. Edited by Christopher Tolkien. Boston: Houghton Mifflin, 2007.

———. *The Lord of the Rings*. 50th anniversary one volume ed. New York: Houghton Mifflin, 2004.

———. *The Silmarillion*. Edited by Christopher Tolkien. Del Rey, 2002. Boston: Houghton Mifflin, 2004.

Tupy, Marian L. "Improvements in Human Well-Being in the New Millennium." *HumanProgress*. April 11, 2019. https://humanprogress.org/article.php?p=1844.

Turkle, Sherry. *Alone Together: Why We Expect More From Technology and Less From Each Other*. New York: Basic Books, 2011.

———. *Reclaiming Conversation: The Power of Talk in a Digital Age*. New York: Penguin Press, 2015.

Twenge, Jean M. "Have Smart Phones Destroyed a Generation?" *Atlantic Monthly*, last modified September 2017. https://www.theatlantic.com/magazine/archive/2017/09/has-the-smartphone-destroyed-a-generation/534198/.

Uhls, Jim. *Fight Club*. Directed by David Fincher. Los Angeles, CA: 20th Century Fox, 1999.

Voegelin, Eric. *Science, Politics and Gnosticism: Two Essays*. New York: Regnery Publishing, 1968.

Wachs, Anthony M. *The New Science of Communication: Reconsidering McLuhan's Message for Our Modern Moment*. Pittsburgh, PA: Duquesne University Press, 2015.

Walker, Jeffrey. *Rhetoric and Poetics in Antiquity*. New York: Oxford University Press, 2000.

———. *The Genuine Teachers of This Art: Rhetorical Education in Antiquity.* Columbia: University of South Carolina Press, 2011.

WALL-E. Directed by Andrew Stanton. Written by Andrew Stanton, Pete Docter, and Jim Reardon. Emeryville, CA: Pixar, 2008.

Weaver, Richard M. *Ideas Have Consequences.* Expanded ed. Chicago: University of Chicago, 2013.

———. "The Phaedrus and the Nature of Rhetoric." *The Ethics of Rhetoric.* Davis, CA: Hermagoras Press, 1985.

Weber, Max. *Science as Vocation.* http://anthropos-lab.net/wp/wpcontent/uploads /2011/12/Weber-Science-as-aVocation.pdf.

———. *The Theory of Social and Economic Organization.* Translated by A. M. Henderson and Talcott Parsons. New York: The Free Press, 1974.

Weinrib, Laura. "The ACLUS's Free Speech Stance Should Be About Social Justice, Not 'Timeless' Principles." *Los Angeles Times*, last modified August 30, 2017. https://www.latimes.com/opinion/op-ed/la-oe-weinrib aclu-speech-history-20170830-story.html (accessed February 14, 2019).

Westworld. Season 1, episode 2. "Chestnut." Directed by Richard J. Lewis. Written by Jonathan Nolan and Lisa Joy. HBO, Aired October 7, 2016.

———. Season 1, episode 3. "The Stray." Directed by Neil Marshall. Written by Daniel T. Thomsen and Lisa Joy. HBO, Aired October 16, 2016.

———. Season 1, episode 4, "Dissonance Theory." directed by Vincenzo Narali, written by Ed Brubaker and Jonathan Nolan, aired on October 23, 2016, on HBO.

———. Season 1, episode 5. "Contrapasso." Directed by Jonny Campbell. Written by Dominic Mitchell and Lisa Joy. HBO, Aired October 30, 2016.

———. Season 1, episode 6. "The Adversary." Directed by Frederick E.O. Toye. Written by Halley Gross and Jonathan Nolan. HBO, Aired November 6, 2016.

———. Season 1, episode 7. "Trompe L'Oeil." Directed by Frederick E.O. Toye. Written by Halley Gross and Jonathan Nolan. HBO, Aired November 13, 2016.

———. Season 1, episode 8, "Trace Decay," directed by Stephen Williams, written by Charles Yu and Lisa Joy, aired on November 20, 2016, on HBO.

———. Season 1, episode 9. "The Well-Tempered Clavier." Directed by Michelle MacLaren. Written by Dan Dietz and Katherine Lingenfelter. HBO, Aired November 27, 2016.

———. Season 1, episode 10. "The Bicameral Mind." Directed by Jonathan Nolan. Written by Lisay Joy and Jonathan Nolan. HBO, Aired December 4, 2016.

———. Season 2, episode 9. "Vanishing Point." Directed by Stephen Williams. Written by Roberto Patino. HBO, Aired June 17, 2018.

Whitson, Steven and John Poulakos. "Nietzsche and the Aesthetics of Rhetoric." *Quarterly Journal of Speech*, v. 79 n. 2 (1993).

Wilson, Woodrow. *Constitutional Government in the United States.* New York: Columbia University Press, 1908. Reprint New Brunswick, NJ: Transaction Publishers, 2002

Wisecrack. "Pride & Prejudice—Thug Notes Summary and Analysis." Filmed [July 2013]. YouTube video, 4:15. Posted [July 8, 2013]. https://www.youtube.com/watch?v=5Nm61IoNdHg.

Wolfe, Cary. *What Is Posthumanism?* Minneapolis: University of Minnesota, 2010.

Wood, Raph. *The Gospel According to Tolkien.* Louisville: Westminster John Knox Press, 2003.

Wosner, Robert and David Boyns. "Between the Living and Undead: How Zombie Cinema Reflects the Social Construction of Risk, the Anxious Self, and Disease Pandemic." *The Sociological Quarterly* 57, no. 4, 2016.

Zetterbaum, Marvin. "Alexis De Tocqueville." In *History of Political Philosophy.* 3rd ed. Edited by Leo Strauss and Joseph Cropsey, 761–801. Chicago: University of Chicago, 1987.

Zombieland. Directed by Ruben Fleischer. Written by Rhett Reese and Paul Wernick. Culver City, CA: Colombia Pictures, 2009. DVD.

Zuckert, Catherine H. "Tocqueville's New Political Science." In *Tocqueville's Voyages: The Evolution of His Ideas and Their Journey Beyond His Time,* edited by Christine Dunn Henderson, 142–176. Indianapolis: Liberty Fund, 2014.

Index

About the Authors

Anthony M. Wachs is assistant professor of rhetoric, communication ethics, and the Catholic intellectual tradition at Duquesne University in Pittsburgh, Pennsylvania, where he teaches courses on the intersections of rhetoric, religion, technology, and human relationships. He has published articles on these topics and is author of *The New Science of Communication: Reconsidering McLuhan's Message for Our Modern Moment*.

Jon D. Schaff is professor of political science at Northern State University in Aberdeen, South Dakota, where he teaches courses on American political thought, politics and religion, and politics and film. He has published on the political thought of Abraham Lincoln and Alexis de Tocqueville. He is the author of *Abraham Lincoln's Statesmanship and the Limits of Liberal Democracy*.

CPSIA information can be obtained
at www.ICGtesting.com
Printed in the USA
LVHW041616021221
705095LV00014B/2245